STAR WARS®

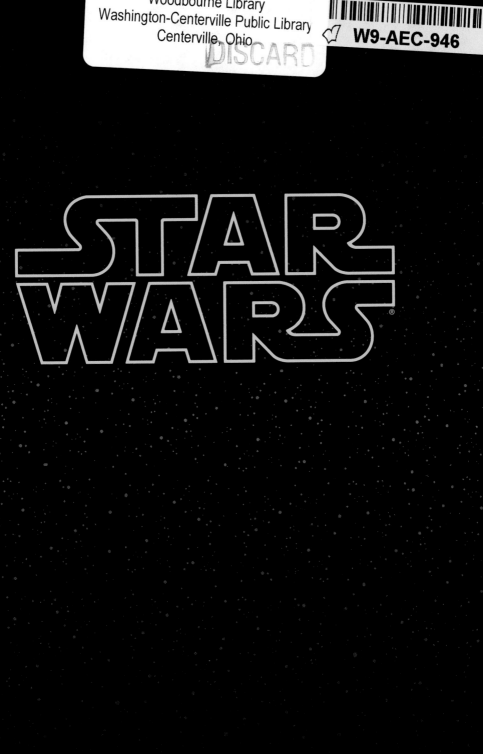

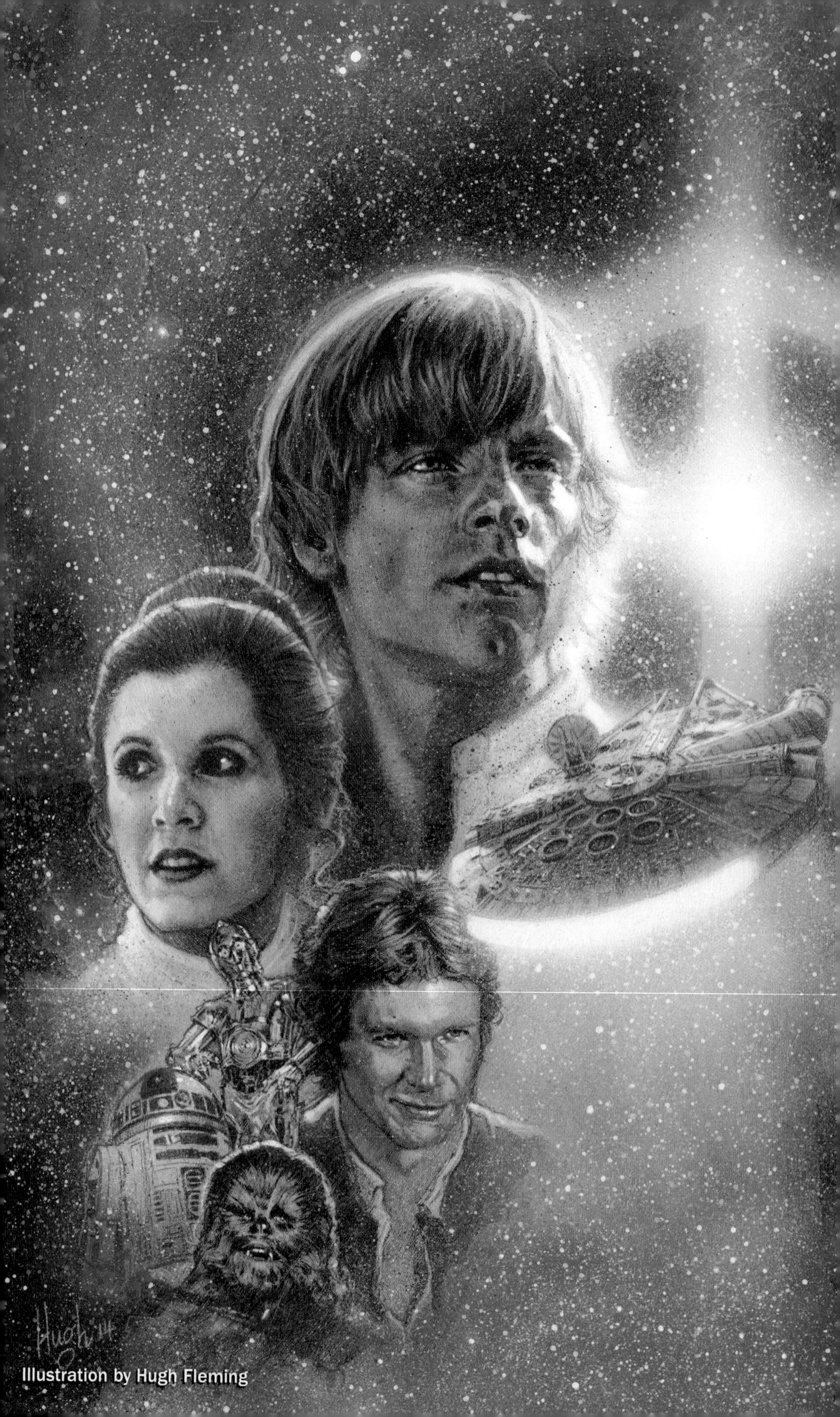
Hugh '14
Illustration by Hugh Fleming

THE REBELLION

FROM THE BATTLE OF YAVIN TO FIVE YEARS AFTER

Open resistance begins to spread across the galaxy in protest of the Empire's tyranny. Rebel groups unite, and the Galactic Civil War begins. This era starts with the Rebel victory that secured the Death Star plans, and ends a year after the death of the Emperor high over the forest moon of Endor. This is the era in which the events in *A New Hope*, *The Empire Strikes Back*, and *Return of the Jedi* take place.

The events in this story take place shortly after the events in *Star Wars:* Episode IV—*A New Hope*.

VOLUME
FOUR | A SHATTERED HOPE

President and Publisher
MIKE RICHARDSON

Collection Designer
RICK DeLUCCO

Editor
RANDY STRADLEY

Assistant Editor
FREDDYE LINS

NEIL HANKERSON . . . . Executive Vice President
TOM WEDDLE . . . . Chief Financial Officer
RANDY STRADLEY . . . . Vice President of Publishing
MICHAEL MARTENS . . . . Vice President of Book Trade Sales
ANITA NELSON . . . . Vice President of Business Affairs
SCOTT ALLIE . . . . Editor in Chief
MATT PARKINSON . . . . Vice President of Marketing
DAVID SCROGGY . . . . Vice President of Product Development
DALE LaFOUNTAIN . . . . Vice President of Information Technology
DARLENE VOGEL . . . . Senior Director of Print, Design, and Production
KEN LIZZI . . . . General Counsel
DAVEY ESTRADA . . . . Editorial Director
CHRIS WARNER . . . . Senior Books Editor
DIANA SCHUTZ . . . . Executive Editor
CARY GRAZZINI . . . . Director of Print and Development
LIA RIBACCHI . . . . Art Director
CARA NIECE . . . . Director of Scheduling
MARK BERNARDI . . . . Director of Digital Publishing

Special thanks to Jennifer Heddle, Leland Chee, Troy Alders, Carol Roeder, Jann Moorhead, and David Anderman at Lucas Licensing.

STAR WARS® VOLUME 4: A SHATTERED HOPE

This volume collects issues #13–#14 and #19–#20 of the comic-book series *Star Wars*, as well as "Star Wars: The Art of the *Bad* Deal" from *Free Comic Book Day 2012*, all from Dark Horse Comics.

Published by Dark Horse Books
A division of Dark Horse Comics, Inc.
10956 SE Main Street
Milwaukie, OR 97222

DarkHorse.com StarWars.com

International Licensing: (503) 905-2377
To find a comics shop in your area, call the Comic Shop Locator Service toll-free at 1-888-266-4226

Library of Congress Cataloging-in-Publication Data

Star wars. Volume 4, A shattered hope.
    pages cm
 "This volume collects issues #13-#14 and #19-#20 of the comic-book series Star Wars, as well as "Star Wars: The Art of the Bad Deal" from Free Comic Book Day 2012, all from Dark Horse Comics"–T.p. verso.
 Summary: ""Darth Vader is on a mission to renew fear and discipline in Imperial ranks. Meanwhile, Han Solo, Chewbacca, Princess Leia, and Luke Skywalker try to locate a Rebel spy in distress"–Provided by publisher.
 ISBN 978-1-61655-554-2 (paperback)
1. Graphic novels. [1. Graphic novels. 2. Science fiction.] I. Wood, Brian, 1972- author. II. Percio, Facundo, illustrator. III. D'Anda, Carlos, illustrator. IV. Whedon, Zack, author. V. Fabbri, Davidé, illustrator. VI. Fleming, Hugh, 1967- illustrator. VII. Title: Shattered hope.

PZ7.7.S723 2014
741.5'973–dc23

                              2014025749

First edition: October 2014
ISBN 978-1-61655-554-2

10 9 8 7 6 5 4 3 2 1
Printed in Canada

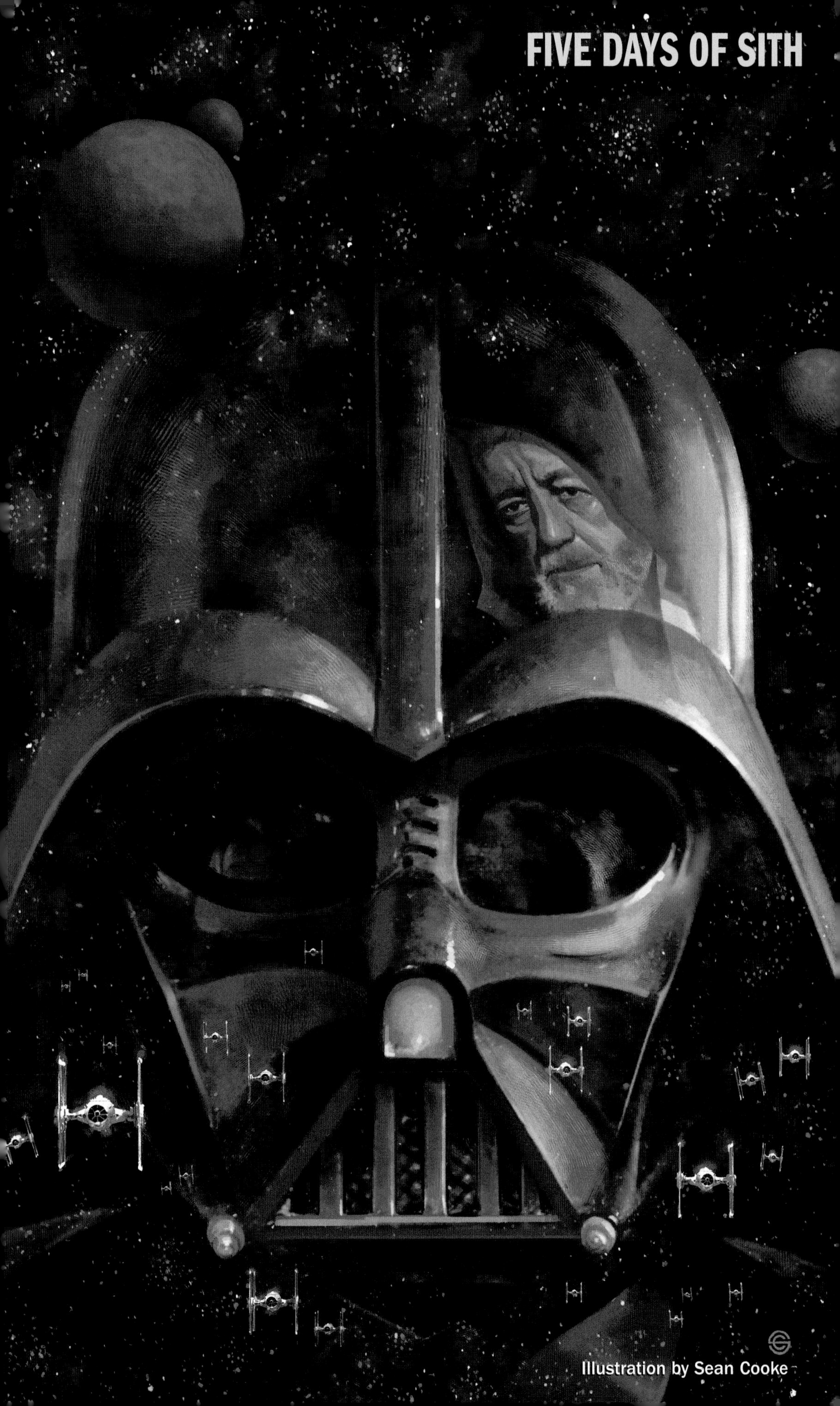
FIVE DAYS OF SITH
Illustration by Sean Cooke

Colonel Bircher, a Rebel spy deeply planted in the Imperial ranks, coordinated an embarrassing defeat for the Star Destroyer *Devastator*—Darth Vader's former flagship. Vader, temporarily diverted by the Emperor to oversee the construction of the second Death Star (as punishment for the destruction of the first one), is determined to get revenge.

But Colonel Bircher is not the only person on Vader's mind. Through Birra Seah, Vader's own spy onboard *Devastator*, he learned of a Rebel prisoner named Luke Skywalker who'd escaped just prior to the Rebels' victory. Now Seah, fearing Vader's wrath has fled.

An elite squad of Stormtroopers has been assembled in secret. Darth Vader is issuing his own orders. A storm of vengeance is coming . . .

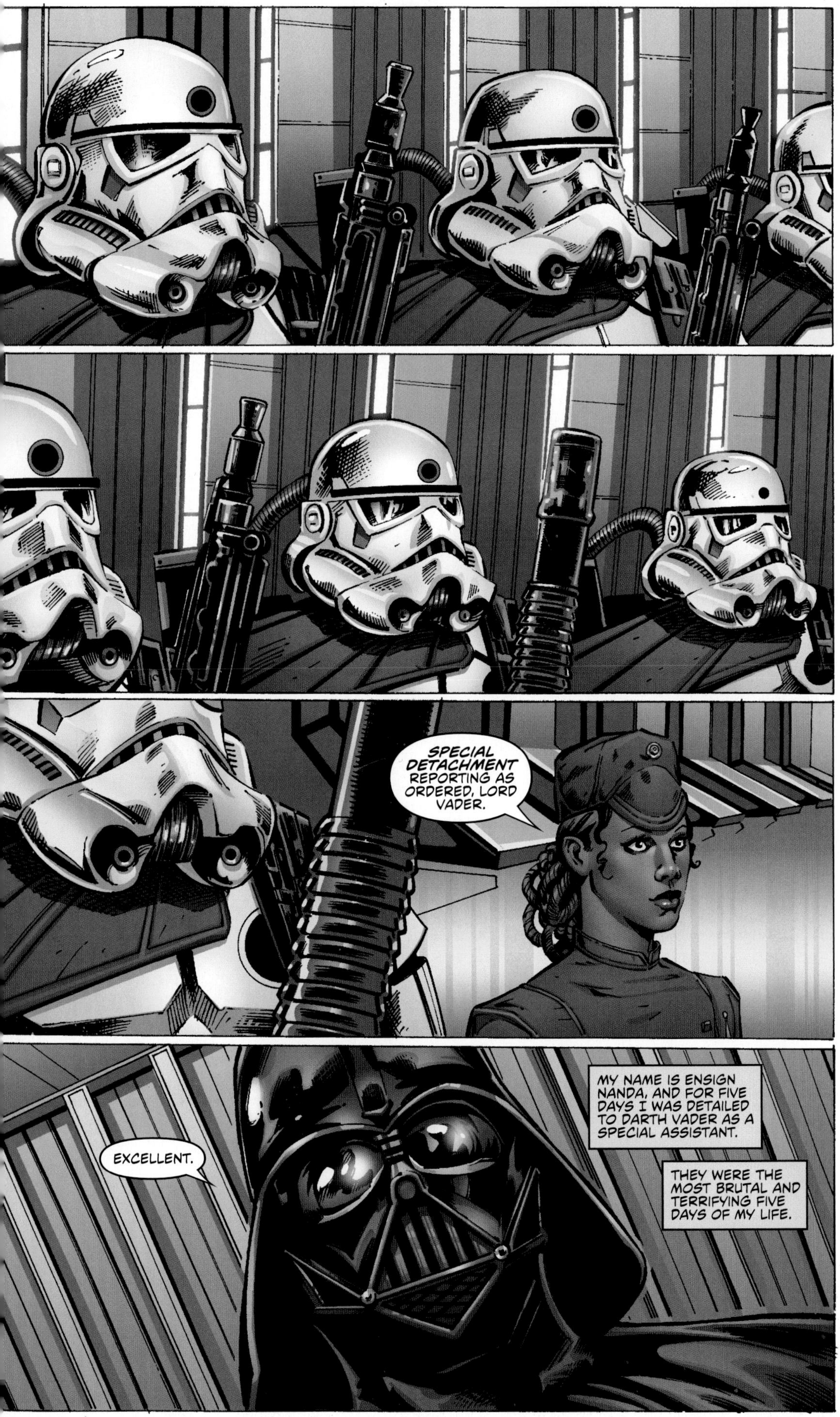
SPECIAL DETACHMENT REPORTING AS ORDERED, LORD VADER.
MY NAME IS ENSIGN NANDA, AND FOR FIVE DAYS I WAS DETAILED TO DARTH VADER AS A SPECIAL ASSISTANT.
EXCELLENT.
THEY WERE THE MOST BRUTAL AND TERRIFYING FIVE DAYS OF MY LIFE.

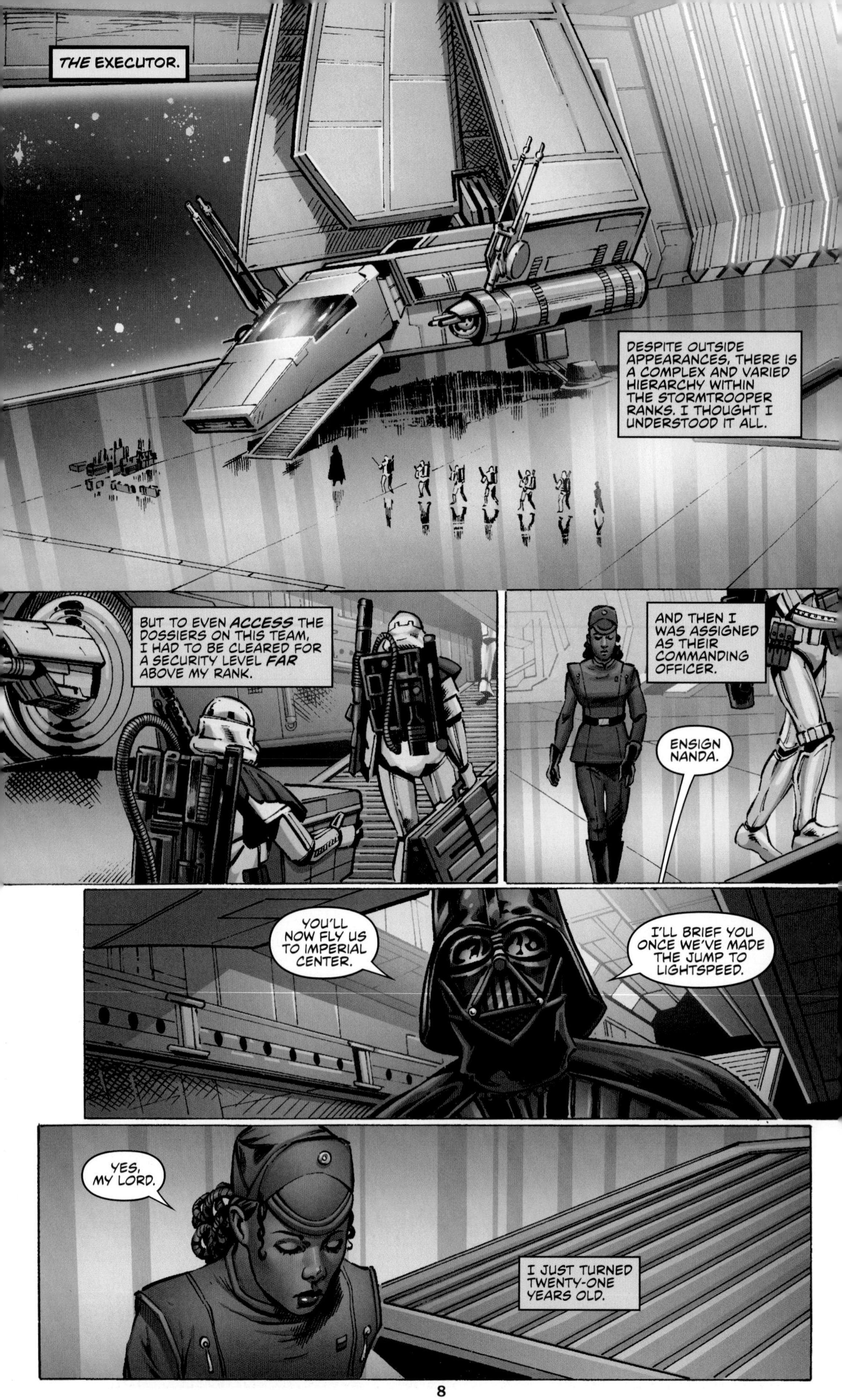
THE EXECUTOR.
DESPITE OUTSIDE APPEARANCES, THERE IS A COMPLEX AND VARIED HIERARCHY WITHIN THE STORMTROOPER RANKS. I THOUGHT I UNDERSTOOD IT ALL.
BUT TO EVEN ACCESS THE DOSSIERS ON THIS TEAM, I HAD TO BE CLEARED FOR A SECURITY LEVEL FAR ABOVE MY RANK.
AND THEN I WAS ASSIGNED AS THEIR COMMANDING OFFICER.
ENSIGN NANDA.
YOU'LL NOW FLY US TO IMPERIAL CENTER.
I'LL BRIEF YOU ONCE WE'VE MADE THE JUMP TO LIGHTSPEED.
YES, MY LORD.
I JUST TURNED TWENTY-ONE YEARS OLD.

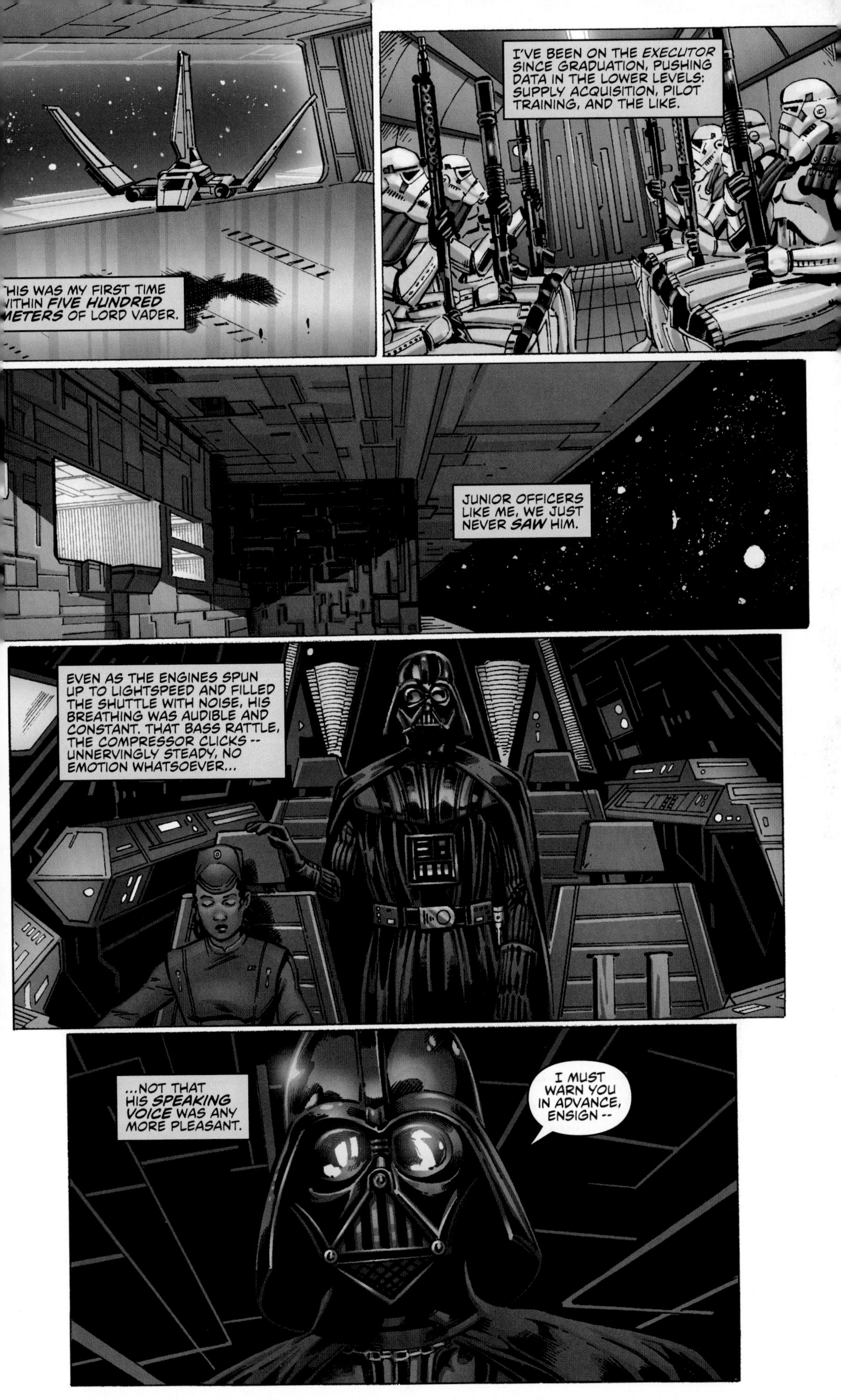

THIS WAS MY FIRST TIME WITHIN FIVE HUNDRED METERS OF LORD VADER.
I'VE BEEN ON THE EXECUTOR SINCE GRADUATION, PUSHING DATA IN THE LOWER LEVELS: SUPPLY ACQUISITION, PILOT TRAINING, AND THE LIKE.
JUNIOR OFFICERS LIKE ME, WE JUST NEVER SAW HIM.
EVEN AS THE ENGINES SPUN UP TO LIGHTSPEED AND FILLED THE SHUTTLE WITH NOISE, HIS BREATHING WAS AUDIBLE AND CONSTANT. THAT BASS RATTLE, THE COMPRESSOR CLICKS -- UNNERVINGLY STEADY, NO EMOTION WHATSOEVER...
...NOT THAT HIS SPEAKING VOICE WAS ANY MORE PLEASANT.
I MUST WARN YOU IN ADVANCE, ENSIGN --

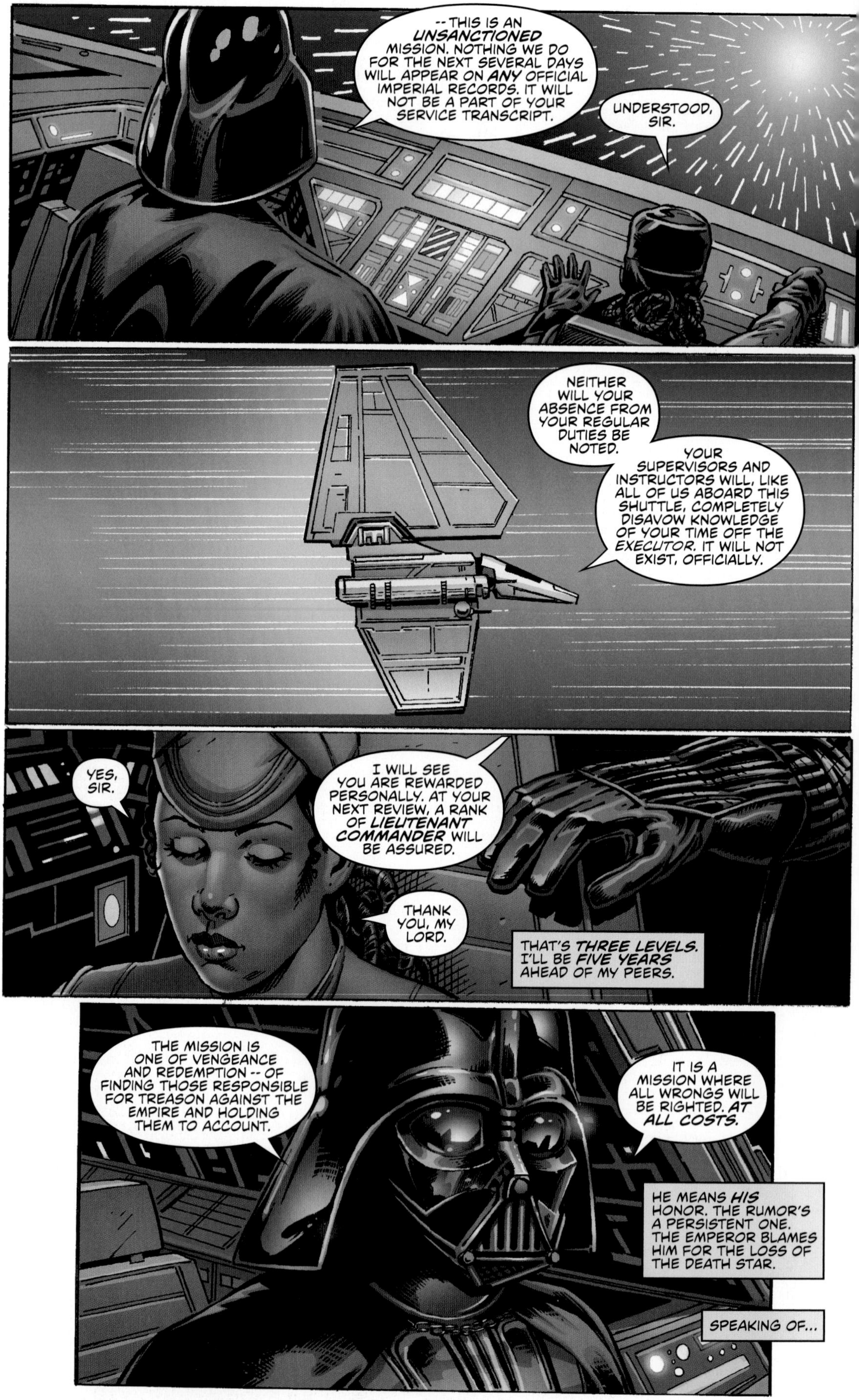
-- THIS IS AN UNSANCTIONED MISSION. NOTHING WE DO FOR THE NEXT SEVERAL DAYS WILL APPEAR ON ANY OFFICIAL IMPERIAL RECORDS. IT WILL NOT BE A PART OF YOUR SERVICE TRANSCRIPT.
UNDERSTOOD, SIR.
NEITHER WILL YOUR ABSENCE FROM YOUR REGULAR DUTIES BE NOTED.
YOUR SUPERVISORS AND INSTRUCTORS WILL, LIKE ALL OF US ABOARD THIS SHUTTLE, COMPLETELY DISAVOW KNOWLEDGE OF YOUR TIME OFF THE EXECUTOR. IT WILL NOT EXIST, OFFICIALLY.
YES, SIR.
I WILL SEE YOU ARE REWARDED PERSONALLY. AT YOUR NEXT REVIEW, A RANK OF LIEUTENANT COMMANDER WILL BE ASSURED.
THANK YOU, MY LORD.
THAT'S THREE LEVELS. I'LL BE FIVE YEARS AHEAD OF MY PEERS.
THE MISSION IS ONE OF VENGEANCE AND REDEMPTION -- OF FINDING THOSE RESPONSIBLE FOR TREASON AGAINST THE EMPIRE AND HOLDING THEM TO ACCOUNT.
IT IS A MISSION WHERE ALL WRONGS WILL BE RIGHTED. AT ALL COSTS.
HE MEANS HIS HONOR. THE RUMOR'S A PERSISTENT ONE. THE EMPEROR BLAMES HIM FOR THE LOSS OF THE DEATH STAR.
SPEAKING OF...

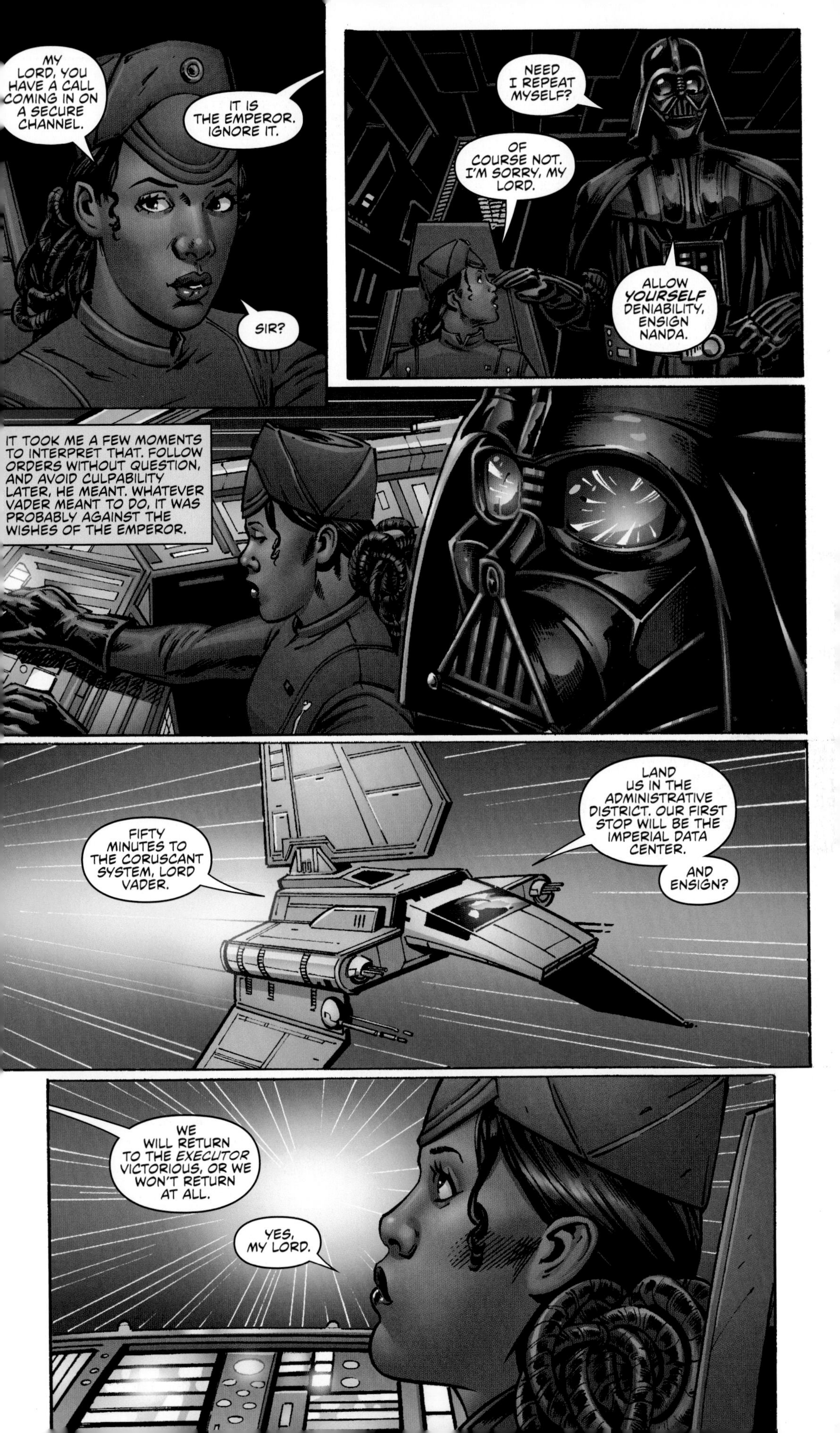
MY LORD, YOU HAVE A CALL COMING IN ON A SECURE CHANNEL.
IT IS THE EMPEROR. IGNORE IT.
SIR?
NEED I REPEAT MYSELF?
OF COURSE NOT. I'M SORRY, MY LORD.
ALLOW *YOURSELF* DENIABILITY, ENSIGN NANDA.
IT TOOK ME A FEW MOMENTS TO INTERPRET THAT. FOLLOW ORDERS WITHOUT QUESTION, AND AVOID CULPABILITY LATER, HE MEANT. WHATEVER VADER MEANT TO DO, IT WAS PROBABLY AGAINST THE WISHES OF THE EMPEROR.
FIFTY MINUTES TO THE CORUSCANT SYSTEM, LORD VADER.
LAND US IN THE ADMINISTRATIVE DISTRICT. OUR FIRST STOP WILL BE THE IMPERIAL DATA CENTER.
AND ENSIGN?
WE WILL RETURN TO THE *EXECUTOR* VICTORIOUS, OR WE WON'T RETURN AT ALL.
YES, MY LORD.

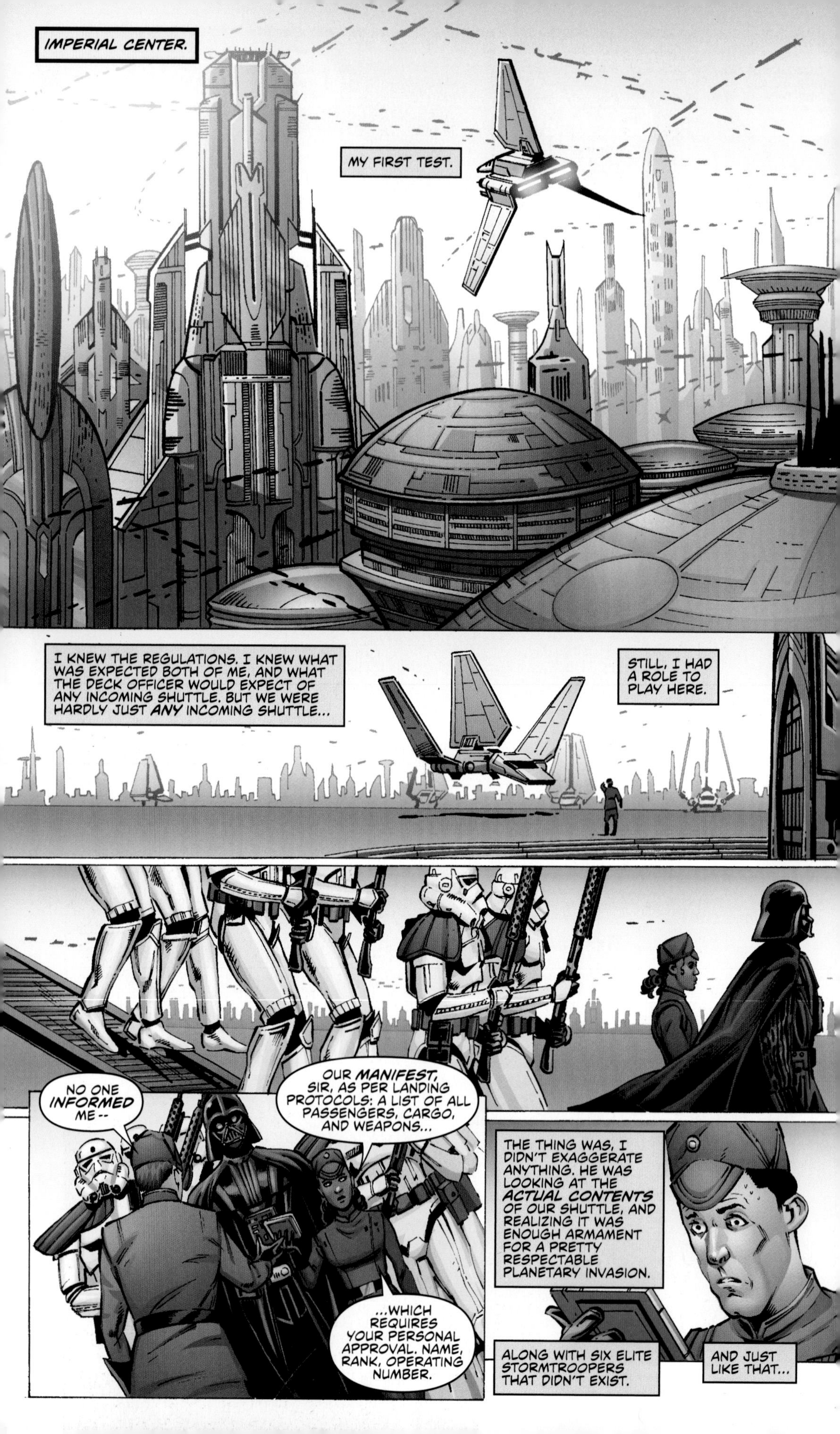
IMPERIAL CENTER.
MY FIRST TEST.
I KNEW THE REGULATIONS. I KNEW WHAT WAS EXPECTED BOTH OF ME, AND WHAT THE DECK OFFICER WOULD EXPECT OF ANY INCOMING SHUTTLE. BUT WE WERE HARDLY JUST ANY INCOMING SHUTTLE...
STILL, I HAD A ROLE TO PLAY HERE.
NO ONE INFORMED ME --
OUR MANIFEST, SIR, AS PER LANDING PROTOCOLS: A LIST OF ALL PASSENGERS, CARGO, AND WEAPONS...
...WHICH REQUIRES YOUR PERSONAL APPROVAL. NAME, RANK, OPERATING NUMBER.
THE THING WAS, I DIDN'T EXAGGERATE ANYTHING. HE WAS LOOKING AT THE ACTUAL CONTENTS OF OUR SHUTTLE, AND REALIZING IT WAS ENOUGH ARMAMENT FOR A PRETTY RESPECTABLE PLANETARY INVASION.
ALONG WITH SIX ELITE STORMTROOPERS THAT DIDN'T EXIST.
AND JUST LIKE THAT...

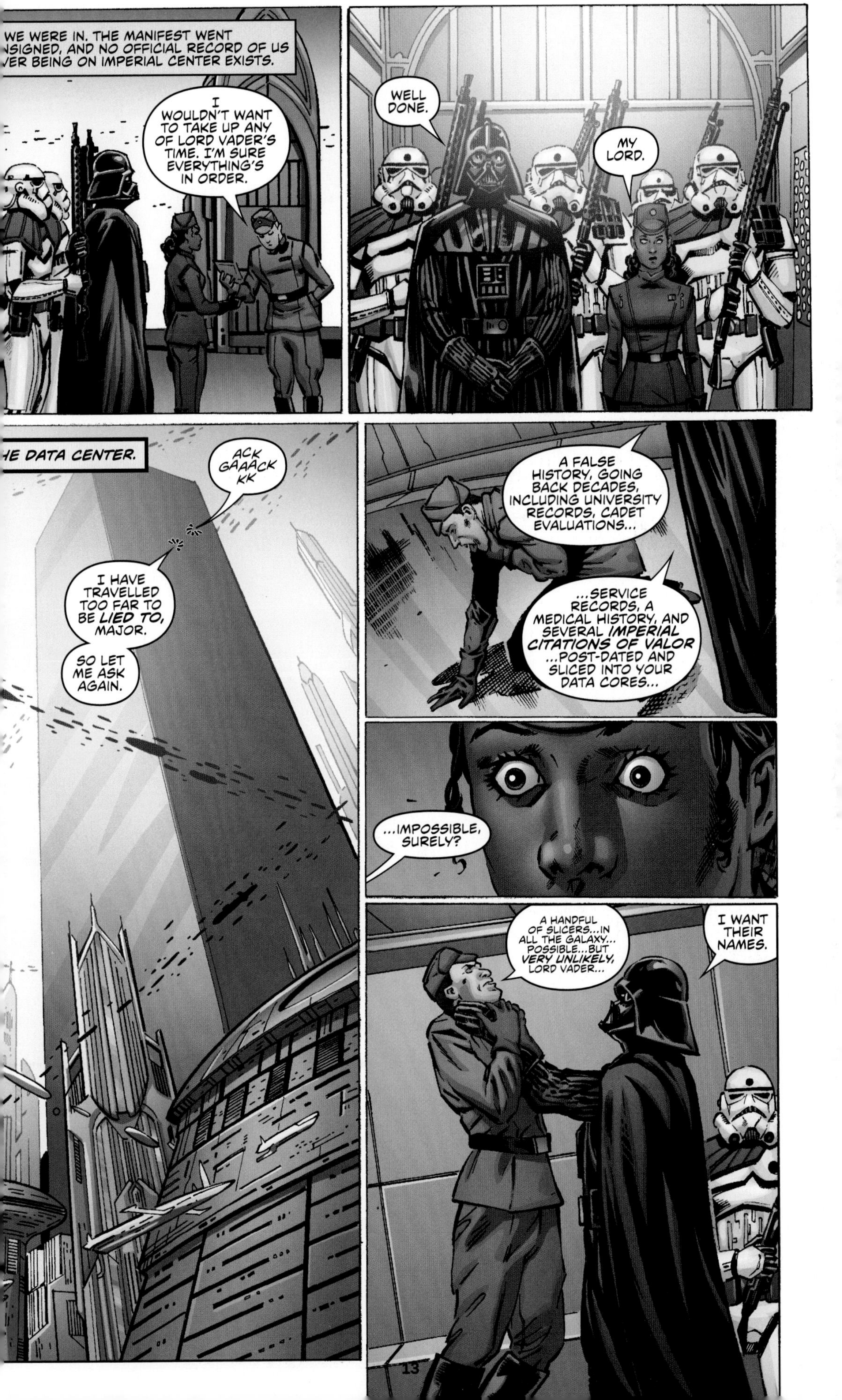
WE WERE IN. THE MANIFEST WENT
NSIGNED, AND NO OFFICIAL RECORD OF US
VER BEING ON IMPERIAL CENTER EXISTS.
I WOULDN'T WANT TO TAKE UP ANY OF LORD VADER'S TIME. I'M SURE EVERYTHING'S IN ORDER.
WELL DONE.
MY LORD.
HE DATA CENTER.
ACK GAAACK KK
I HAVE TRAVELLED TOO FAR TO BE LIED TO, MAJOR.
SO LET ME ASK AGAIN.
A FALSE HISTORY, GOING BACK DECADES, INCLUDING UNIVERSITY RECORDS, CADET EVALUATIONS...
...SERVICE RECORDS, A MEDICAL HISTORY, AND SEVERAL IMPERIAL CITATIONS OF VALOR ...POST-DATED AND SLICED INTO YOUR DATA CORES...
...IMPOSSIBLE, SURELY?
A HANDFUL OF SLICERS...IN ALL THE GALAXY... POSSIBLE...BUT VERY UNLIKELY, LORD VADER...
I WANT THEIR NAMES.

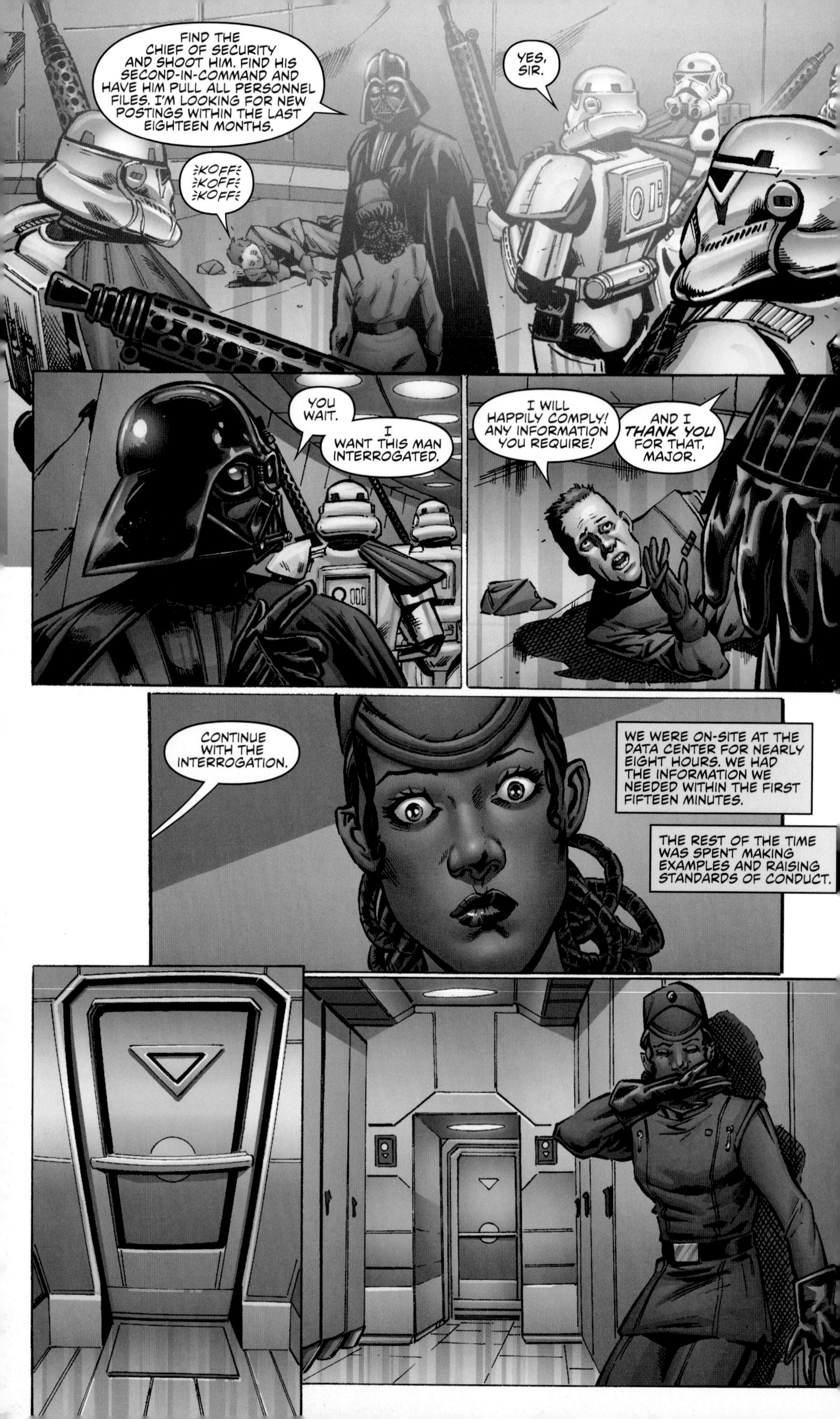
FIND THE CHIEF OF SECURITY AND SHOOT HIM. FIND HIS SECOND-IN-COMMAND AND HAVE HIM PULL ALL PERSONNEL FILES. I'M LOOKING FOR NEW POSTINGS WITHIN THE LAST EIGHTEEN MONTHS.
YES, SIR.
KOFF KOFF KOFF
YOU WAIT.
I WANT THIS MAN INTERROGATED.
I WILL HAPPILY COMPLY! ANY INFORMATION YOU REQUIRE!
AND I THANK YOU FOR THAT, MAJOR.
CONTINUE WITH THE INTERROGATION.
WE WERE ON-SITE AT THE DATA CENTER FOR NEARLY EIGHT HOURS. WE HAD THE INFORMATION WE NEEDED WITHIN THE FIRST FIFTEEN MINUTES.
THE REST OF THE TIME WAS SPENT MAKING EXAMPLES AND RAISING STANDARDS OF CONDUCT.

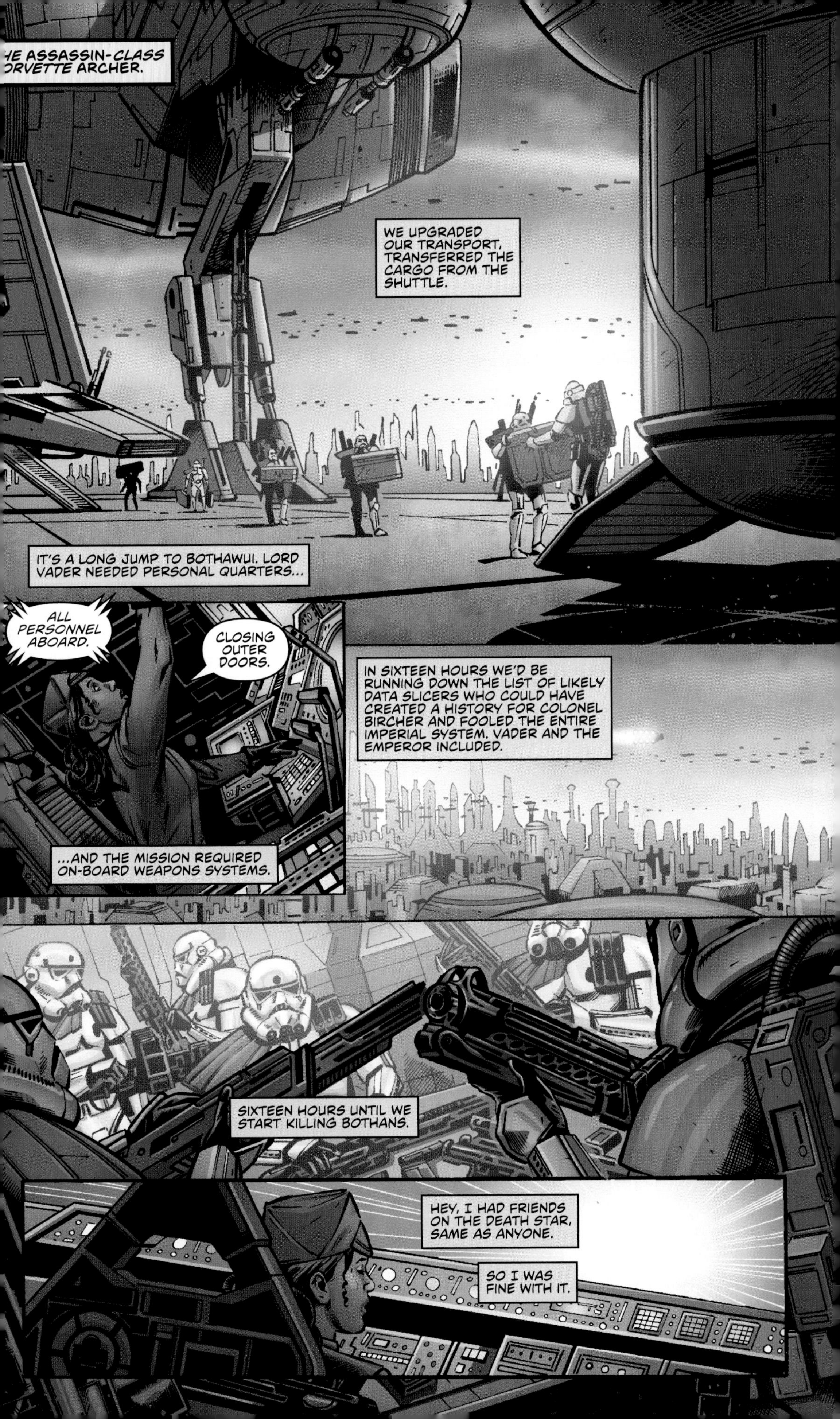

HE ASSASSIN-CLASS ORVETTE ARCHER.
WE UPGRADED OUR TRANSPORT, TRANSFERRED THE CARGO FROM THE SHUTTLE.
IT'S A LONG JUMP TO BOTHAWUI. LORD VADER NEEDED PERSONAL QUARTERS...
ALL PERSONNEL ABOARD.
CLOSING OUTER DOORS.
...AND THE MISSION REQUIRED ON-BOARD WEAPONS SYSTEMS.
IN SIXTEEN HOURS WE'D BE RUNNING DOWN THE LIST OF LIKELY DATA SLICERS WHO COULD HAVE CREATED A HISTORY FOR COLONEL BIRCHER AND FOOLED THE ENTIRE IMPERIAL SYSTEM. VADER AND THE EMPEROR INCLUDED.
SIXTEEN HOURS UNTIL WE START KILLING BOTHANS.
HEY, I HAD FRIENDS ON THE DEATH STAR, SAME AS ANYONE.
SO I WAS FINE WITH IT.

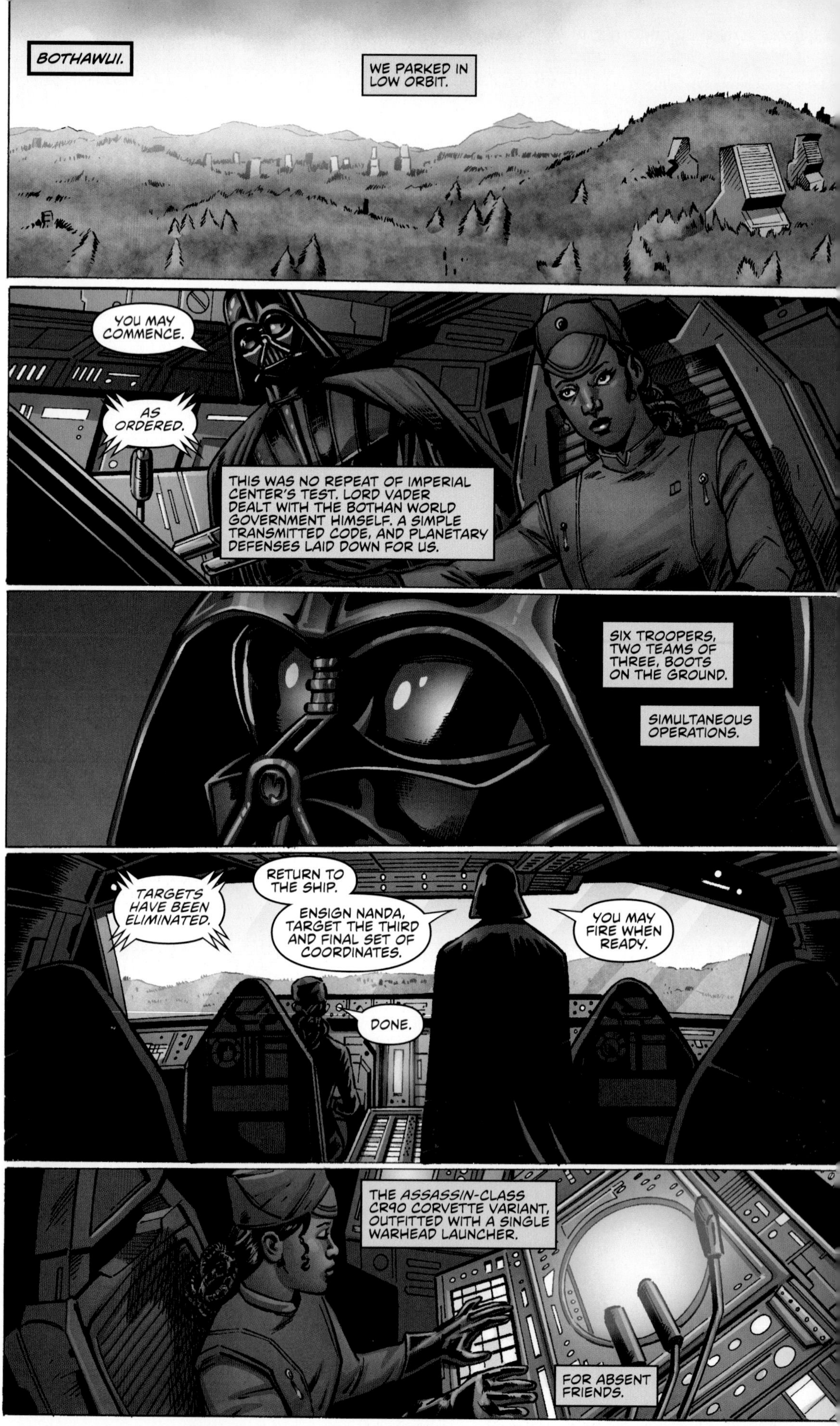
BOTHAWUI.
WE PARKED IN LOW ORBIT.
YOU MAY COMMENCE.
AS ORDERED.
THIS WAS NO REPEAT OF IMPERIAL CENTER'S TEST. LORD VADER DEALT WITH THE BOTHAN WORLD GOVERNMENT HIMSELF. A SIMPLE TRANSMITTED CODE, AND PLANETARY DEFENSES LAID DOWN FOR US.
SIX TROOPERS, TWO TEAMS OF THREE, BOOTS ON THE GROUND.
SIMULTANEOUS OPERATIONS.
TARGETS HAVE BEEN ELIMINATED.
RETURN TO THE SHIP.
ENSIGN NANDA, TARGET THE THIRD AND FINAL SET OF COORDINATES.
DONE.
YOU MAY FIRE WHEN READY.
THE *ASSASSIN*-CLASS CR90 CORVETTE VARIANT, OUTFITTED WITH A SINGLE WARHEAD LAUNCHER.
FOR ABSENT FRIENDS.

I AM FROM NABOO. I DID MY MANDATORY RESERVIST TRAINING. I'M NOT MUCH OF A SOLDIER, BUT I'M FAMILIAR WITH THE EMOTIONS.

THE ADRENALINE HIGH, ALWAYS LAGGING BEHIND THE ACTUAL ACTION. IT KICKS IN MIDWAY THROUGH THE MISSION, AND STAYS WITH YOU LONG AFTER.

LEAVES YOU ON EDGE. UNFULFILLED.

ALL I DID WAS HIT A BUTTON. THESE MEN CONDUCTED HOME INVASIONS, UP-CLOSE MURDER, PROBABLY ARSON TO CLEAN UP. COLLECTIVE PUNISHMENT. THE WRATH OF THE EMPIRE: SUDDEN, UNEXPECTED, AND FULLY OUT OF ALL PROPORTION.

ARE YOU ALL RIGHT?

BACK TO YOUR COCKPIT, LITTLE GIRL.

NEXT STOP -- KUAT.

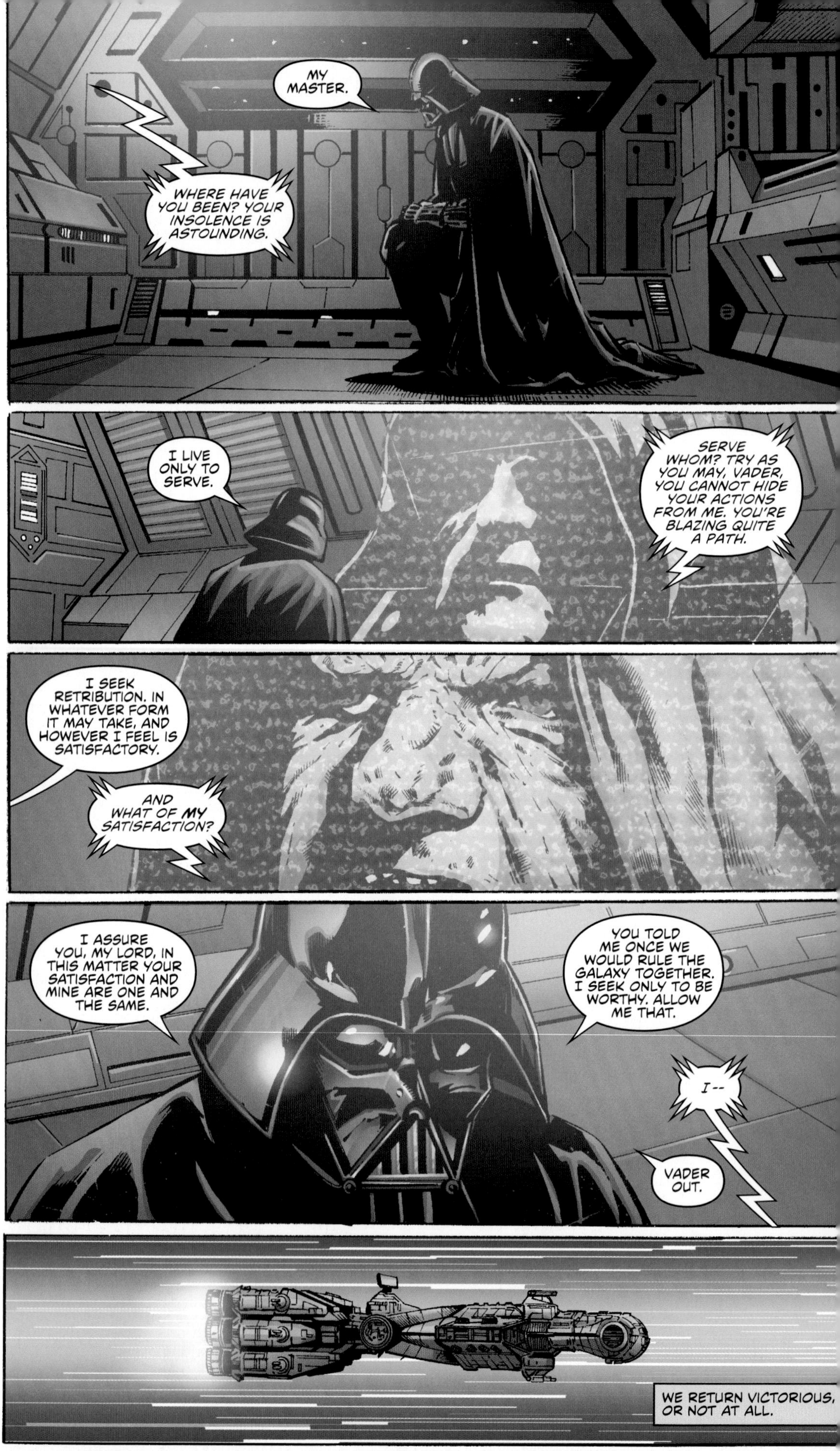
MY MASTER.
WHERE HAVE YOU BEEN? YOUR INSOLENCE IS ASTOUNDING.
I LIVE ONLY TO SERVE.
SERVE WHOM? TRY AS YOU MAY, VADER, YOU CANNOT HIDE YOUR ACTIONS FROM ME. YOU'RE BLAZING QUITE A PATH.
I SEEK RETRIBUTION. IN WHATEVER FORM IT MAY TAKE, AND HOWEVER I FEEL IS SATISFACTORY.
AND WHAT OF MY SATISFACTION?
I ASSURE YOU, MY LORD, IN THIS MATTER YOUR SATISFACTION AND MINE ARE ONE AND THE SAME.
YOU TOLD ME ONCE WE WOULD RULE THE GALAXY TOGETHER. I SEEK ONLY TO BE WORTHY. ALLOW ME THAT.
I --
VADER OUT.
WE RETURN VICTORIOUS, OR NOT AT ALL.

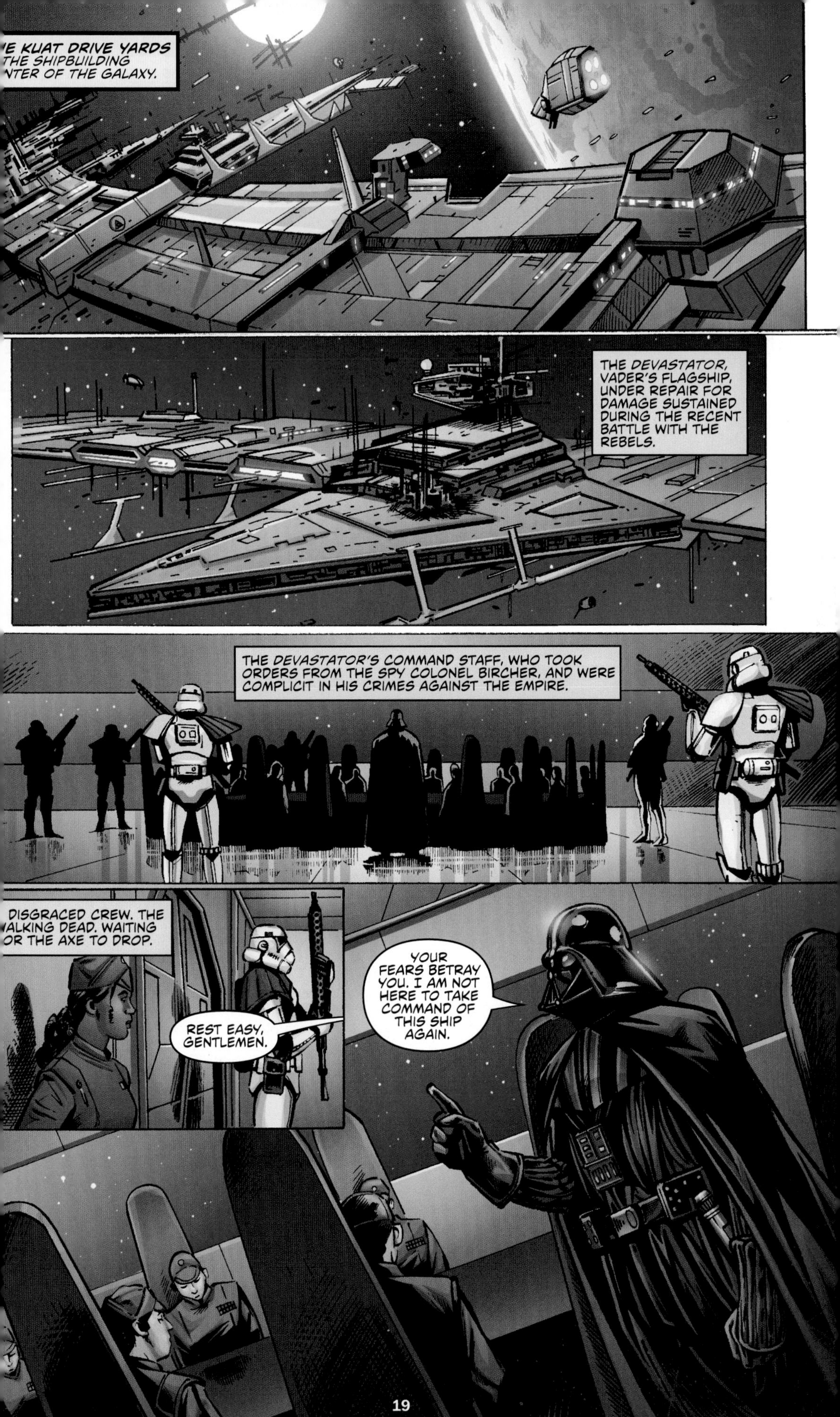

E KUAT DRIVE YARDS
THE SHIPBUILDING
NTER OF THE GALAXY.
THE *DEVASTATOR*, VADER'S FLAGSHIP, UNDER REPAIR FOR DAMAGE SUSTAINED DURING THE RECENT BATTLE WITH THE REBELS.
THE *DEVASTATOR'S* COMMAND STAFF, WHO TOOK ORDERS FROM THE SPY COLONEL BIRCHER, AND WERE COMPLICIT IN HIS CRIMES AGAINST THE EMPIRE.
DISGRACED CREW. THE
ALKING DEAD. WAITING
OR THE AXE TO DROP.
REST EASY, GENTLEMEN.
YOUR FEARS BETRAY YOU. I AM NOT HERE TO TAKE COMMAND OF THIS SHIP AGAIN.

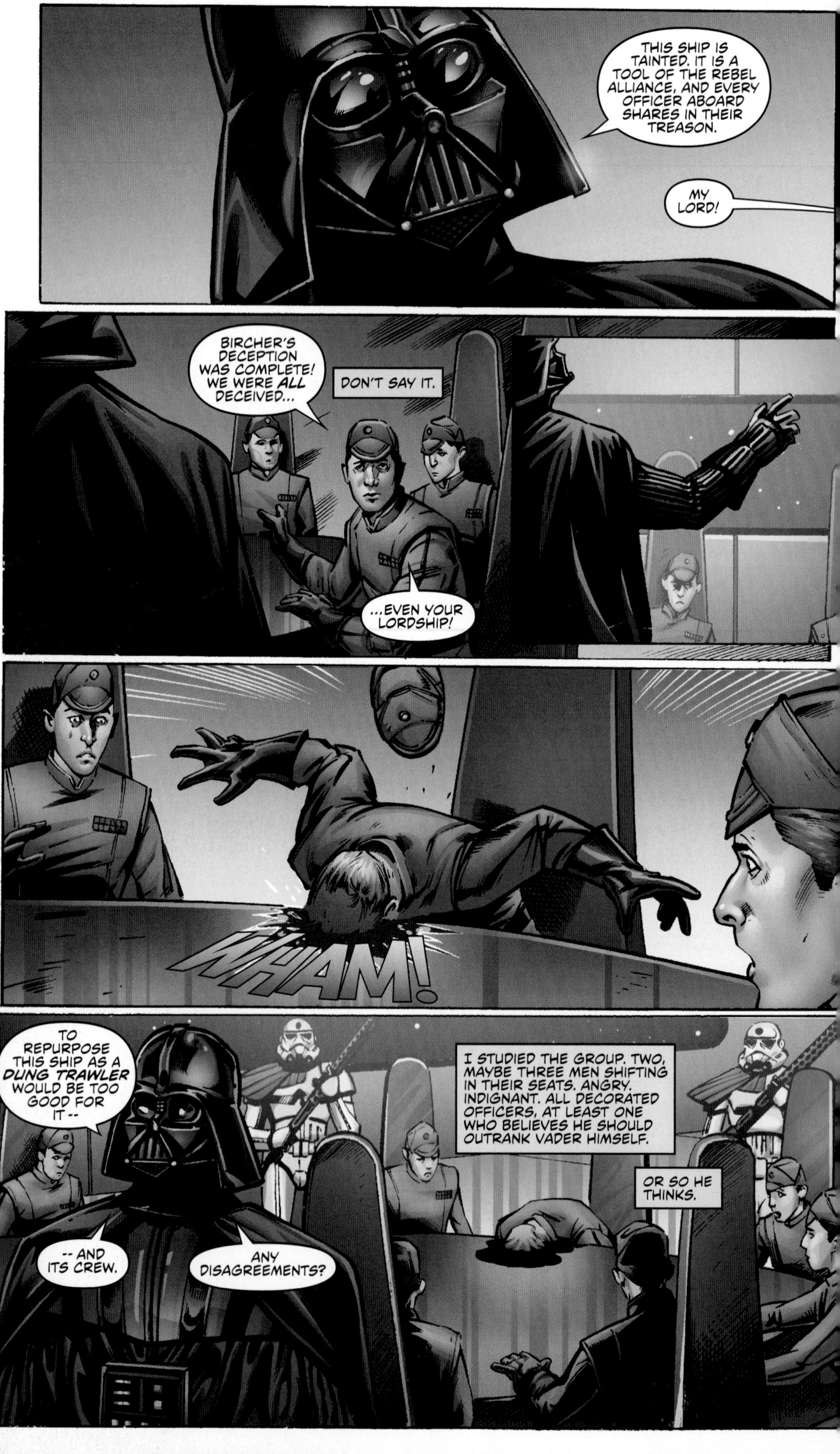
THIS SHIP IS TAINTED. IT IS A TOOL OF THE REBEL ALLIANCE, AND EVERY OFFICER ABOARD SHARES IN THEIR TREASON.
MY LORD!
BIRCHER'S DECEPTION WAS COMPLETE! WE WERE ALL DECEIVED...
DON'T SAY IT.
...EVEN YOUR LORDSHIP!
WHAM!
TO REPURPOSE THIS SHIP AS A DUNG TRAWLER WOULD BE TOO GOOD FOR IT --
I STUDIED THE GROUP. TWO, MAYBE THREE MEN SHIFTING IN THEIR SEATS. ANGRY. INDIGNANT. ALL DECORATED OFFICERS, AT LEAST ONE WHO BELIEVES HE SHOULD OUTRANK VADER HIMSELF.
OR SO HE THINKS.
-- AND ITS CREW.
ANY DISAGREEMENTS?

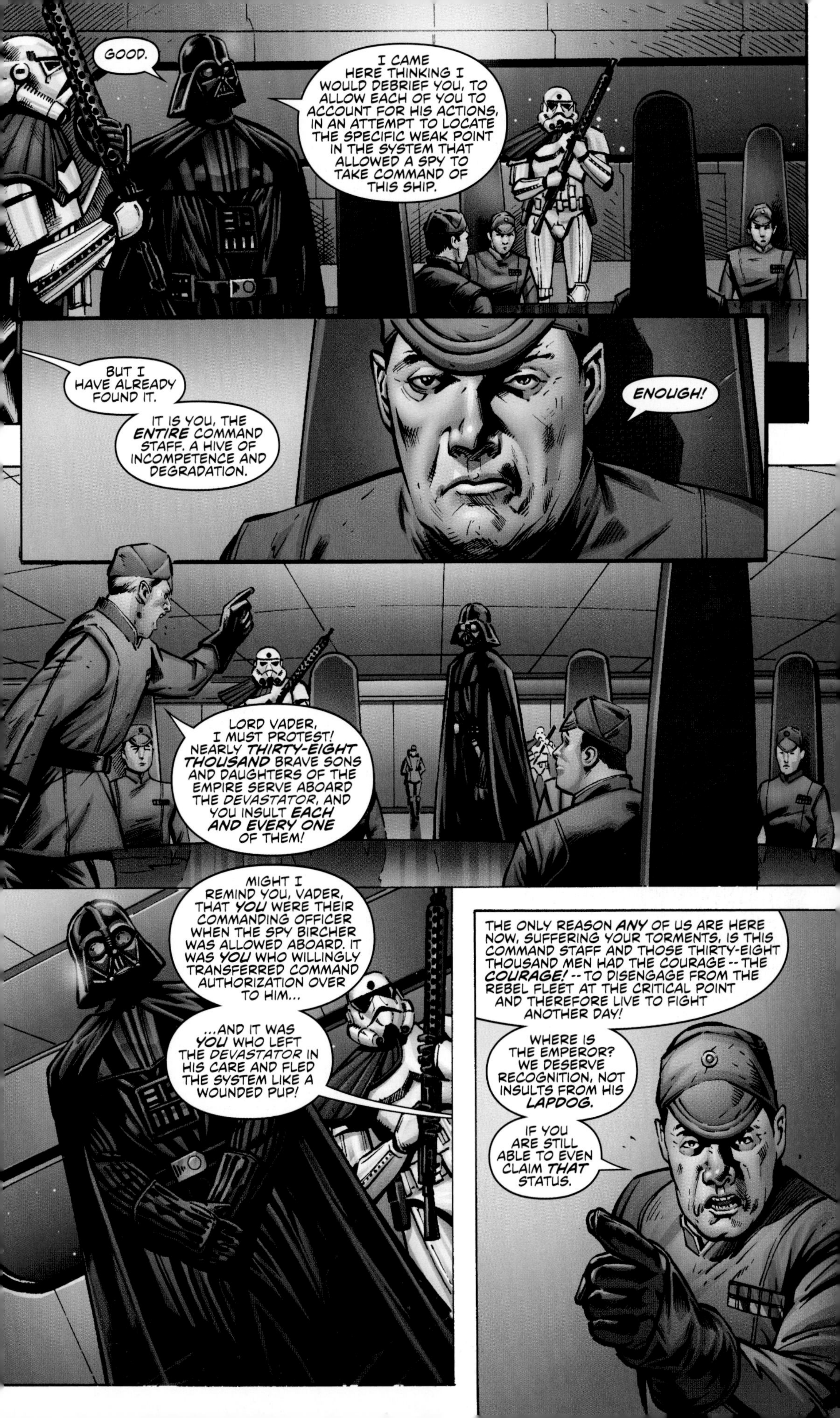
GOOD.
I CAME HERE THINKING I WOULD DEBRIEF YOU, TO ALLOW EACH OF YOU TO ACCOUNT FOR HIS ACTIONS, IN AN ATTEMPT TO LOCATE THE SPECIFIC WEAK POINT IN THE SYSTEM THAT ALLOWED A SPY TO TAKE COMMAND OF THIS SHIP.
BUT I HAVE ALREADY FOUND IT.
IT IS YOU, THE *ENTIRE* COMMAND STAFF. A HIVE OF INCOMPETENCE AND DEGRADATION.
ENOUGH!
LORD VADER, I MUST PROTEST! NEARLY *THIRTY-EIGHT THOUSAND* BRAVE SONS AND DAUGHTERS OF THE EMPIRE SERVE ABOARD THE *DEVASTATOR*, AND YOU INSULT *EACH AND EVERY ONE* OF THEM!
MIGHT I REMIND YOU, VADER, THAT *YOU* WERE THEIR COMMANDING OFFICER WHEN THE SPY BIRCHER WAS ALLOWED ABOARD. IT WAS *YOU* WHO WILLINGLY TRANSFERRED COMMAND AUTHORIZATION OVER TO HIM...
...AND IT WAS *YOU* WHO LEFT THE *DEVASTATOR* IN HIS CARE AND FLED THE SYSTEM LIKE A WOUNDED PUP!
THE ONLY REASON *ANY* OF US ARE HERE NOW, SUFFERING YOUR TORMENTS, IS THIS COMMAND STAFF AND THOSE THIRTY-EIGHT THOUSAND MEN HAD THE COURAGE -- THE *COURAGE!* -- TO DISENGAGE FROM THE REBEL FLEET AT THE CRITICAL POINT AND THEREFORE LIVE TO FIGHT ANOTHER DAY!
WHERE IS THE EMPEROR? WE DESERVE RECOGNITION, NOT INSULTS FROM HIS *LAPDOG.*
IF YOU ARE STILL ABLE TO EVEN CLAIM *THAT* STATUS.

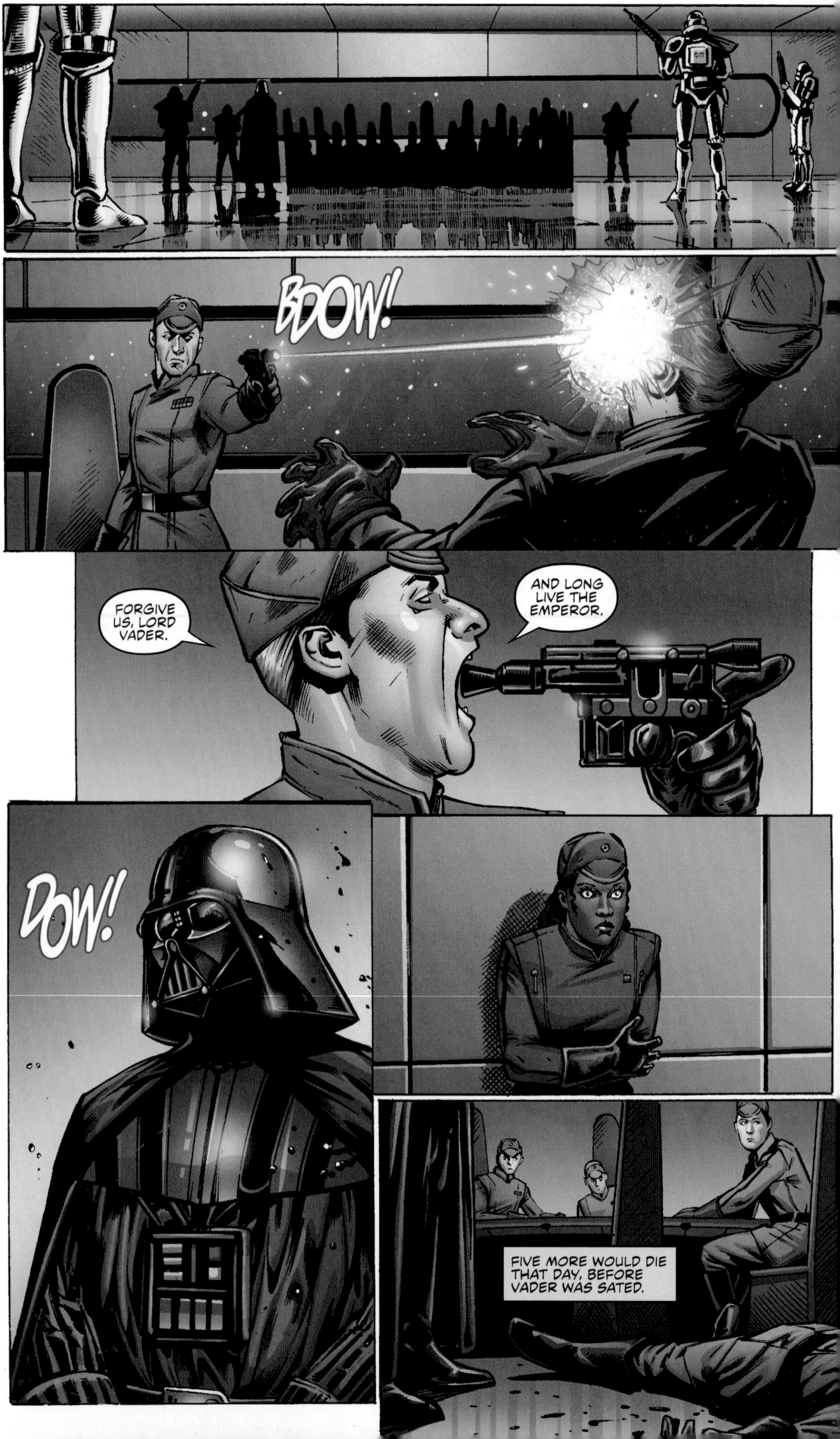
BDOW!
FORGIVE US, LORD VADER.
AND LONG LIVE THE EMPEROR.
DOW!
FIVE MORE WOULD DIE THAT DAY, BEFORE VADER WAS SATED.

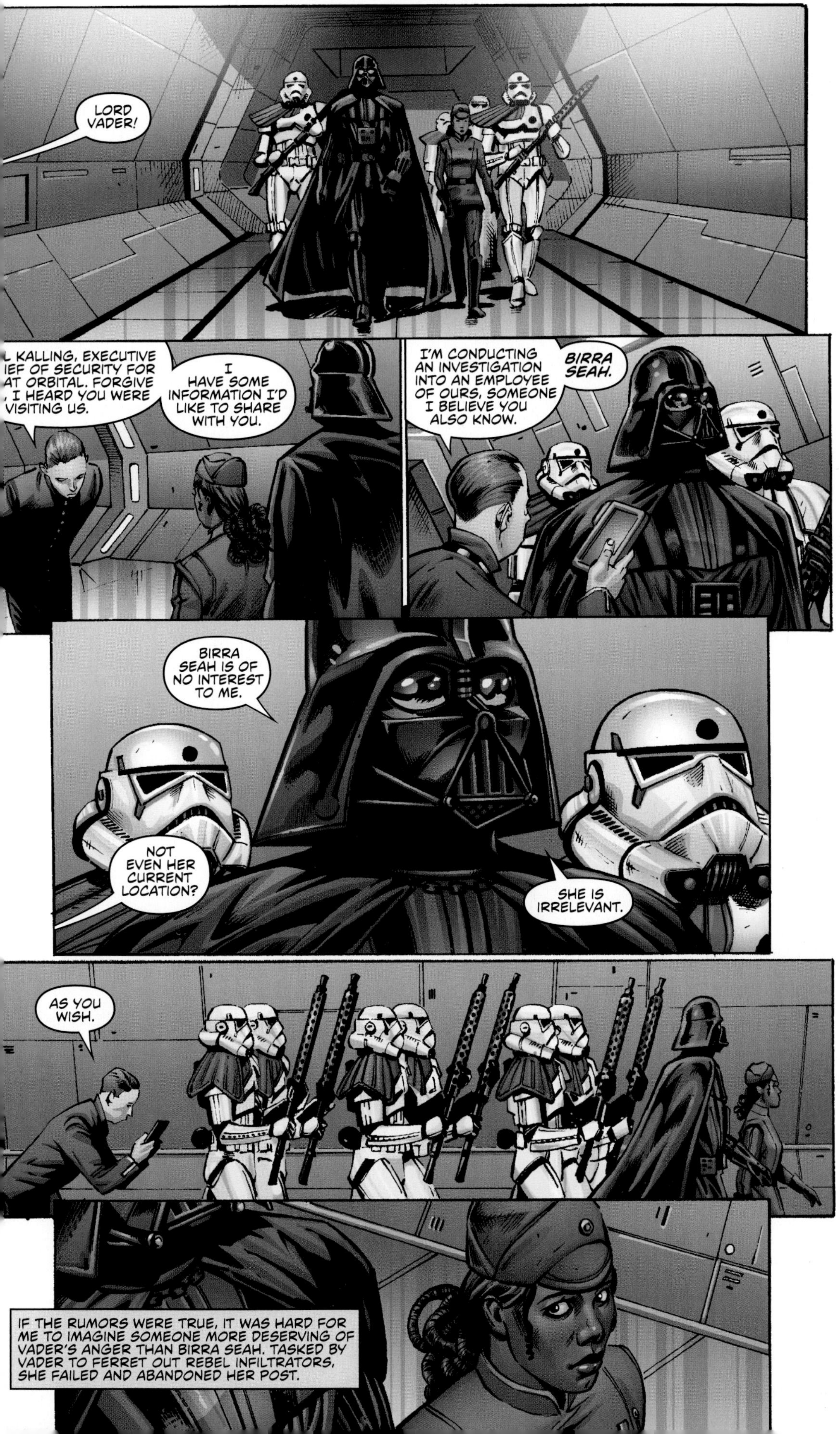
LORD VADER!
L KALLING, EXECUTIVE IEF OF SECURITY FOR AT ORBITAL. FORGIVE , I HEARD YOU WERE VISITING US.
I HAVE SOME INFORMATION I'D LIKE TO SHARE WITH YOU.
I'M CONDUCTING AN INVESTIGATION INTO AN EMPLOYEE OF OURS, SOMEONE I BELIEVE YOU ALSO KNOW.
BIRRA SEAH.
BIRRA SEAH IS OF NO INTEREST TO ME.
NOT EVEN HER CURRENT LOCATION?
SHE IS IRRELEVANT.
AS YOU WISH.
IF THE RUMORS WERE TRUE, IT WAS HARD FOR ME TO IMAGINE SOMEONE MORE DESERVING OF VADER'S ANGER THAN BIRRA SEAH. TASKED BY VADER TO FERRET OUT REBEL INFILTRATORS, SHE FAILED AND ABANDONED HER POST.

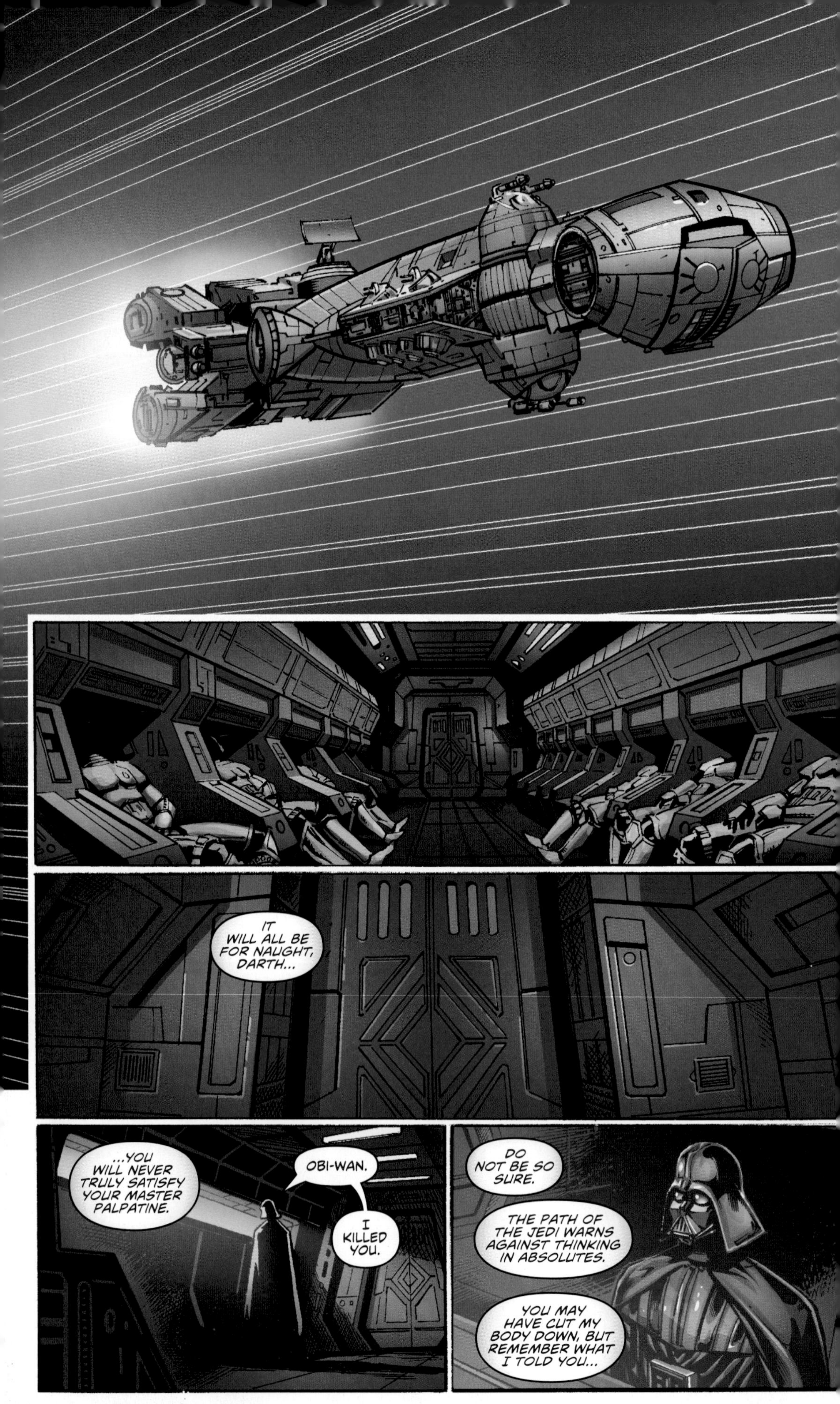
IT WILL ALL BE FOR NAUGHT, DARTH...
...YOU WILL NEVER TRULY SATISFY YOUR MASTER PALPATINE.
OBI-WAN.
I KILLED YOU.
DO NOT BE SO SURE.
THE PATH OF THE JEDI WARNS AGAINST THINKING IN ABSOLUTES.
YOU MAY HAVE CUT MY BODY DOWN, BUT REMEMBER WHAT I TOLD YOU...

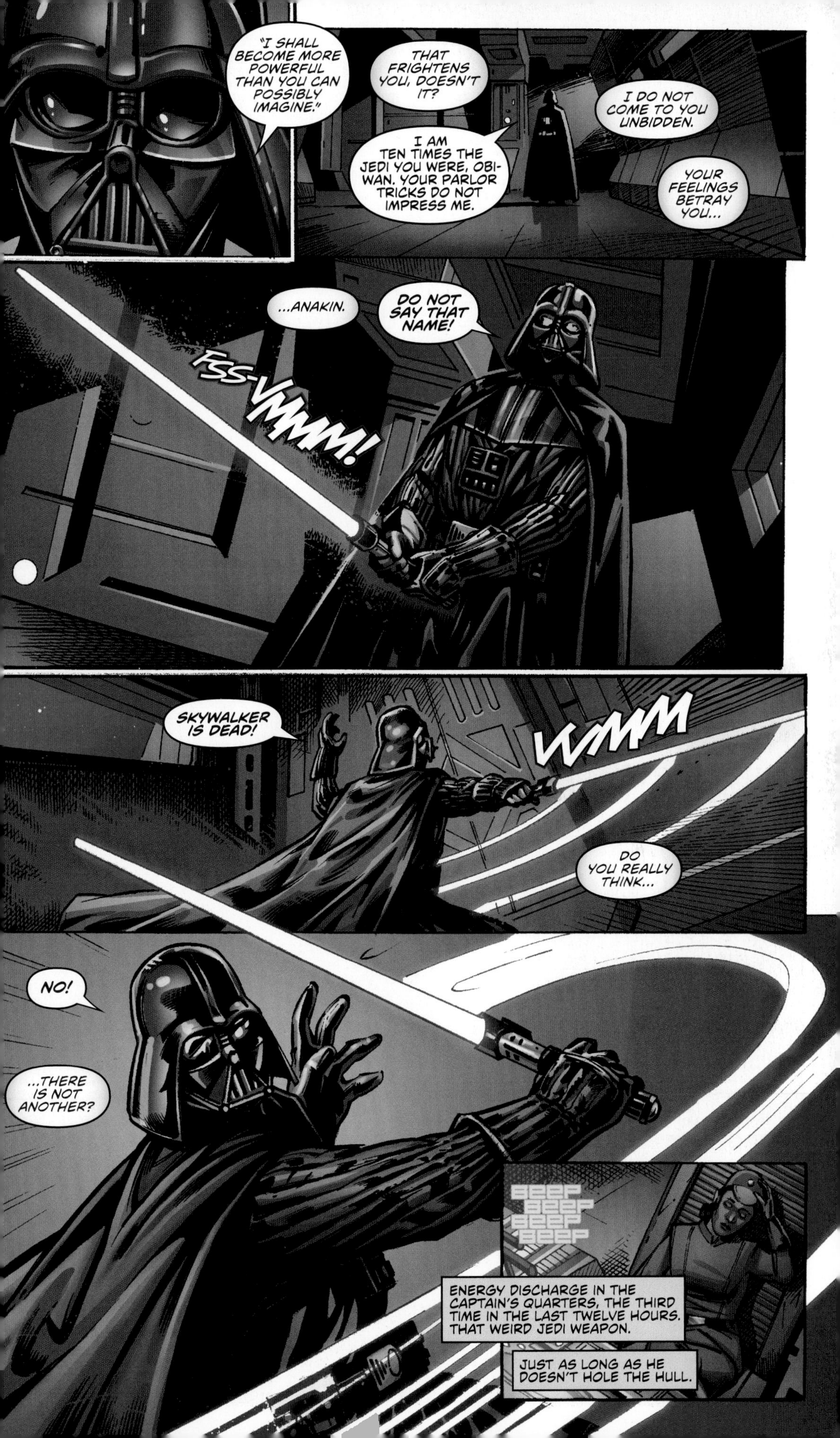
"I SHALL BECOME MORE POWERFUL THAN YOU CAN POSSIBLY IMAGINE."
THAT FRIGHTENS YOU, DOESN'T IT?
I AM TEN TIMES THE JEDI YOU WERE, OBI-WAN. YOUR PARLOR TRICKS DO NOT IMPRESS ME.
I DO NOT COME TO YOU UNBIDDEN.
YOUR FEELINGS BETRAY YOU...
...ANAKIN.
DO NOT SAY THAT NAME!
FSS-VMMMM!
SKYWALKER IS DEAD!
VVMM
DO YOU REALLY THINK...
NO!
...THERE IS NOT ANOTHER?
BEEP BEEP BEEP BEEP
ENERGY DISCHARGE IN THE CAPTAIN'S QUARTERS, THE THIRD TIME IN THE LAST TWELVE HOURS. THAT WEIRD JEDI WEAPON.
JUST AS LONG AS HE DOESN'T HOLE THE HULL.

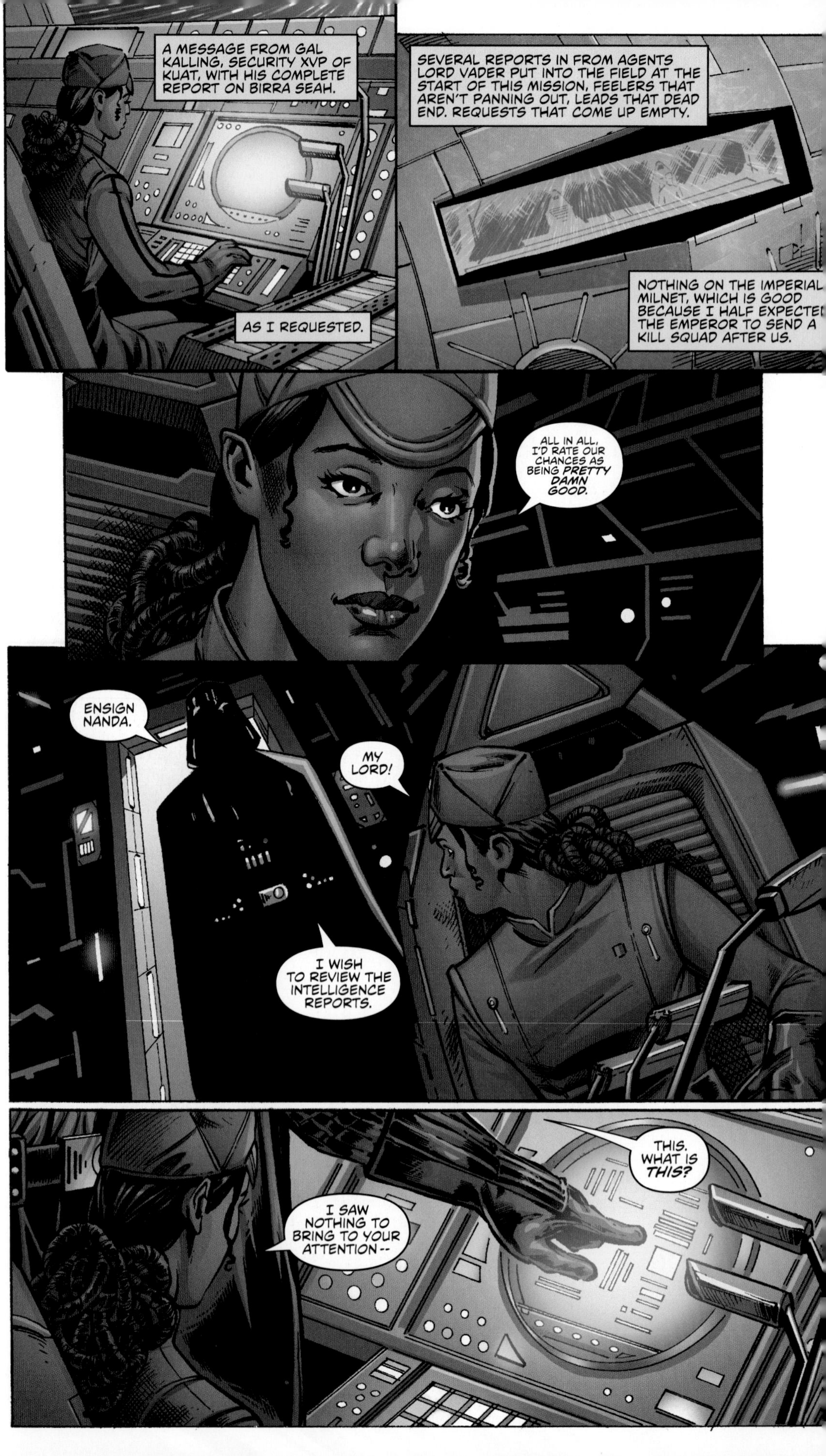
A MESSAGE FROM GAL KALLING, SECURITY XVP OF KUAT, WITH HIS COMPLETE REPORT ON BIRRA SEAH.
AS I REQUESTED.
SEVERAL REPORTS IN FROM AGENTS LORD VADER PUT INTO THE FIELD AT THE START OF THIS MISSION. FEELERS THAT AREN'T PANNING OUT, LEADS THAT DEAD END. REQUESTS THAT COME UP EMPTY.
NOTHING ON THE IMPERIAL MILNET, WHICH IS GOOD BECAUSE I HALF EXPECTED THE EMPEROR TO SEND A KILL SQUAD AFTER US.
ALL IN ALL, I'D RATE OUR CHANCES AS BEING *PRETTY DAMN* GOOD.
ENSIGN NANDA.
MY LORD!
I WISH TO REVIEW THE INTELLIGENCE REPORTS.
THIS. WHAT IS *THIS?*
I SAW NOTHING TO BRING TO YOUR ATTENTION --

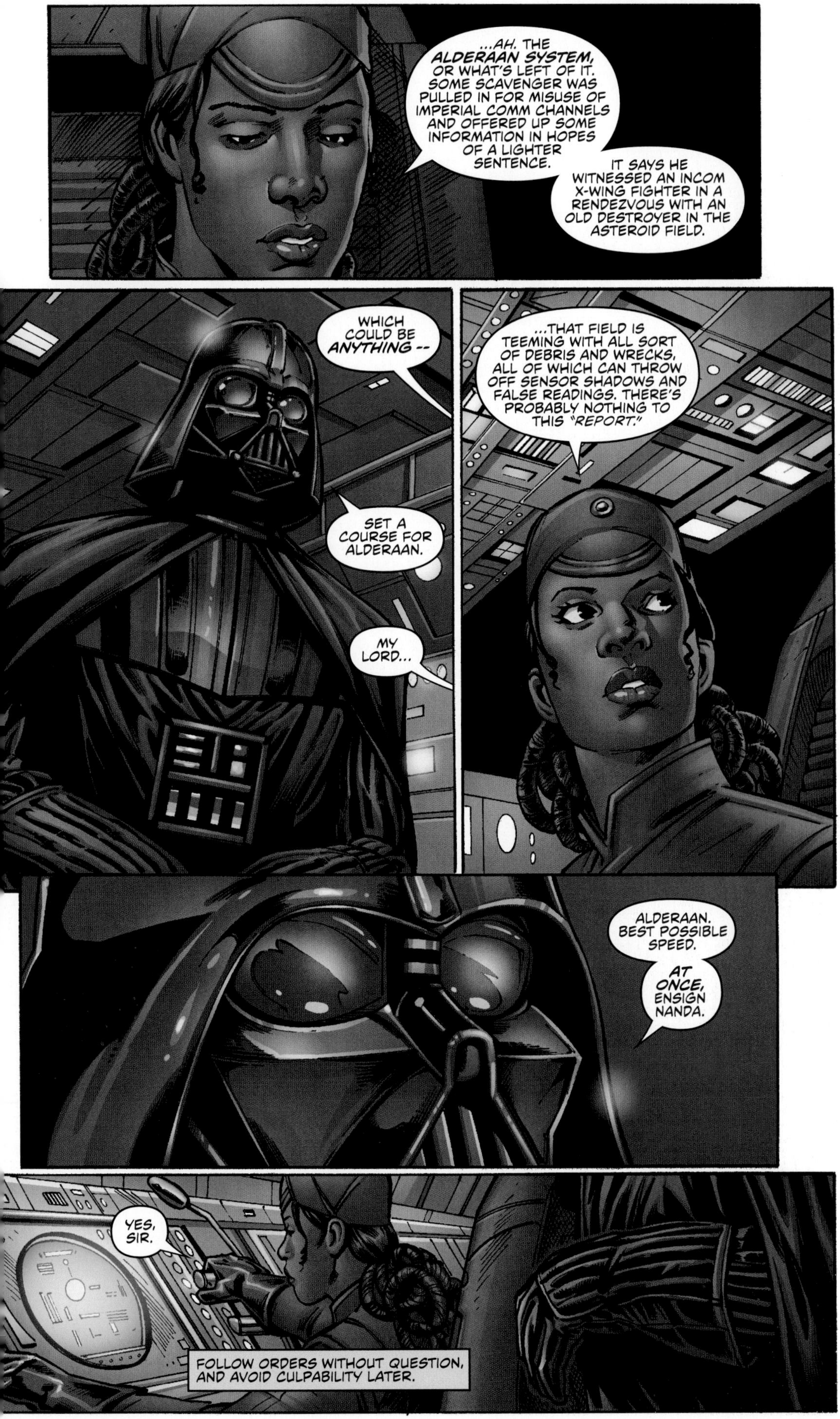
...AH. THE ALDERAAN SYSTEM, OR WHAT'S LEFT OF IT. SOME SCAVENGER WAS PULLED IN FOR MISUSE OF IMPERIAL COMM CHANNELS AND OFFERED UP SOME INFORMATION IN HOPES OF A LIGHTER SENTENCE.
IT SAYS HE WITNESSED AN INCOM X-WING FIGHTER IN A RENDEZVOUS WITH AN OLD DESTROYER IN THE ASTEROID FIELD.
WHICH COULD BE ANYTHING --
...THAT FIELD IS TEEMING WITH ALL SORT OF DEBRIS AND WRECKS, ALL OF WHICH CAN THROW OFF SENSOR SHADOWS AND FALSE READINGS. THERE'S PROBABLY NOTHING TO THIS "REPORT."
SET A COURSE FOR ALDERAAN.
MY LORD...
ALDERAAN. BEST POSSIBLE SPEED.
AT ONCE, ENSIGN NANDA.
YES, SIR.
FOLLOW ORDERS WITHOUT QUESTION, AND AVOID CULPABILITY LATER.

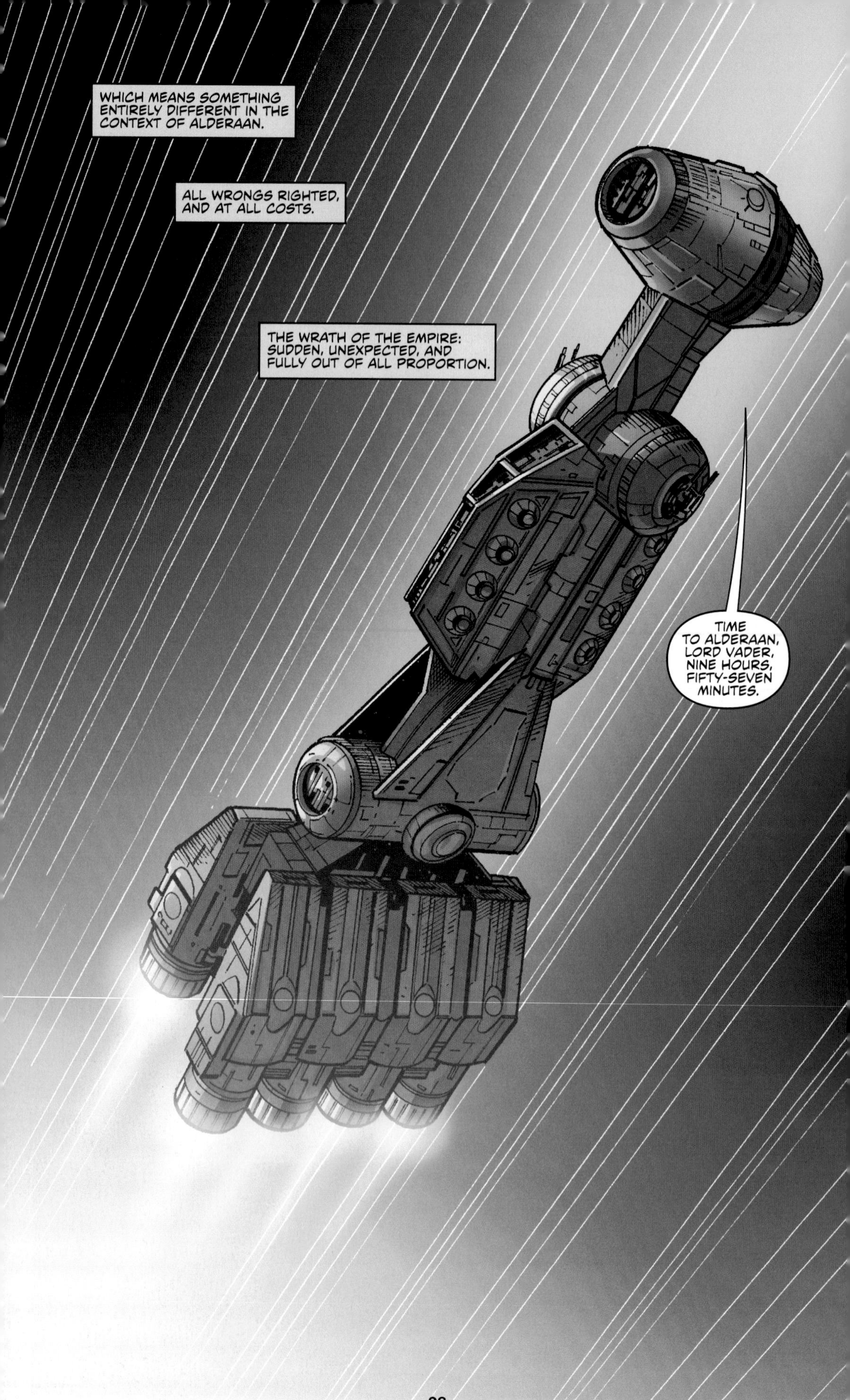
WHICH MEANS SOMETHING ENTIRELY DIFFERENT IN THE CONTEXT OF ALDERAAN.
ALL WRONGS RIGHTED, AND AT ALL COSTS.
THE WRATH OF THE EMPIRE: SUDDEN, UNEXPECTED, AND FULLY OUT OF ALL PROPORTION.
TIME TO ALDERAAN, LORD VADER, NINE HOURS, FIFTY-SEVEN MINUTES.

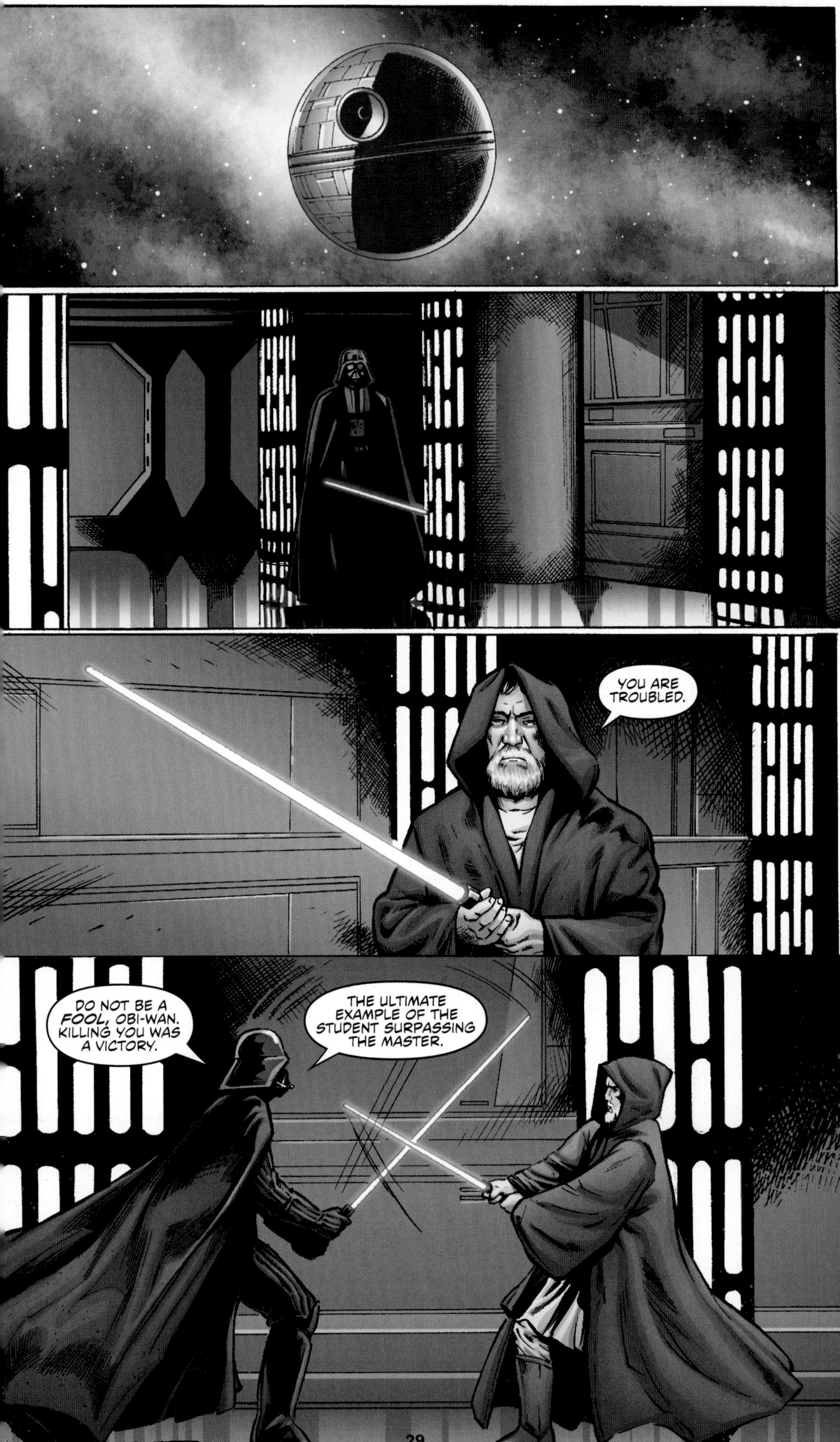
YOU ARE TROUBLED.
DO NOT BE A FOOL, OBI-WAN. KILLING YOU WAS A VICTORY.
THE ULTIMATE EXAMPLE OF THE STUDENT SURPASSING THE MASTER.

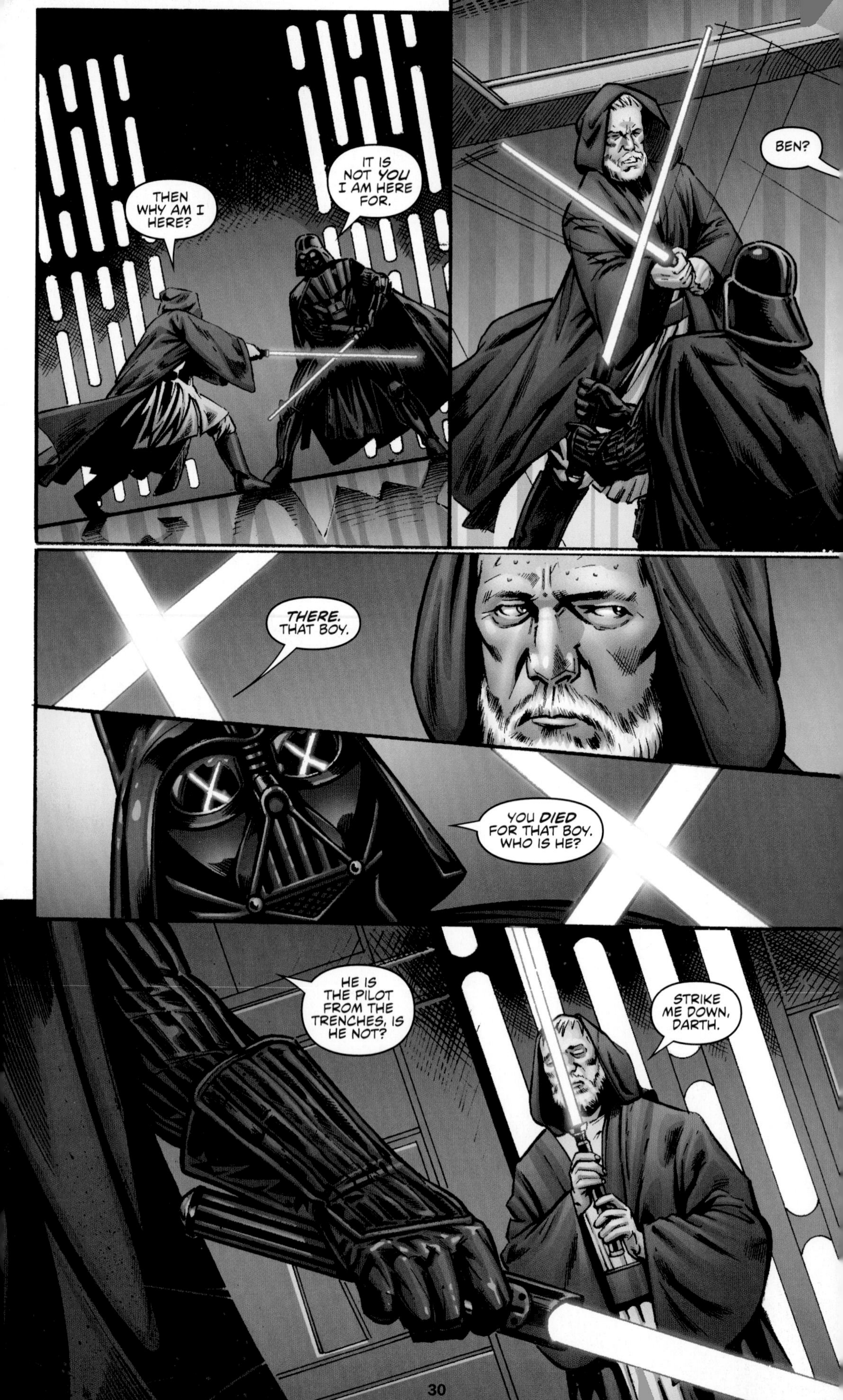
THEN WHY AM I HERE?
IT IS NOT YOU I AM HERE FOR.
BEN?
THERE. THAT BOY.
YOU DIED FOR THAT BOY. WHO IS HE?
HE IS THE PILOT FROM THE TRENCHES, IS HE NOT?
STRIKE ME DOWN, DARTH.

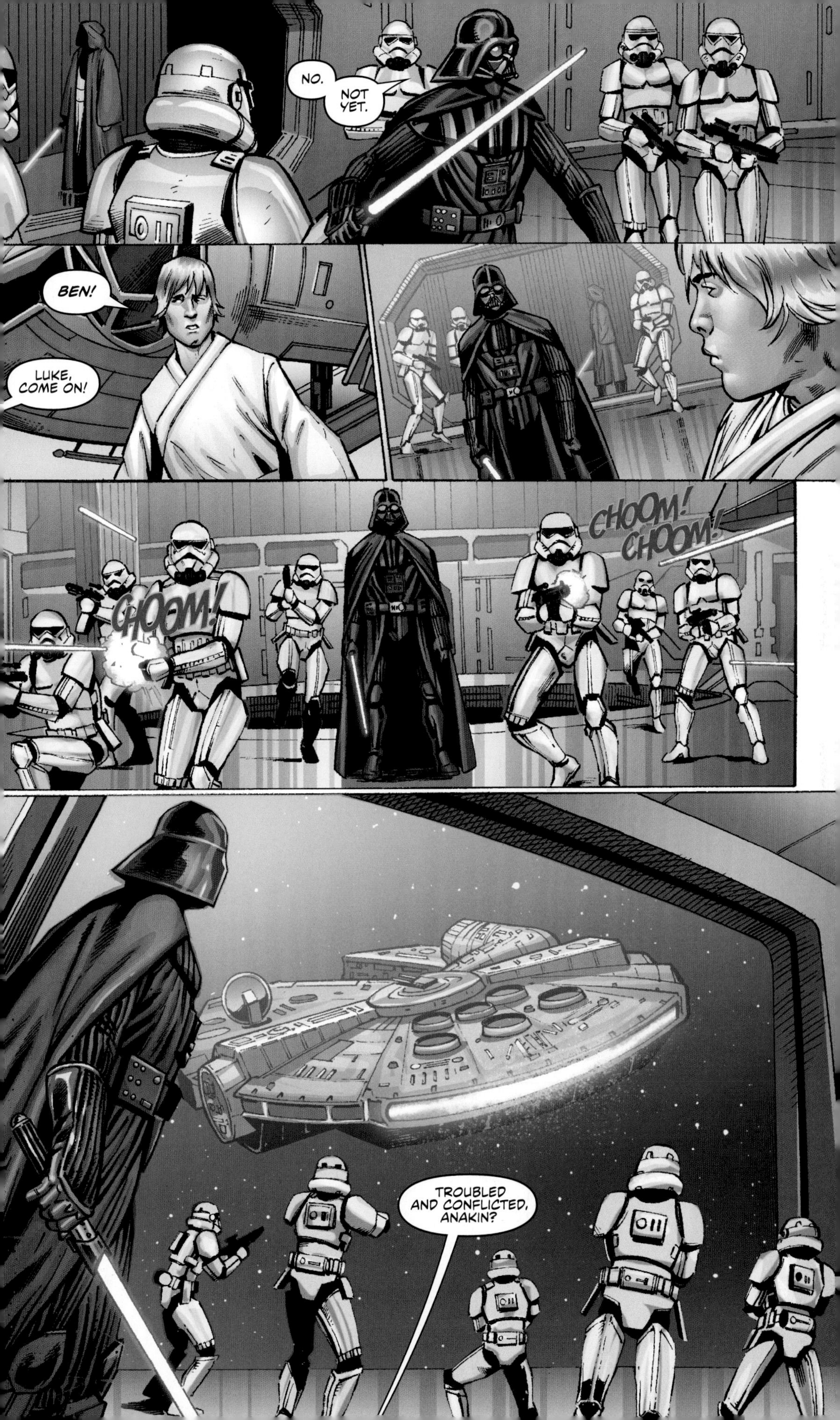
NO.
NOT YET.
BEN!
LUKE, COME ON!
CHOOM!
CHOOM!
CHOOM!
TROUBLED AND CONFLICTED, ANAKIN?

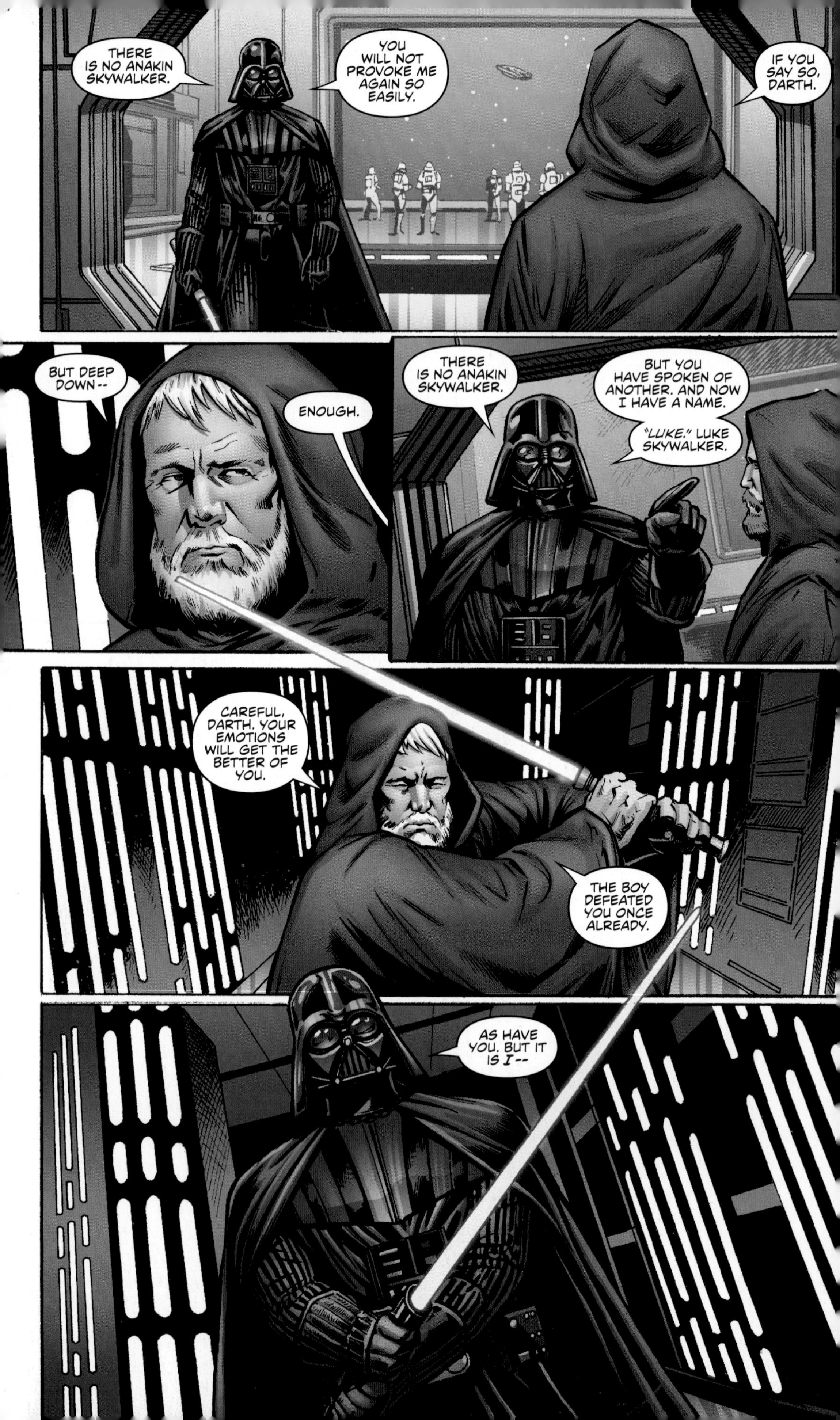
THERE IS NO ANAKIN SKYWALKER.
YOU WILL NOT PROVOKE ME AGAIN SO EASILY.
IF YOU SAY SO, DARTH.
BUT DEEP DOWN--
ENOUGH.
THERE IS NO ANAKIN SKYWALKER.
BUT YOU HAVE SPOKEN OF ANOTHER. AND NOW I HAVE A NAME.
"LUKE." LUKE SKYWALKER.
CAREFUL, DARTH. YOUR EMOTIONS WILL GET THE BETTER OF YOU.
THE BOY DEFEATED YOU ONCE ALREADY.
AS HAVE YOU. BUT IT IS *I*--

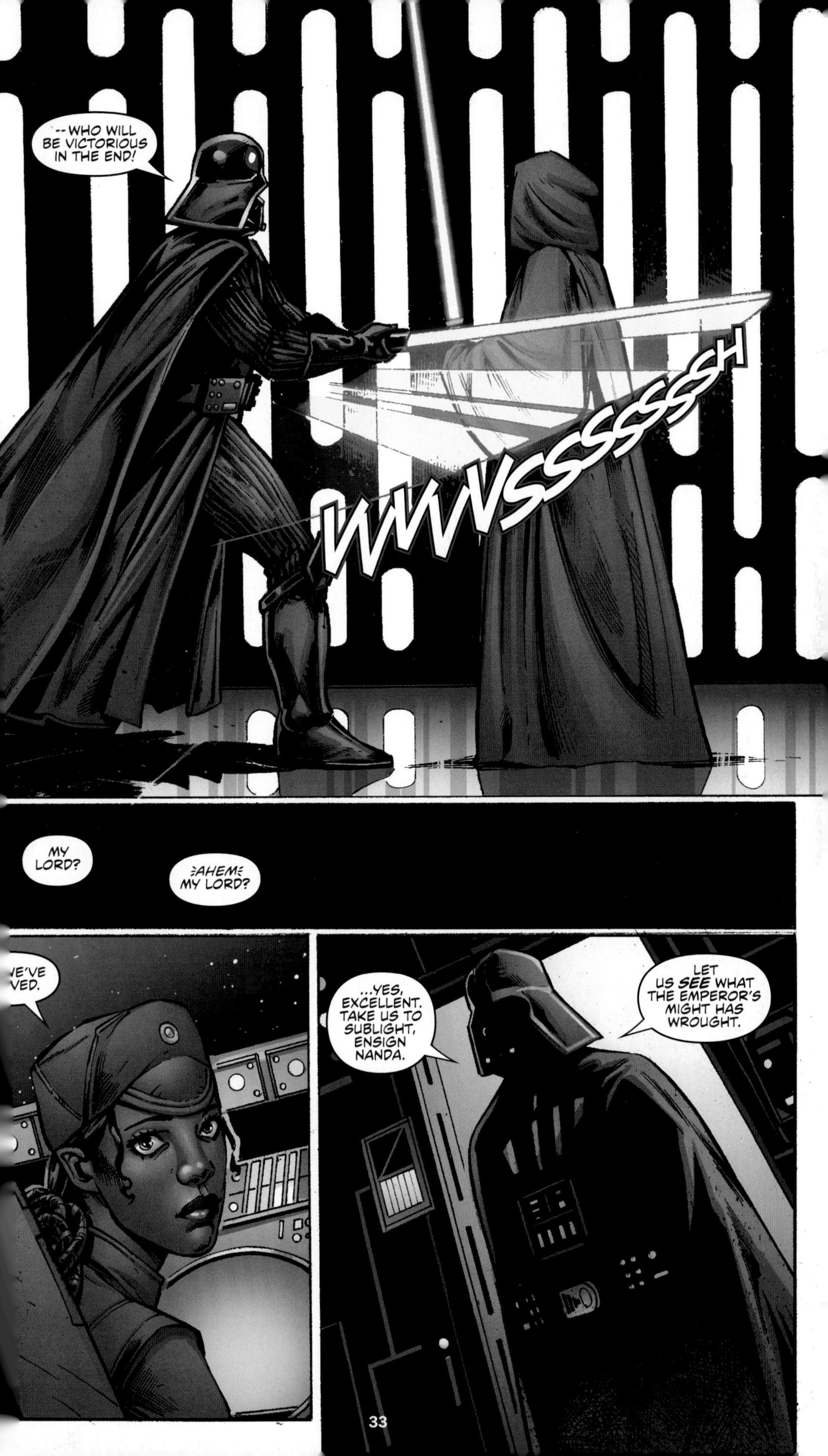
--WHO WILL BE VICTORIOUS IN THE END!
WWVSSSSSSH
MY LORD?
AHEM MY LORD?
E'VE VED.
...YES, EXCELLENT. TAKE US TO SUBLIGHT, ENSIGN NANDA.
LET US **SEE** WHAT THE EMPEROR'S MIGHT HAS WROUGHT.

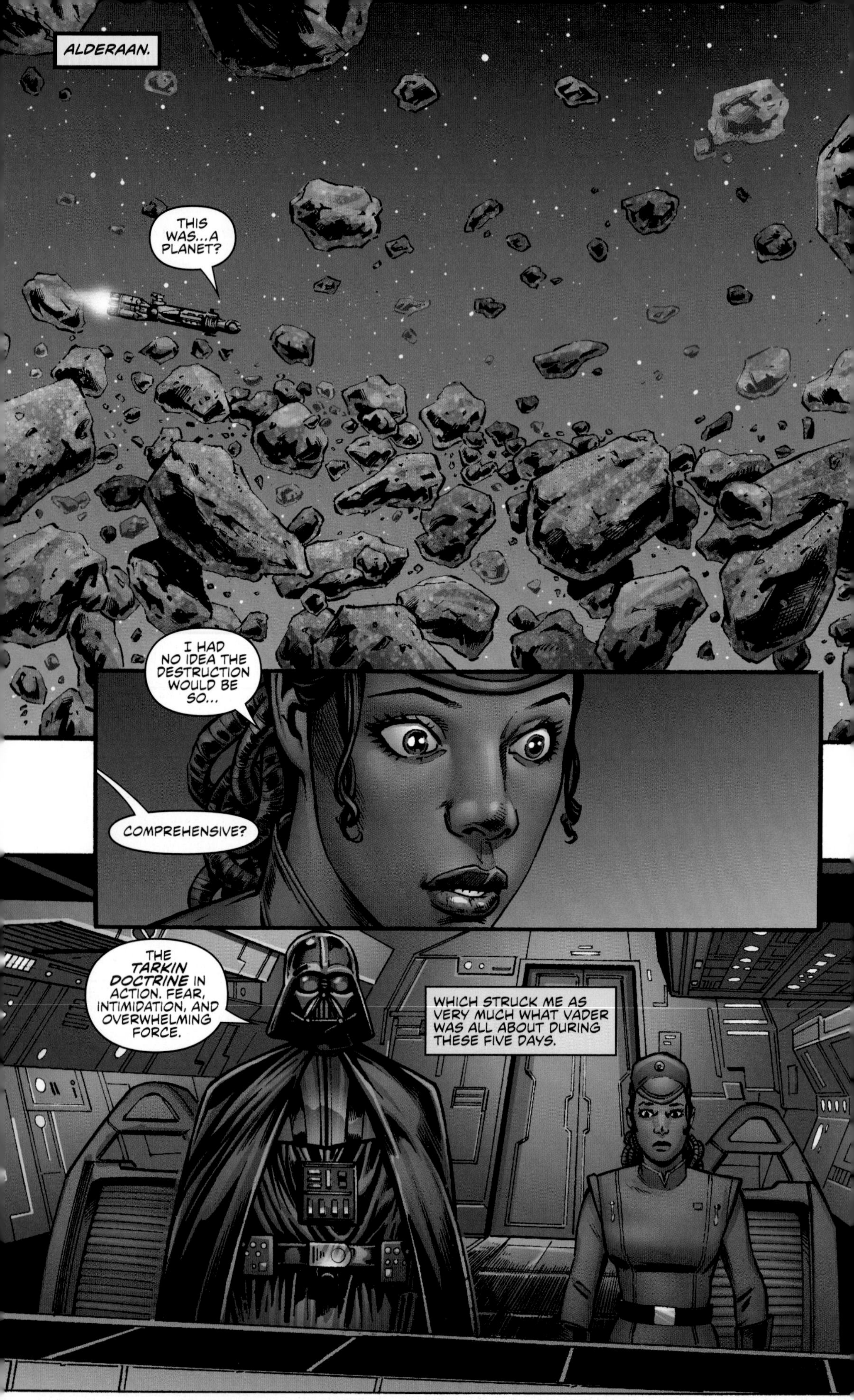
ALDERAAN.
THIS WAS...A PLANET?
I HAD NO IDEA THE DESTRUCTION WOULD BE SO...
COMPREHENSIVE?
THE TARKIN DOCTRINE IN ACTION. FEAR, INTIMIDATION, AND OVERWHELMING FORCE.
WHICH STRUCK ME AS VERY MUCH WHAT VADER WAS ALL ABOUT DURING THESE FIVE DAYS.

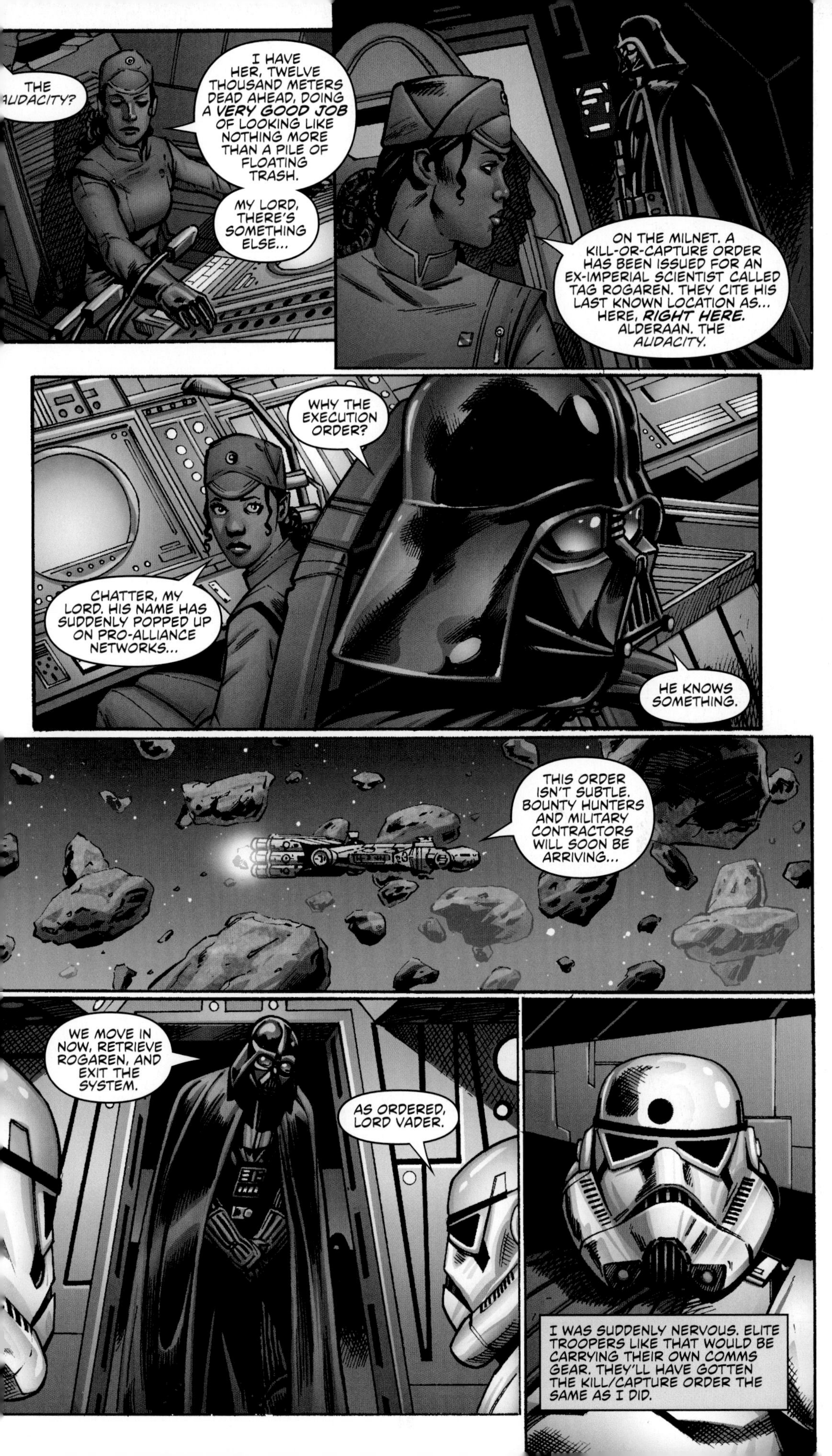
THE AUDACITY?
I HAVE HER, TWELVE THOUSAND METERS DEAD AHEAD, DOING A VERY GOOD JOB OF LOOKING LIKE NOTHING MORE THAN A PILE OF FLOATING TRASH.
MY LORD, THERE'S SOMETHING ELSE...
ON THE MILNET. A KILL-OR-CAPTURE ORDER HAS BEEN ISSUED FOR AN EX-IMPERIAL SCIENTIST CALLED TAG ROGAREN. THEY CITE HIS LAST KNOWN LOCATION AS... HERE, RIGHT HERE. ALDERAAN. THE AUDACITY.
WHY THE EXECUTION ORDER?
CHATTER, MY LORD. HIS NAME HAS SUDDENLY POPPED UP ON PRO-ALLIANCE NETWORKS...
HE KNOWS SOMETHING.
THIS ORDER ISN'T SUBTLE. BOUNTY HUNTERS AND MILITARY CONTRACTORS WILL SOON BE ARRIVING...
WE MOVE IN NOW, RETRIEVE ROGAREN, AND EXIT THE SYSTEM.
AS ORDERED, LORD VADER.
I WAS SUDDENLY NERVOUS. ELITE TROOPERS LIKE THAT WOULD BE CARRYING THEIR OWN COMMS GEAR. THEY'LL HAVE GOTTEN THE KILL/CAPTURE ORDER THE SAME AS I DID.

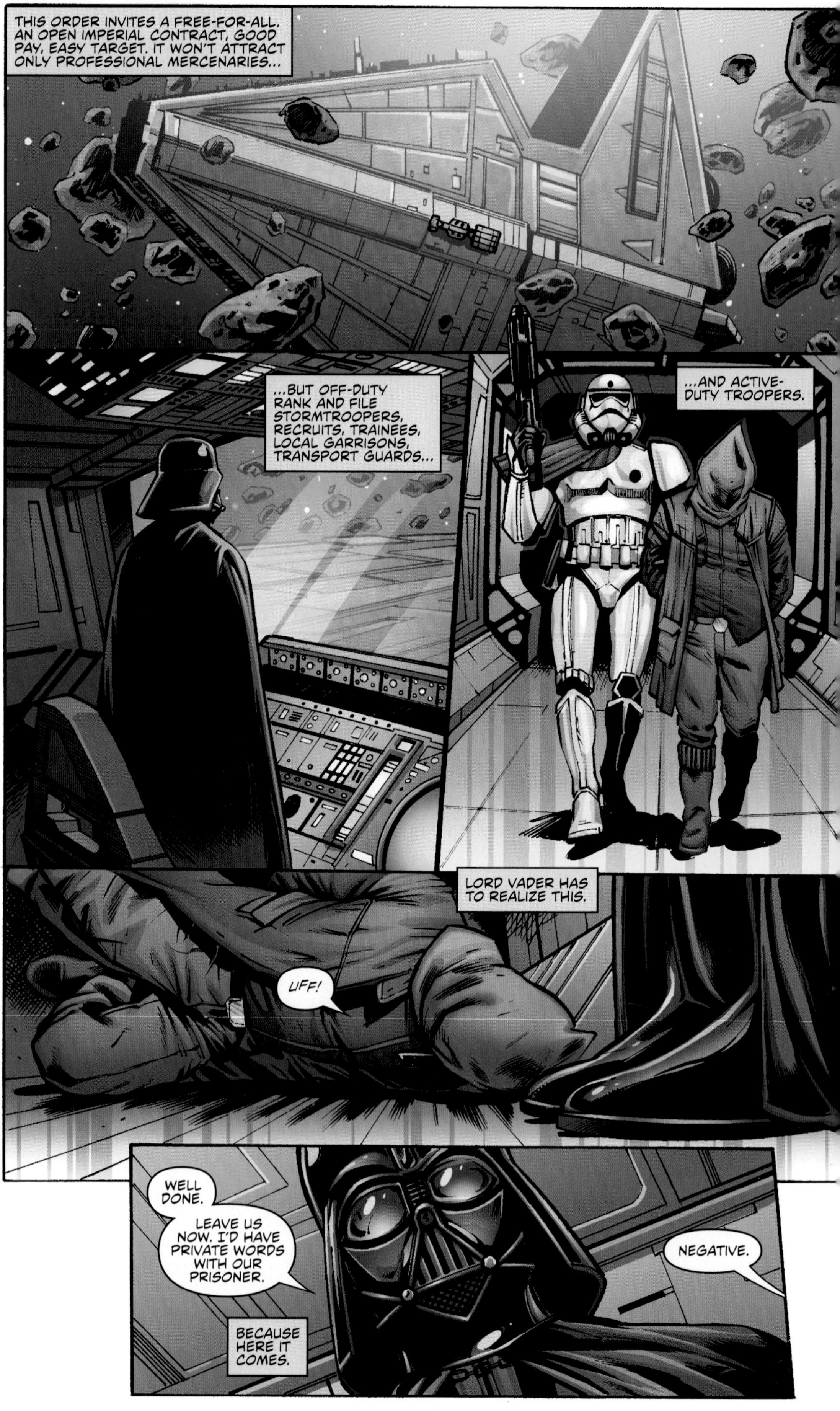
THIS ORDER INVITES A FREE-FOR-ALL. AN OPEN IMPERIAL CONTRACT, GOOD PAY, EASY TARGET. IT WON'T ATTRACT ONLY PROFESSIONAL MERCENARIES...
...BUT OFF-DUTY RANK AND FILE STORMTROOPERS, RECRUITS, TRAINEES, LOCAL GARRISONS, TRANSPORT GUARDS...
...AND ACTIVE-DUTY TROOPERS.
LORD VADER HAS TO REALIZE THIS.
UFF!
WELL DONE.
LEAVE US NOW. I'D HAVE PRIVATE WORDS WITH OUR PRISONER.
NEGATIVE.
BECAUSE HERE IT COMES.

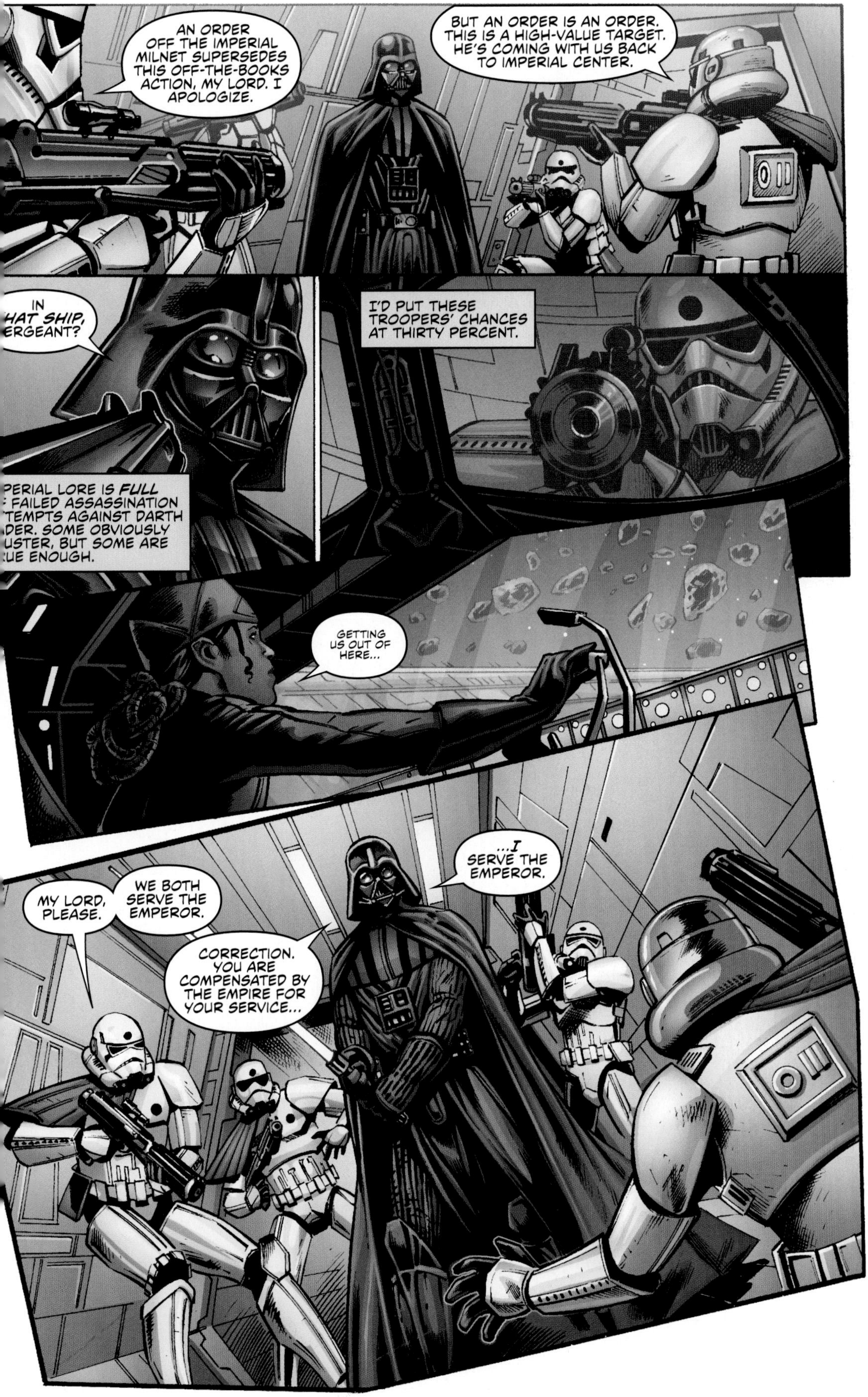
AN ORDER OFF THE IMPERIAL MILNET SUPERSEDES THIS OFF-THE-BOOKS ACTION, MY LORD. I APOLOGIZE.
BUT AN ORDER IS AN ORDER. THIS IS A HIGH-VALUE TARGET. HE'S COMING WITH US BACK TO IMPERIAL CENTER.
IN HAT SHIP, ERGEANT?
PERIAL LORE IS FULL F FAILED ASSASSINATION TEMPTS AGAINST DARTH DER. SOME OBVIOUSLY USTER, BUT SOME ARE UE ENOUGH.
I'D PUT THESE TROOPERS' CHANCES AT THIRTY PERCENT.
GETTING US OUT OF HERE...
MY LORD, PLEASE.
WE BOTH SERVE THE EMPEROR.
CORRECTION. YOU ARE COMPENSATED BY THE EMPIRE FOR YOUR SERVICE...
...I SERVE THE EMPEROR.

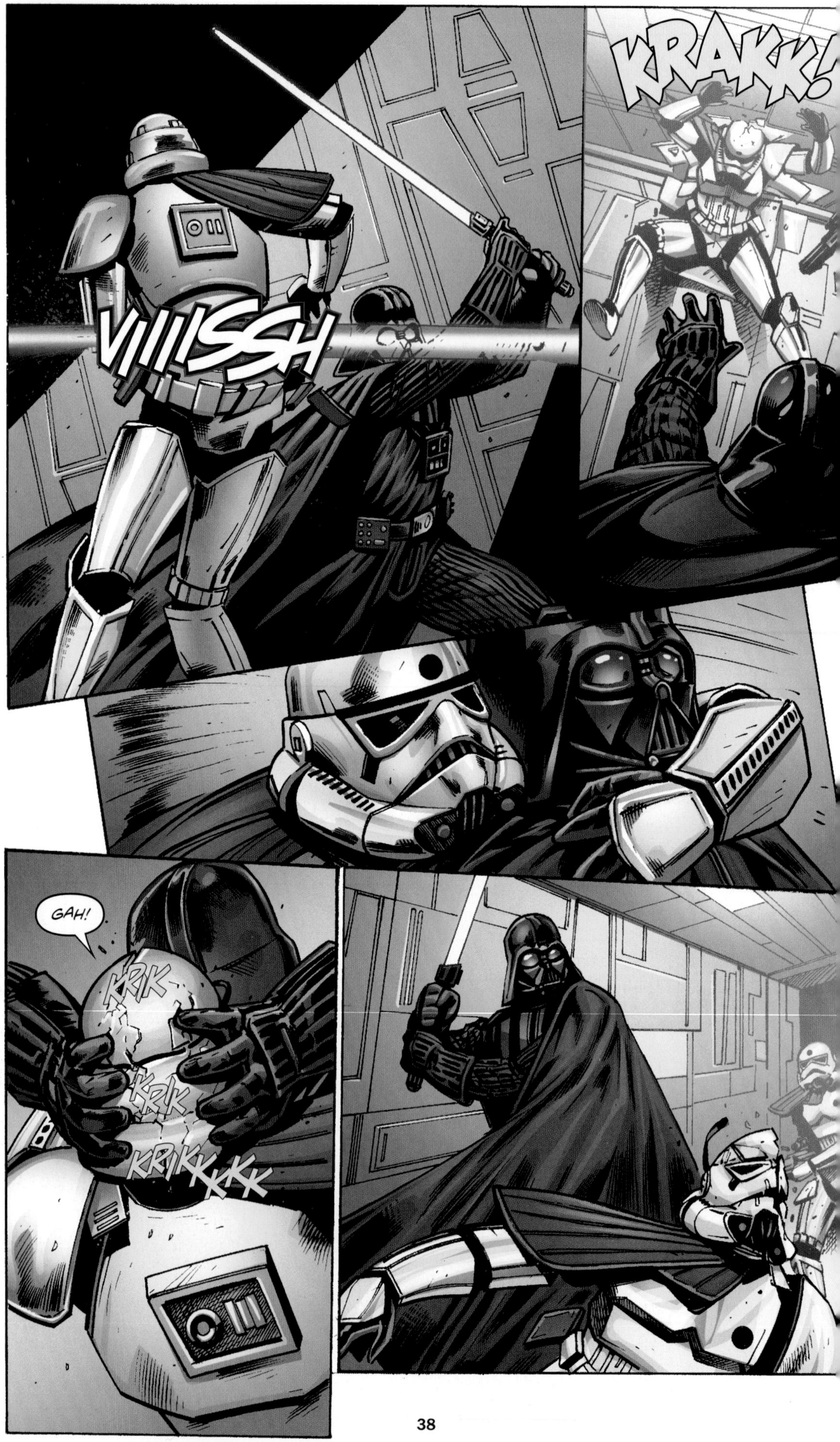
VIIISSH
KRAKK!
GAH!
KRIK-
KRIK
KRIKKKKK

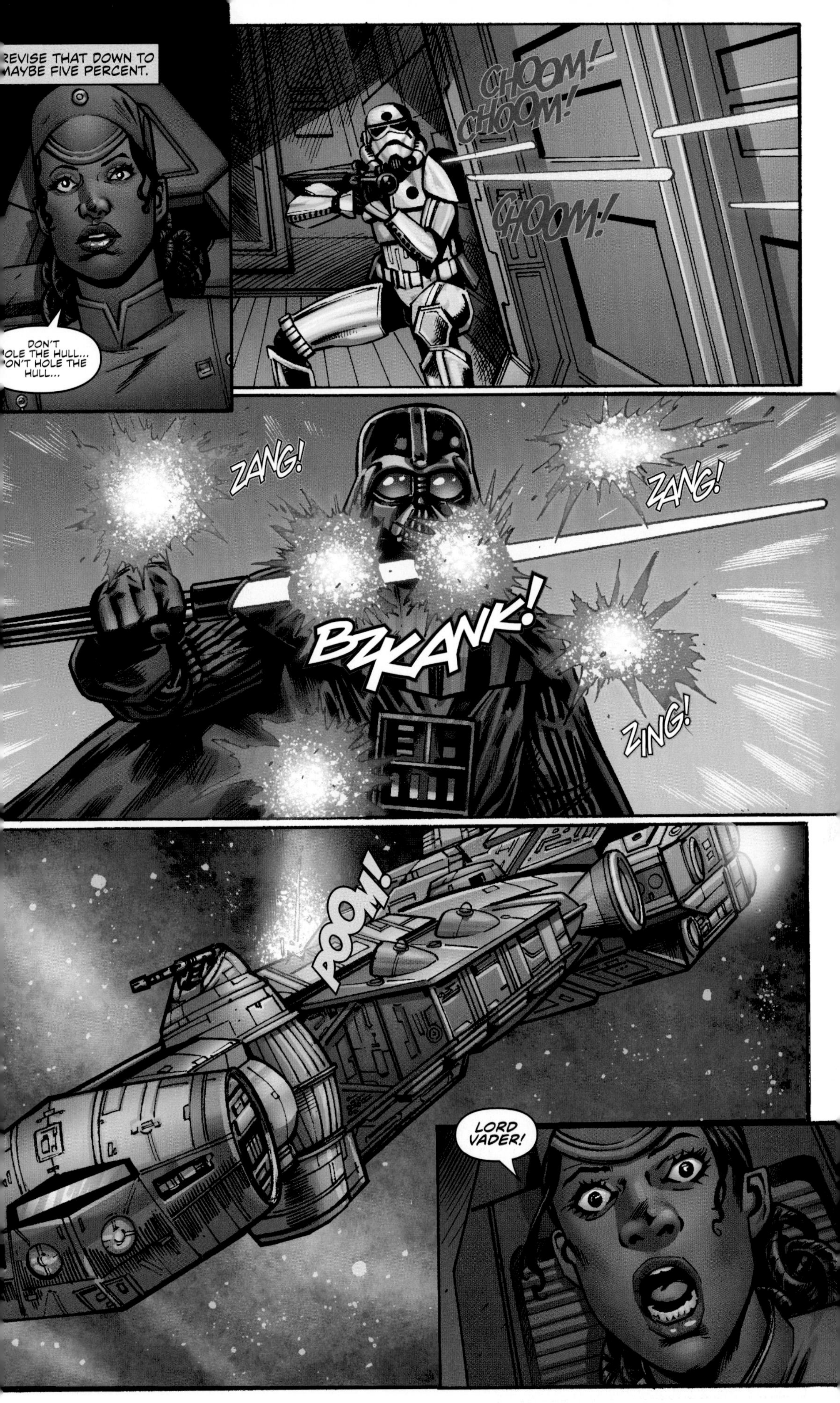
REVISE THAT DOWN TO MAYBE FIVE PERCENT.
DON'T HOLE THE HULL... DON'T HOLE THE HULL...
CHOOM! CHOOM!
CHOOM!
ZANG!
ZANG!
BZKANK!
ZING!
POOM!
LORD VADER!

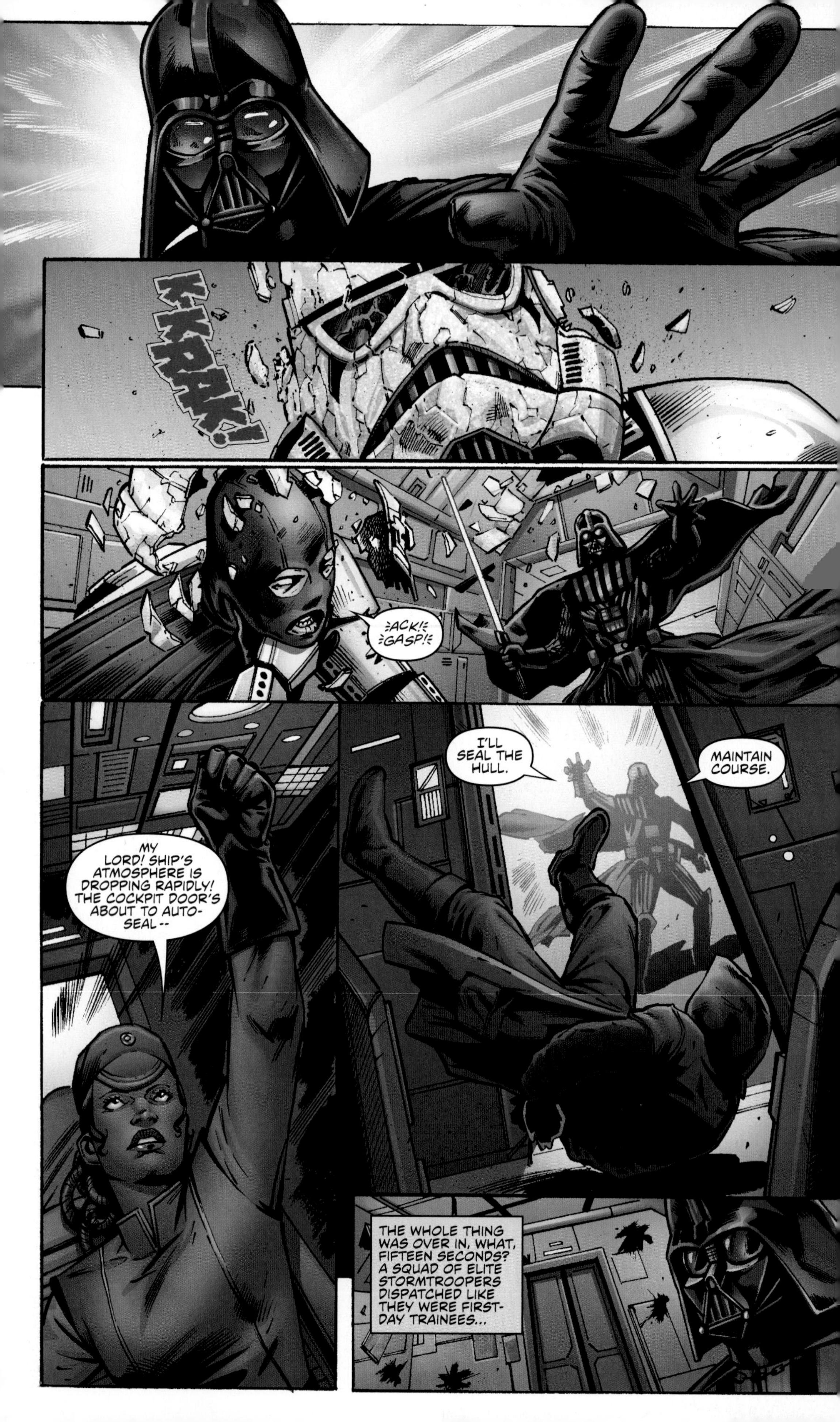
K-KRAK!
ACK! GASP!
MY LORD! SHIP'S ATMOSPHERE IS DROPPING RAPIDLY! THE COCKPIT DOOR'S ABOUT TO AUTO-SEAL --
I'LL SEAL THE HULL.
MAINTAIN COURSE.
THE WHOLE THING WAS OVER IN, WHAT, FIFTEEN SECONDS? A SQUAD OF ELITE STORMTROOPERS DISPATCHED LIKE THEY WERE FIRST-DAY TRAINEES...

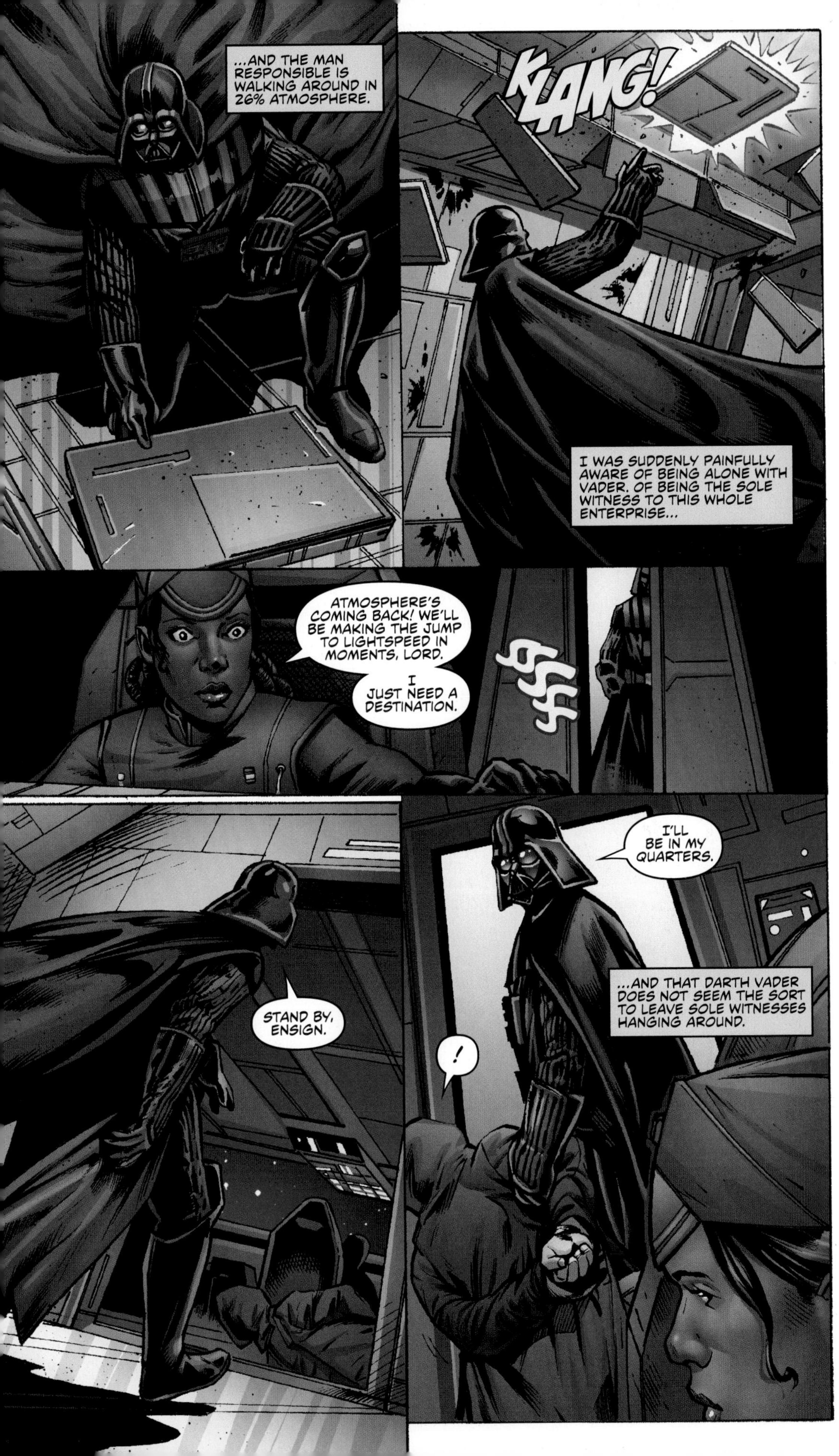
...AND THE MAN RESPONSIBLE IS WALKING AROUND IN 26% ATMOSPHERE.
KLANG!
I WAS SUDDENLY PAINFULLY AWARE OF BEING ALONE WITH VADER. OF BEING THE SOLE WITNESS TO THIS WHOLE ENTERPRISE...
ATMOSPHERE'S COMING BACK! WE'LL BE MAKING THE JUMP TO LIGHTSPEED IN MOMENTS, LORD.
I JUST NEED A DESTINATION.
SSSH
STAND BY, ENSIGN.
I'LL BE IN MY QUARTERS.
...AND THAT DARTH VADER DOES NOT SEEM THE SORT TO LEAVE SOLE WITNESSES HANGING AROUND.
!

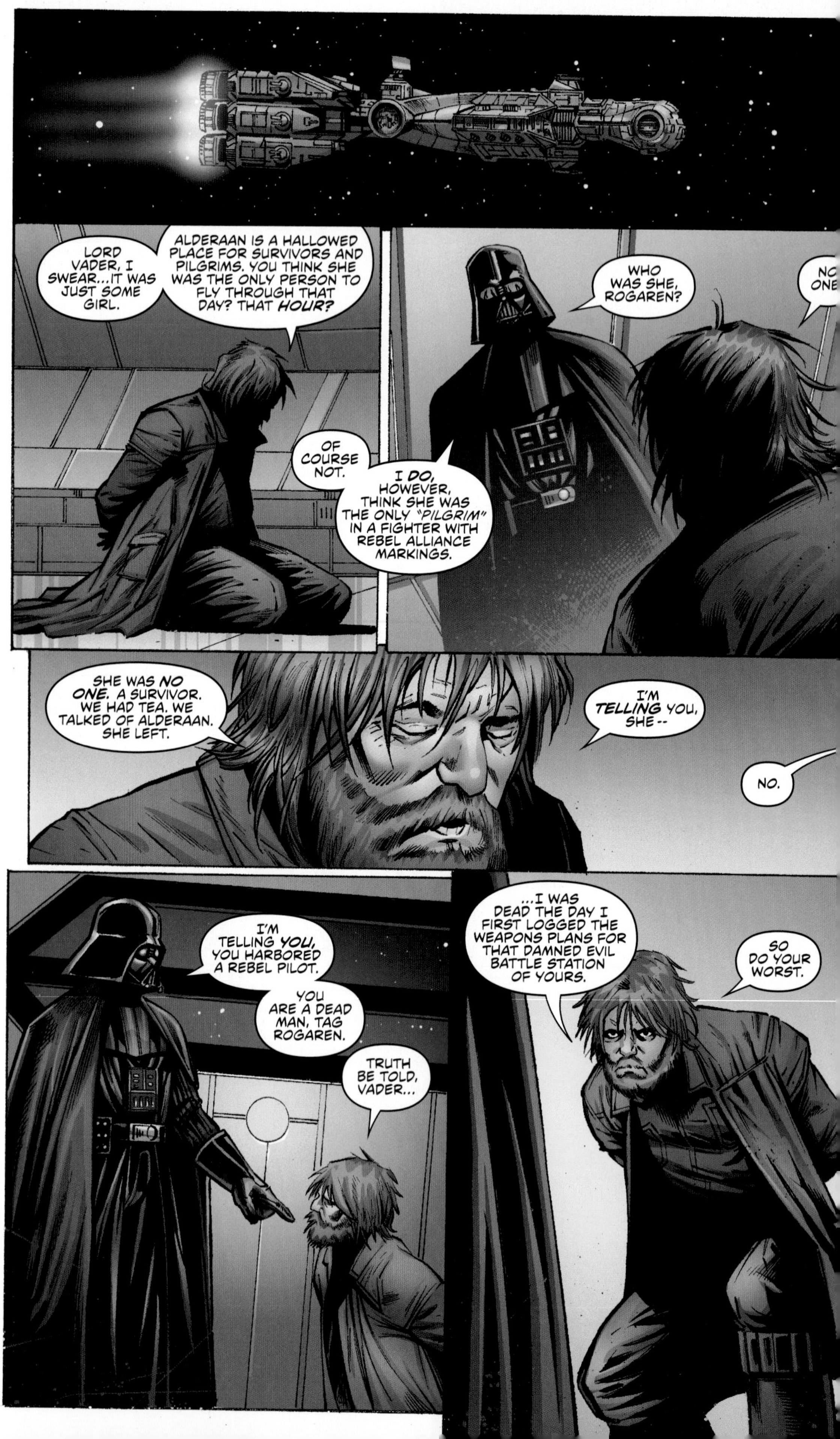
LORD VADER, I SWEAR...IT WAS JUST SOME GIRL.
ALDERAAN IS A HALLOWED PLACE FOR SURVIVORS AND PILGRIMS. YOU THINK SHE WAS THE ONLY PERSON TO FLY THROUGH THAT DAY? THAT HOUR?
OF COURSE NOT.
I DO, HOWEVER, THINK SHE WAS THE ONLY "PILGRIM" IN A FIGHTER WITH REBEL ALLIANCE MARKINGS.
WHO WAS SHE, ROGAREN?
SHE WAS NO ONE. A SURVIVOR. WE HAD TEA. WE TALKED OF ALDERAAN. SHE LEFT.
I'M TELLING YOU, SHE --
NO.
I'M TELLING YOU, YOU HARBORED A REBEL PILOT.
YOU ARE A DEAD MAN, TAG ROGAREN.
TRUTH BE TOLD, VADER...
...I WAS DEAD THE DAY I FIRST LOGGED THE WEAPONS PLANS FOR THAT DAMNED EVIL BATTLE STATION OF YOURS.
SO DO YOUR WORST.

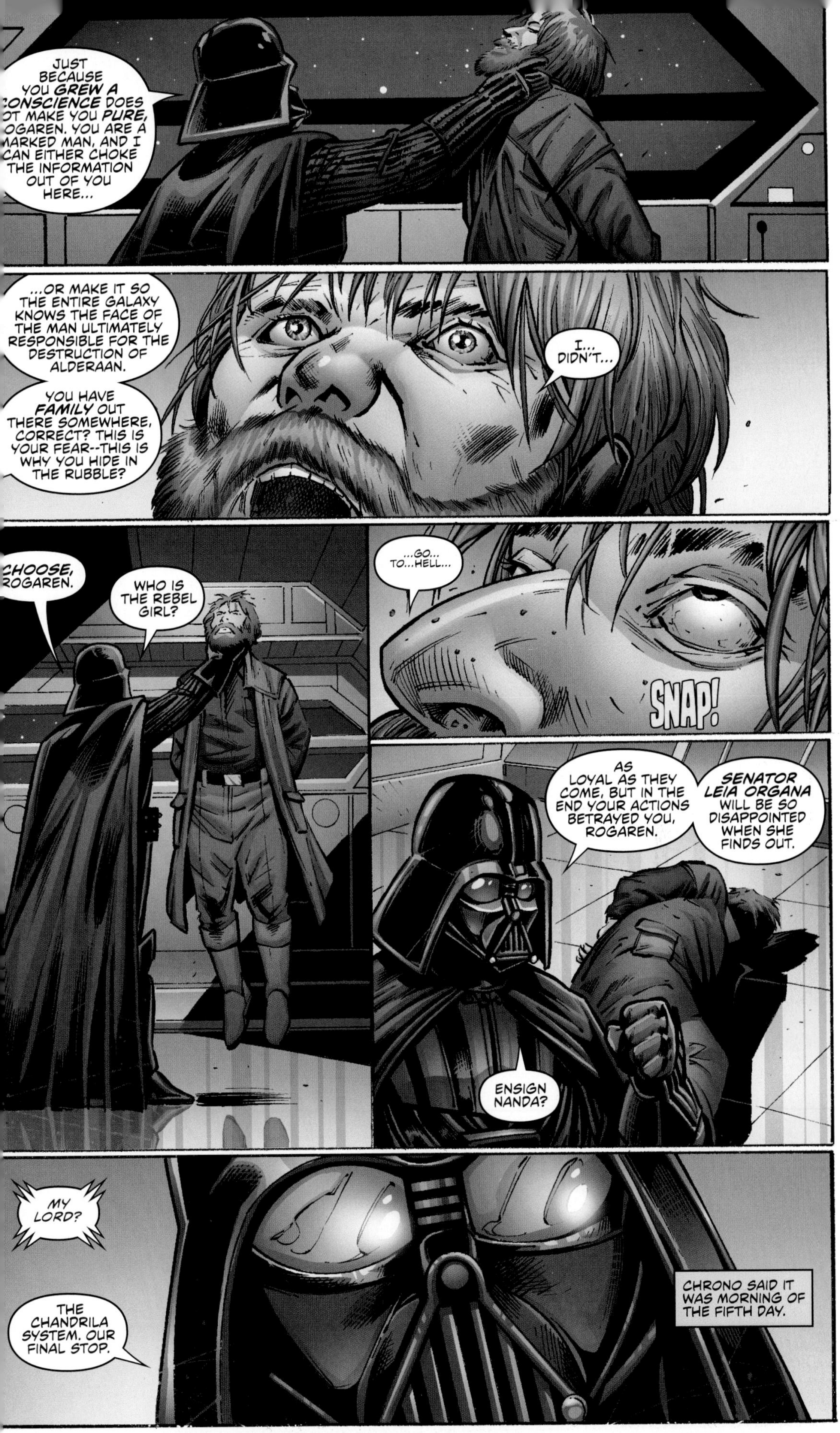
JUST BECAUSE YOU GREW A CONSCIENCE DOES NOT MAKE YOU PURE, ROGAREN. YOU ARE A MARKED MAN, AND I CAN EITHER CHOKE THE INFORMATION OUT OF YOU HERE...
...OR MAKE IT SO THE ENTIRE GALAXY KNOWS THE FACE OF THE MAN ULTIMATELY RESPONSIBLE FOR THE DESTRUCTION OF ALDERAAN.
YOU HAVE FAMILY OUT THERE SOMEWHERE, CORRECT? THIS IS YOUR FEAR--THIS IS WHY YOU HIDE IN THE RUBBLE?
I... DIDN'T...
CHOOSE, ROGAREN.
WHO IS THE REBEL GIRL?
...GO... TO...HELL...
SNAP!
AS LOYAL AS THEY COME, BUT IN THE END YOUR ACTIONS BETRAYED YOU, ROGAREN.
SENATOR LEIA ORGANA WILL BE SO DISAPPOINTED WHEN SHE FINDS OUT.
ENSIGN NANDA?
MY LORD?
THE CHANDRILA SYSTEM. OUR FINAL STOP.
CHRONO SAID IT WAS MORNING OF THE FIFTH DAY.

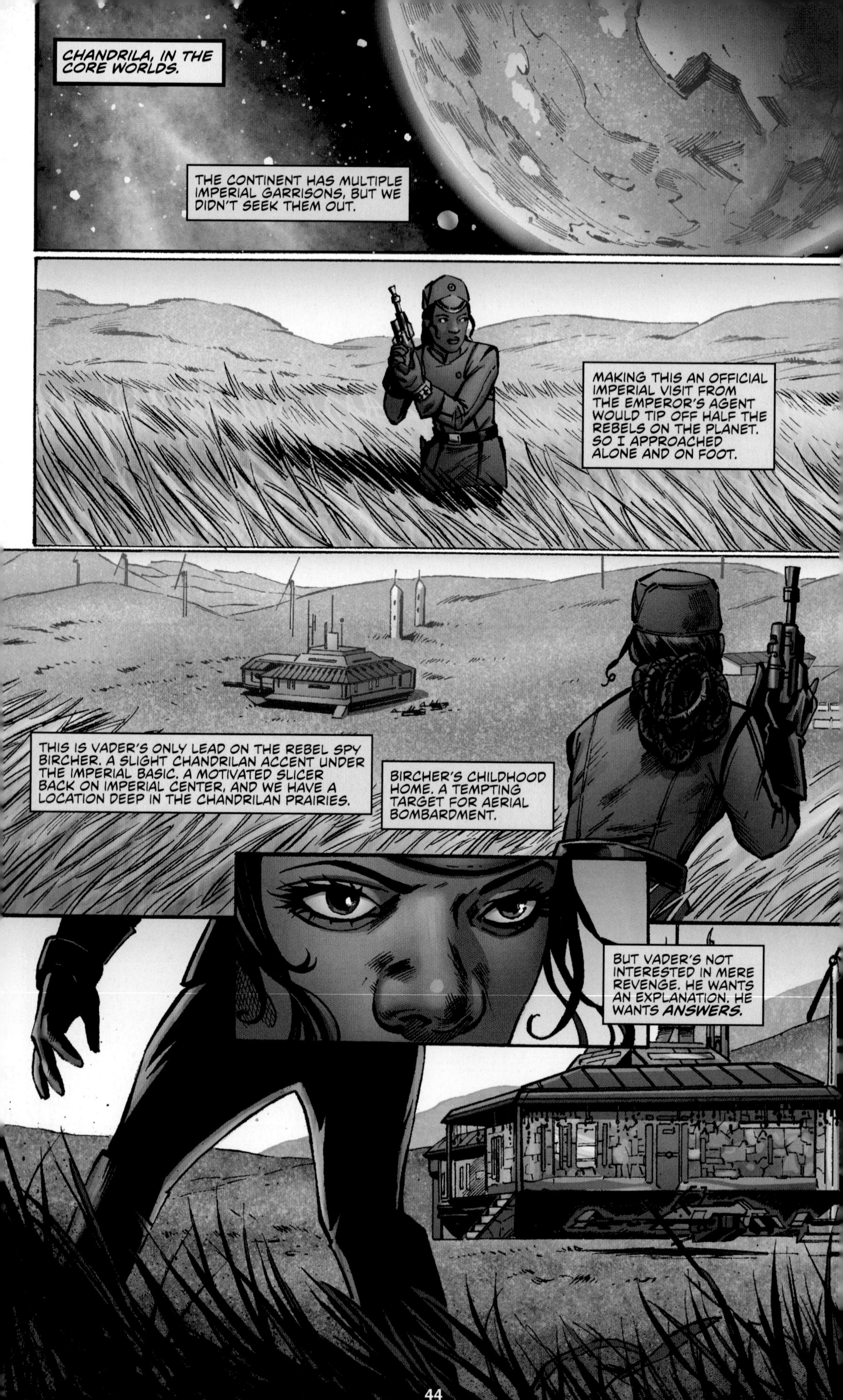

CHANDRILA, IN THE CORE WORLDS.
THE CONTINENT HAS MULTIPLE IMPERIAL GARRISONS, BUT WE DIDN'T SEEK THEM OUT.
MAKING THIS AN OFFICIAL IMPERIAL VISIT FROM THE EMPEROR'S AGENT WOULD TIP OFF HALF THE REBELS ON THE PLANET. SO I APPROACHED ALONE AND ON FOOT.
THIS IS VADER'S ONLY LEAD ON THE REBEL SPY BIRCHER. A SLIGHT CHANDRILAN ACCENT UNDER THE IMPERIAL BASIC. A MOTIVATED SLICER BACK ON IMPERIAL CENTER, AND WE HAVE A LOCATION DEEP IN THE CHANDRILAN PRAIRIES.
BIRCHER'S CHILDHOOD HOME. A TEMPTING TARGET FOR AERIAL BOMBARDMENT.
BUT VADER'S NOT INTERESTED IN MERE REVENGE. HE WANTS AN EXPLANATION. HE WANTS ***ANSWERS.***

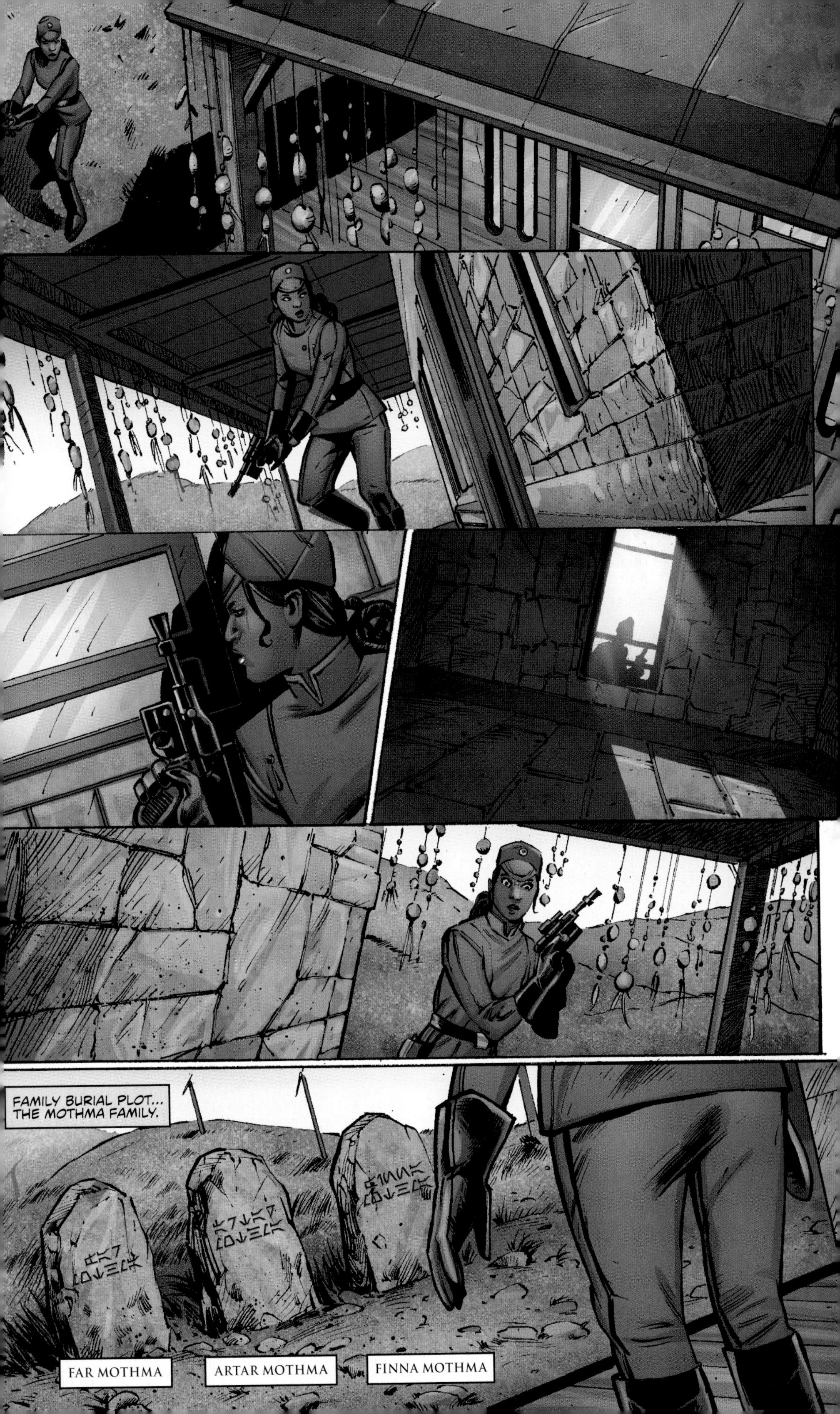
FAMILY BURIAL PLOT... THE MOTHMA FAMILY.
FAR MOTHMA
ARTAR MOTHMA
FINNA MOTHMA

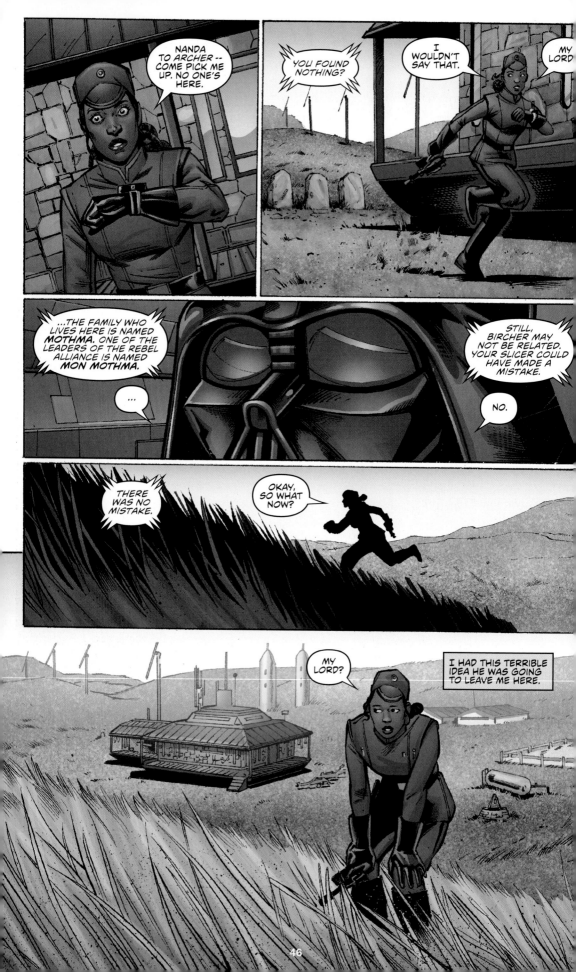

NANDA TO ARCHER -- COME PICK ME UP. NO ONE'S HERE.

YOU FOUND NOTHING?

I WOULDN'T SAY THAT.

MY LORD

...THE FAMILY WHO LIVES HERE IS NAMED MOTHMA. ONE OF THE LEADERS OF THE REBEL ALLIANCE IS NAMED MON MOTHMA.

...

STILL, BIRCHER MAY NOT BE RELATED. YOUR SLICER COULD HAVE MADE A MISTAKE.

NO.

THERE WAS NO MISTAKE.

OKAY, SO WHAT NOW?

MY LORD?

I HAD THIS TERRIBLE IDEA HE WAS GOING TO LEAVE ME HERE.

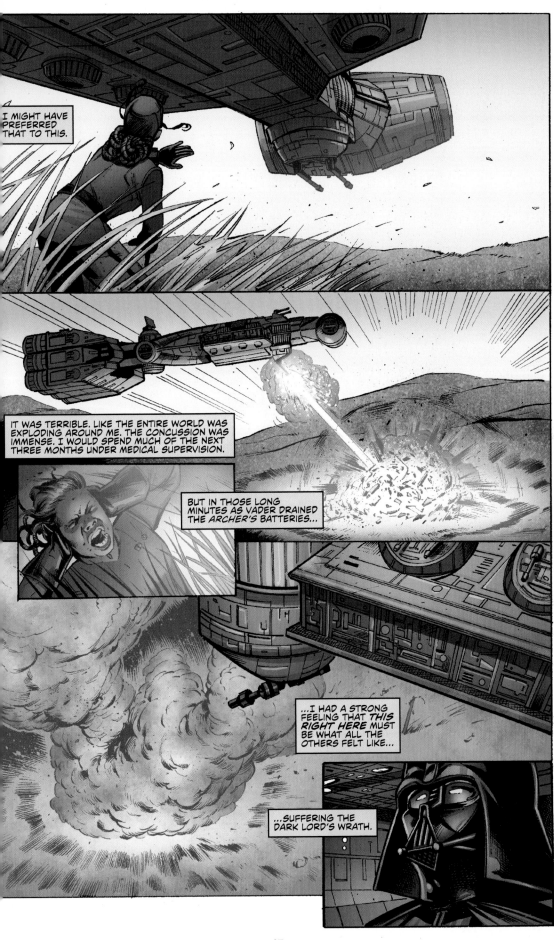

I MIGHT HAVE PREFERRED THAT TO THIS.

IT WAS TERRIBLE. LIKE THE ENTIRE WORLD WAS EXPLODING AROUND ME. THE CONCUSSION WAS IMMENSE. I WOULD SPEND MUCH OF THE NEXT THREE MONTHS UNDER MEDICAL SUPERVISION.

BUT IN THOSE LONG MINUTES AS VADER DRAINED THE *ARCHER'S* BATTERIES...

...I HAD A STRONG FEELING THAT *THIS RIGHT HERE* MUST BE WHAT ALL THE OTHERS FELT LIKE...

...SUFFERING THE DARK LORD'S WRATH.

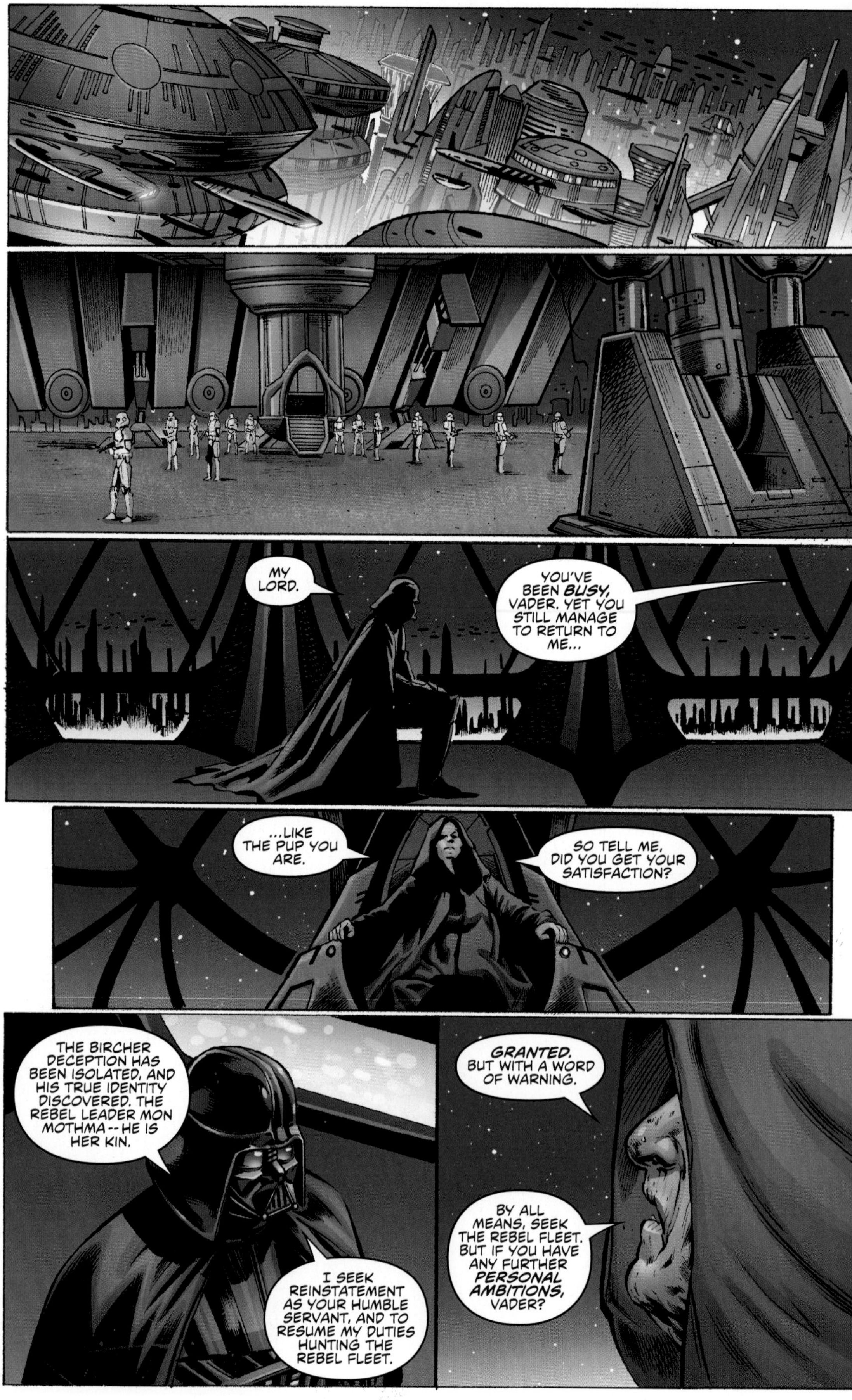

MY LORD.
YOU'VE BEEN BUSY, VADER. YET YOU STILL MANAGE TO RETURN TO ME...
...LIKE THE PUP YOU ARE.
SO TELL ME, DID YOU GET YOUR SATISFACTION?
THE BIRCHER DECEPTION HAS BEEN ISOLATED, AND HIS TRUE IDENTITY DISCOVERED. THE REBEL LEADER MON MOTHMA--HE IS HER KIN.
I SEEK REINSTATEMENT AS YOUR HUMBLE SERVANT, AND TO RESUME MY DUTIES HUNTING THE REBEL FLEET.
GRANTED. BUT WITH A WORD OF WARNING.
BY ALL MEANS, SEEK THE REBEL FLEET. BUT IF YOU HAVE ANY FURTHER PERSONAL AMBITIONS, VADER?

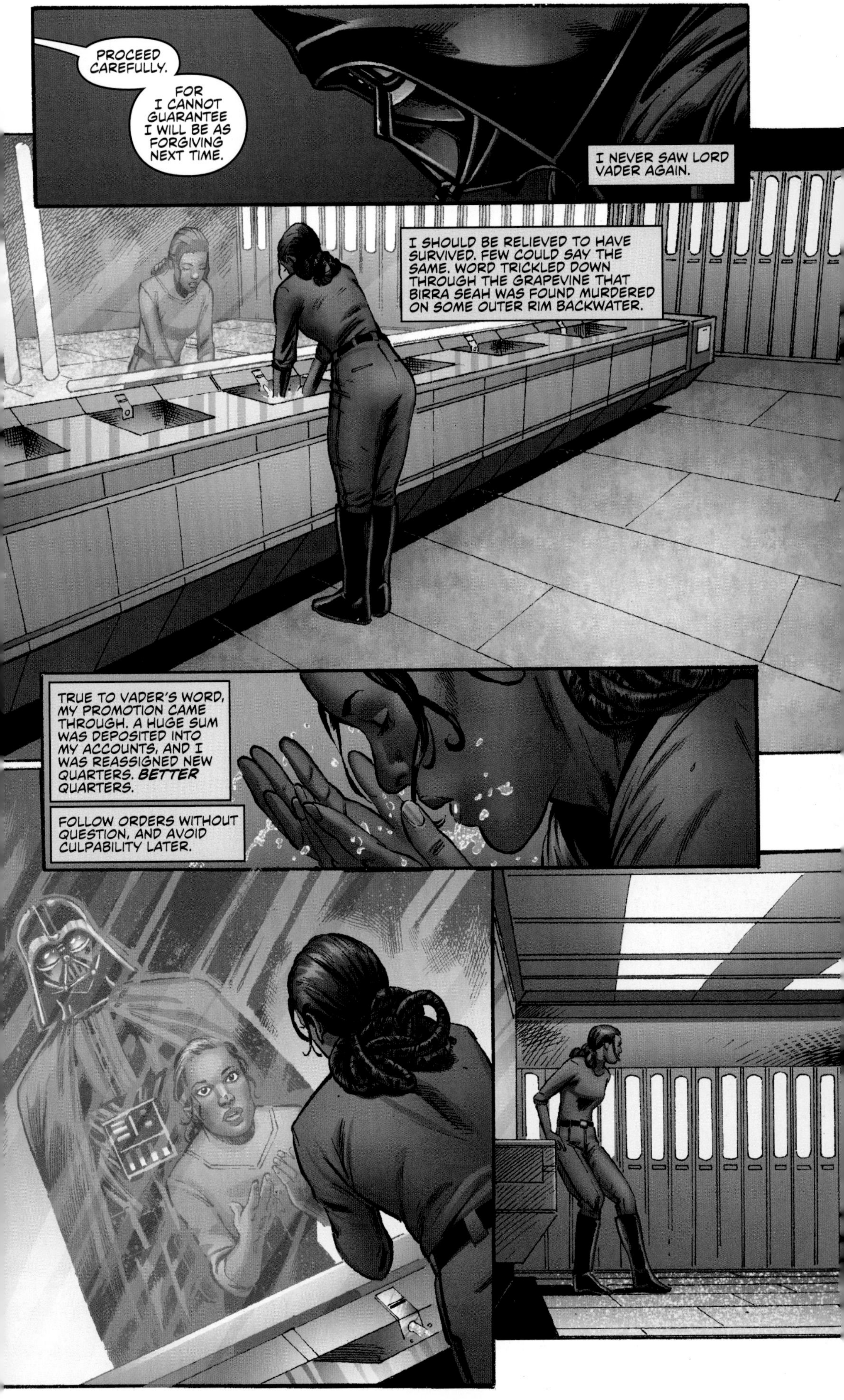
PROCEED CAREFULLY.
FOR I CANNOT GUARANTEE I WILL BE AS FORGIVING NEXT TIME.
I NEVER SAW LORD VADER AGAIN.
I SHOULD BE RELIEVED TO HAVE SURVIVED. FEW COULD SAY THE SAME. WORD TRICKLED DOWN THROUGH THE GRAPEVINE THAT BIRRA SEAH WAS FOUND MURDERED ON SOME OUTER RIM BACKWATER.
TRUE TO VADER'S WORD, MY PROMOTION CAME THROUGH. A HUGE SUM WAS DEPOSITED INTO MY ACCOUNTS, AND I WAS REASSIGNED NEW QUARTERS. *BETTER* QUARTERS.
FOLLOW ORDERS WITHOUT QUESTION, AND AVOID CULPABILITY LATER.

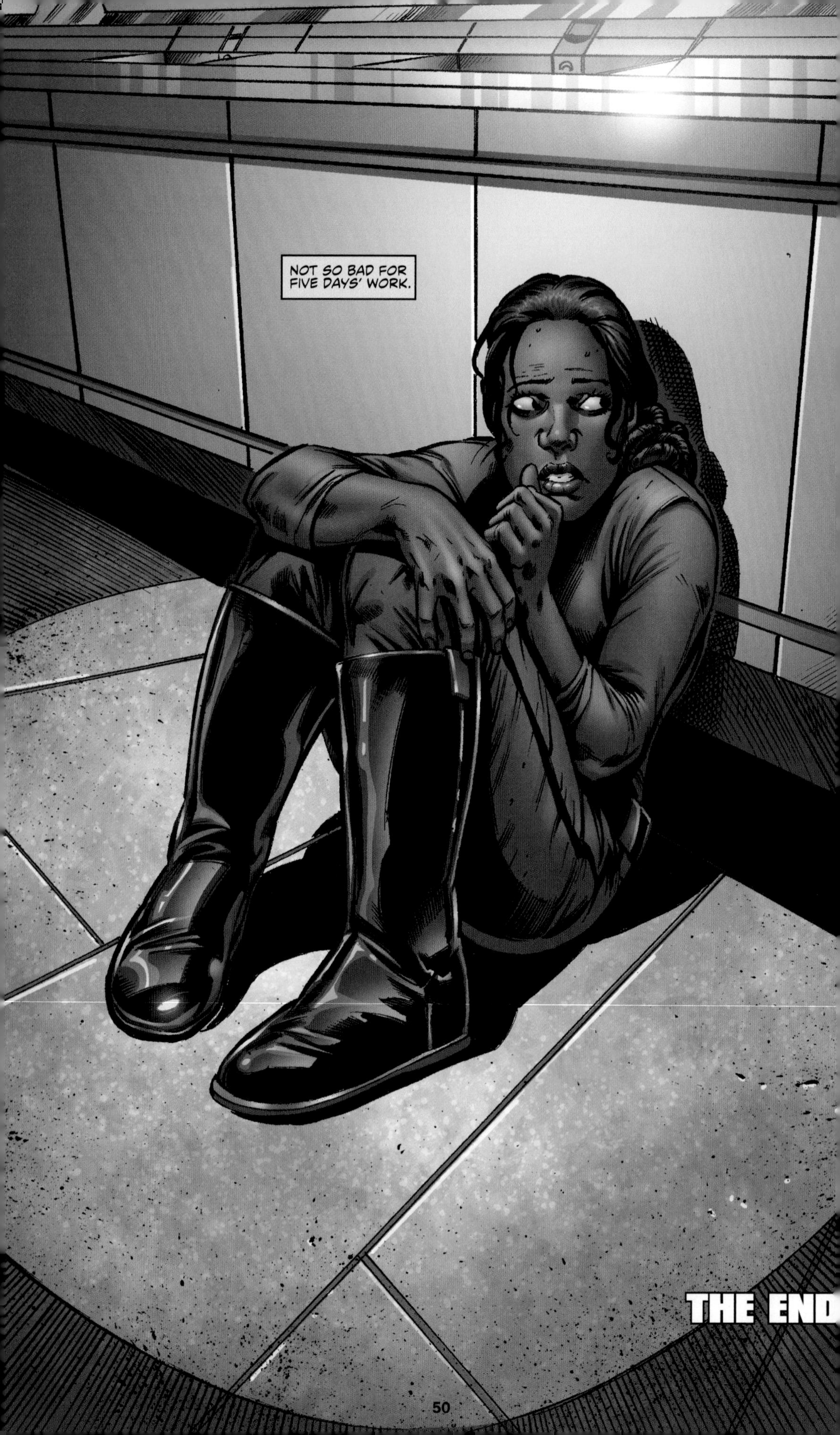
NOT SO BAD FOR FIVE DAYS' WORK.
THE END

WHERE DROIDS GO TO DIE

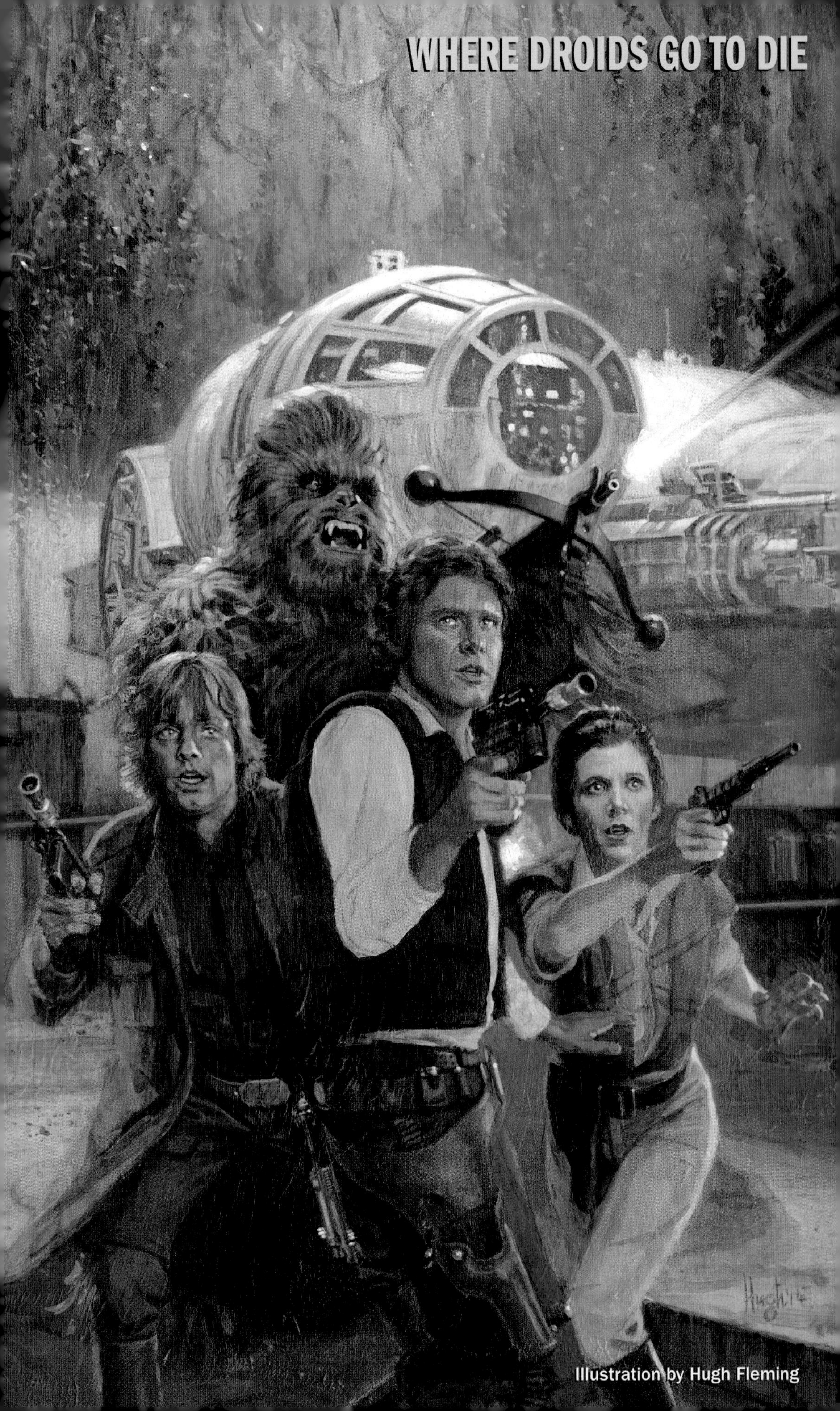

Illustration by Hugh Fleming

After a long search, it seemed that the Rebel Alliance had found a planet to call home—Arrochar, where it could establish a permanent base. All that was required was for Princess Leia to marry that world's prince. But though the prince's intentions were pure, those with the true power on Arrochar had struck a deal with the Empire to help destroy the Rebellion.

After narrowly escaping the Empire's trap, the Rebels are safe—though they are once again homeless. Leia, blaming herself for the disaster on Arrochar, has withdrawn from her friends . . . while rededicating herself to the future of the Alliance.

But across the galaxy, events are unfolding which will require Leia's attention—and the help of those closest to her . . .

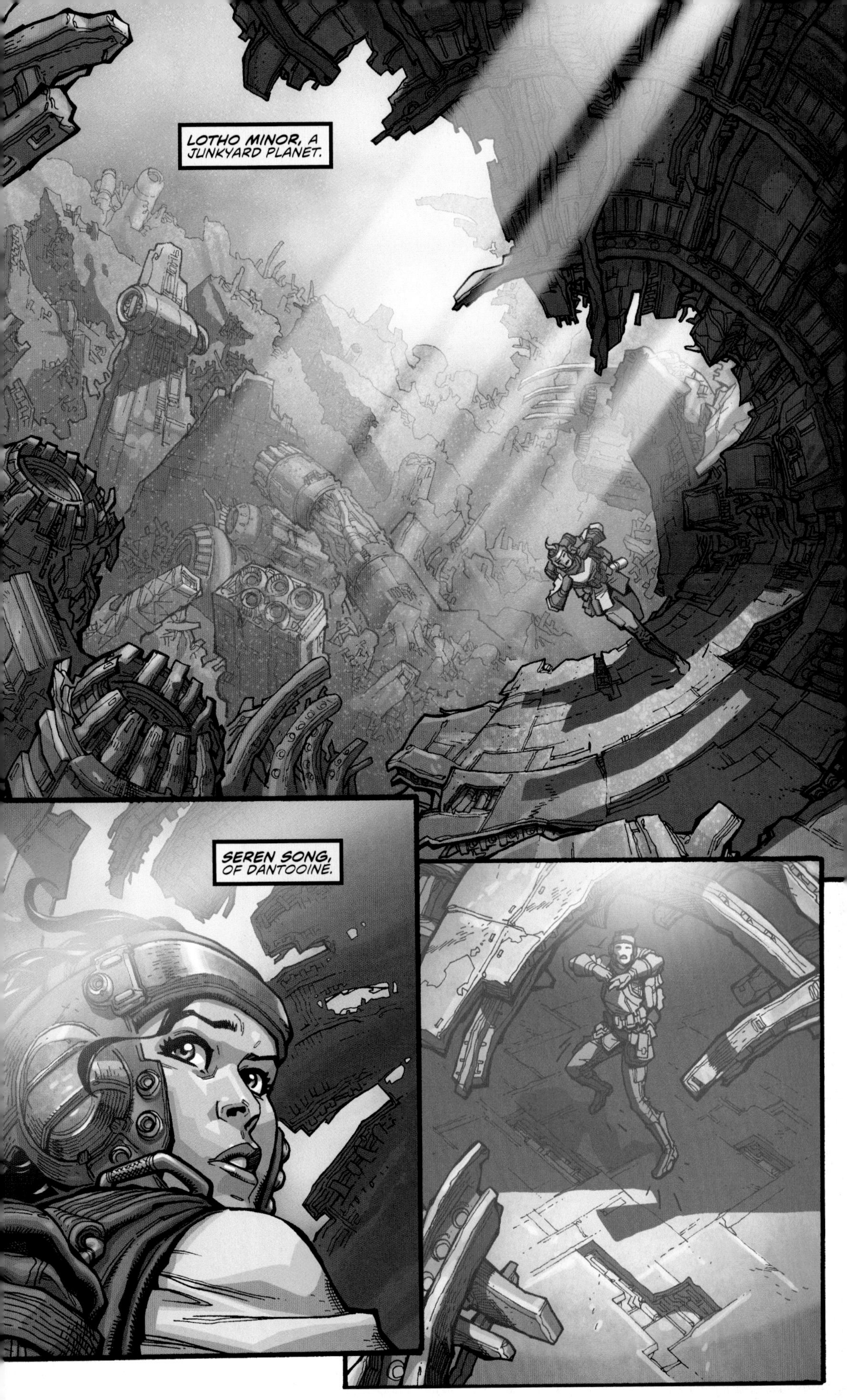

LOTHO MINOR, A JUNKYARD PLANET.
SEREN SONG, OF DANTOOINE.

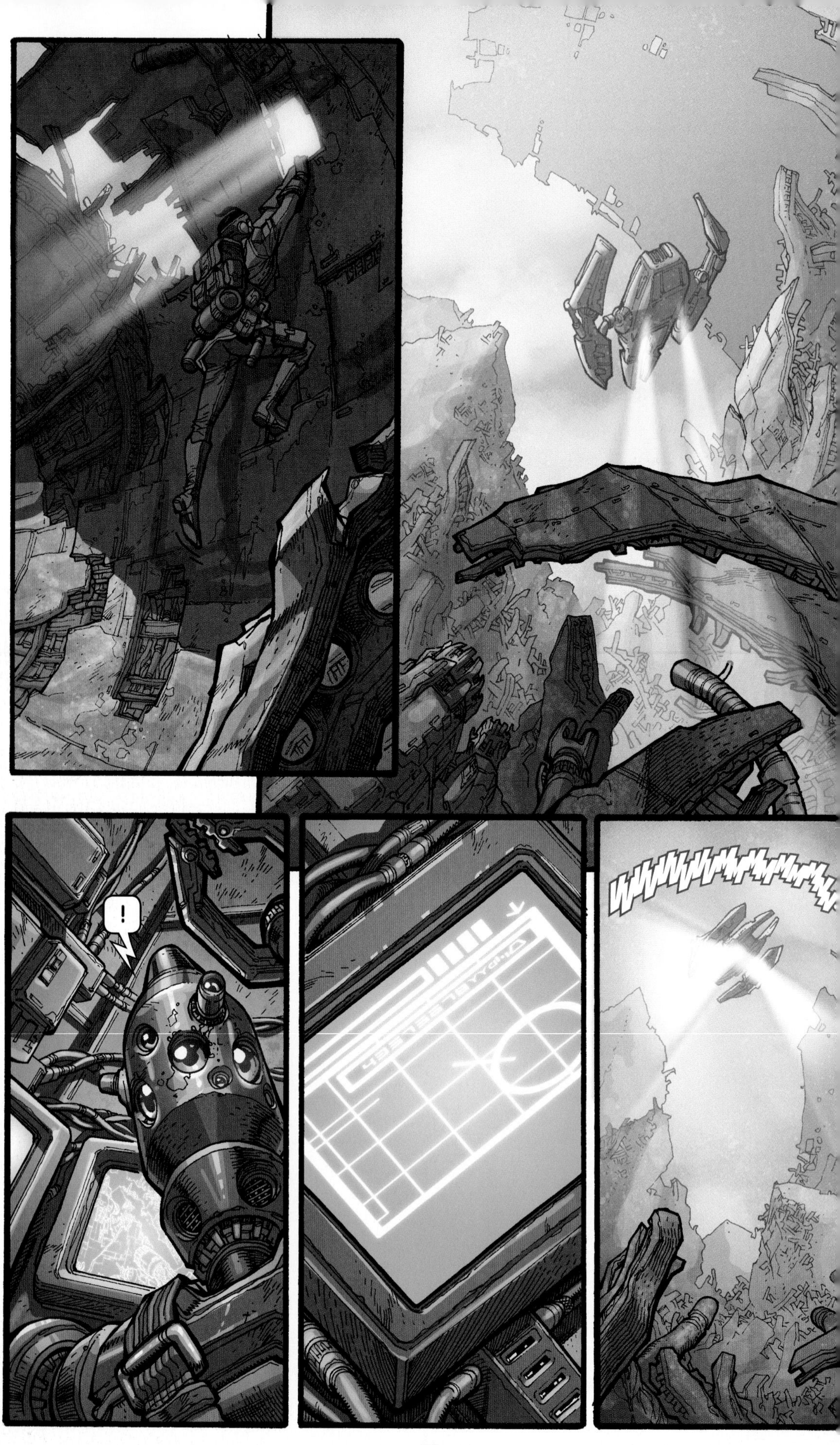
!

BLAST!

190002445B

VIP VIP VIP VIP VIP VIP VIP VIP VIP VIP

VIP VIP VIP VIP VIP VIP

VIP

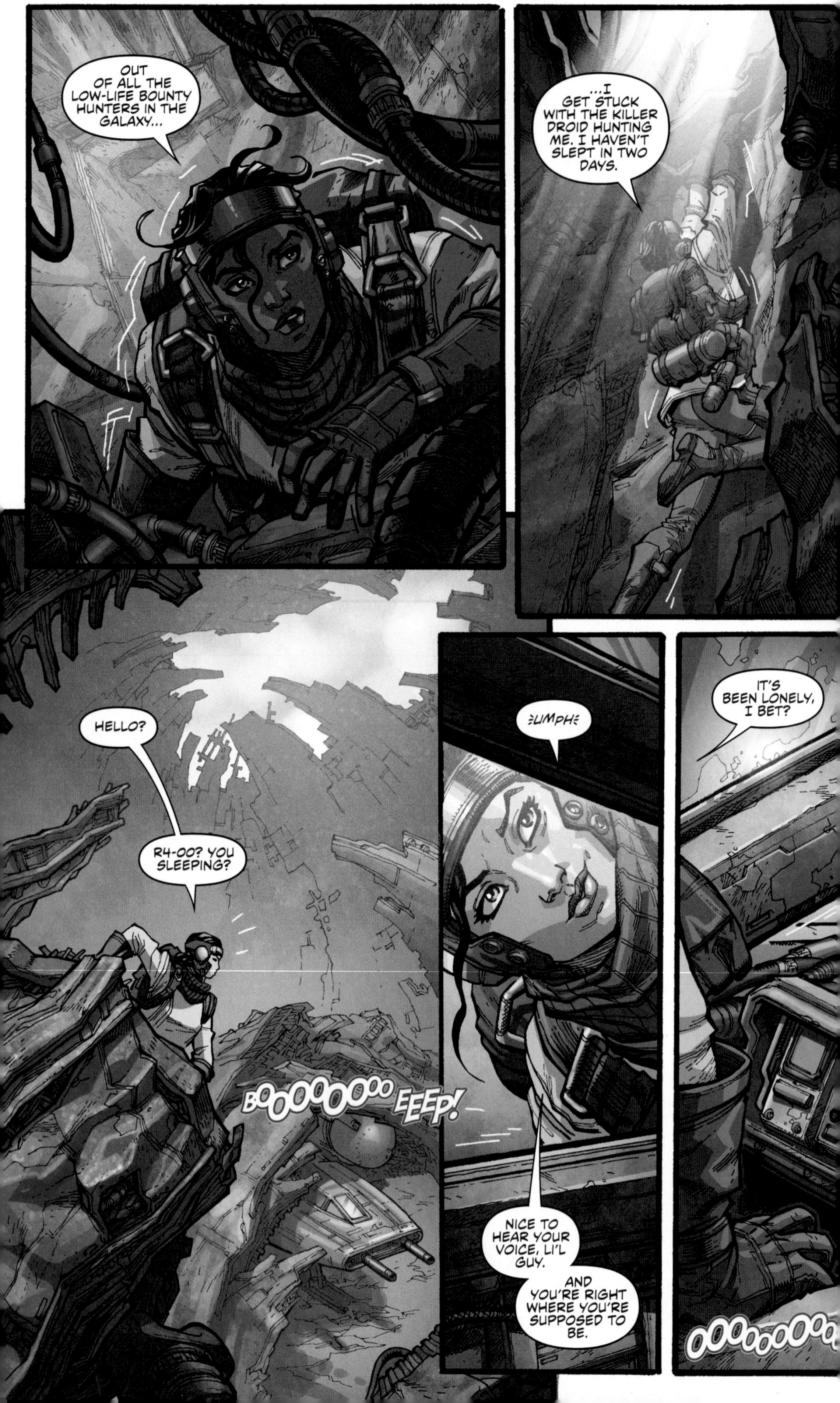
OUT OF ALL THE LOW-LIFE BOUNTY HUNTERS IN THE GALAXY...
...I GET STUCK WITH THE KILLER DROID HUNTING ME. I HAVEN'T SLEPT IN TWO DAYS.
HELLO?
R4-00? YOU SLEEPING?
BOOOOOOOO EEEP!
UMPH
NICE TO HEAR YOUR VOICE, LI'L GUY.
AND YOU'RE RIGHT WHERE YOU'RE SUPPOSED TO BE.
IT'S BEEN LONELY, I BET?
OOOOOOOOO

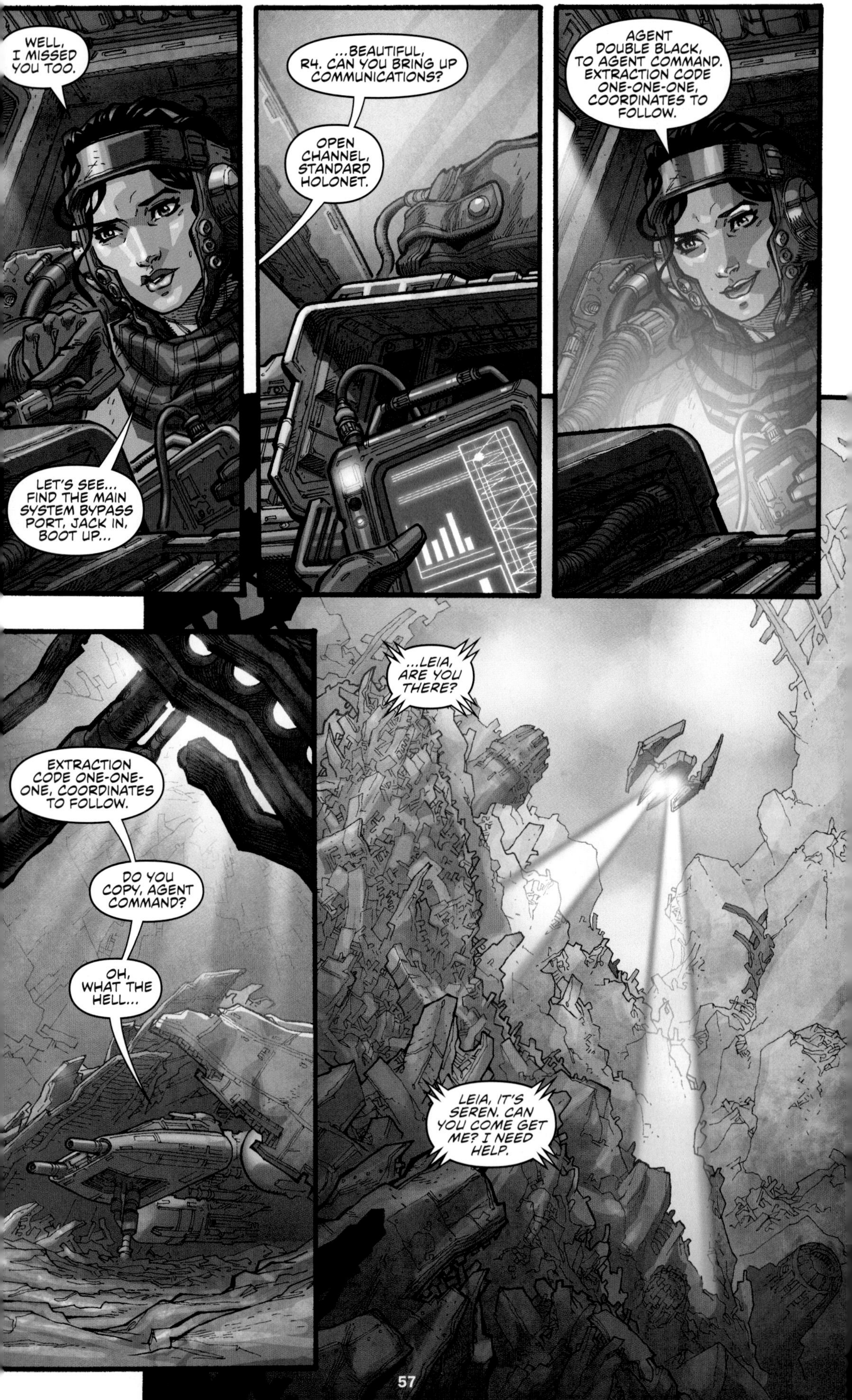
WELL, I MISSED YOU TOO.
LET'S SEE... FIND THE MAIN SYSTEM BYPASS PORT, JACK IN, BOOT UP...
...BEAUTIFUL, R4. CAN YOU BRING UP COMMUNICATIONS?
OPEN CHANNEL, STANDARD HOLONET.
AGENT DOUBLE BLACK, TO AGENT COMMAND. EXTRACTION CODE ONE-ONE-ONE, COORDINATES TO FOLLOW.
EXTRACTION CODE ONE-ONE-ONE, COORDINATES TO FOLLOW.
DO YOU COPY, AGENT COMMAND?
OH, WHAT THE HELL...
...LEIA, ARE YOU THERE?
LEIA, IT'S SEREN. CAN YOU COME GET ME? I NEED HELP.

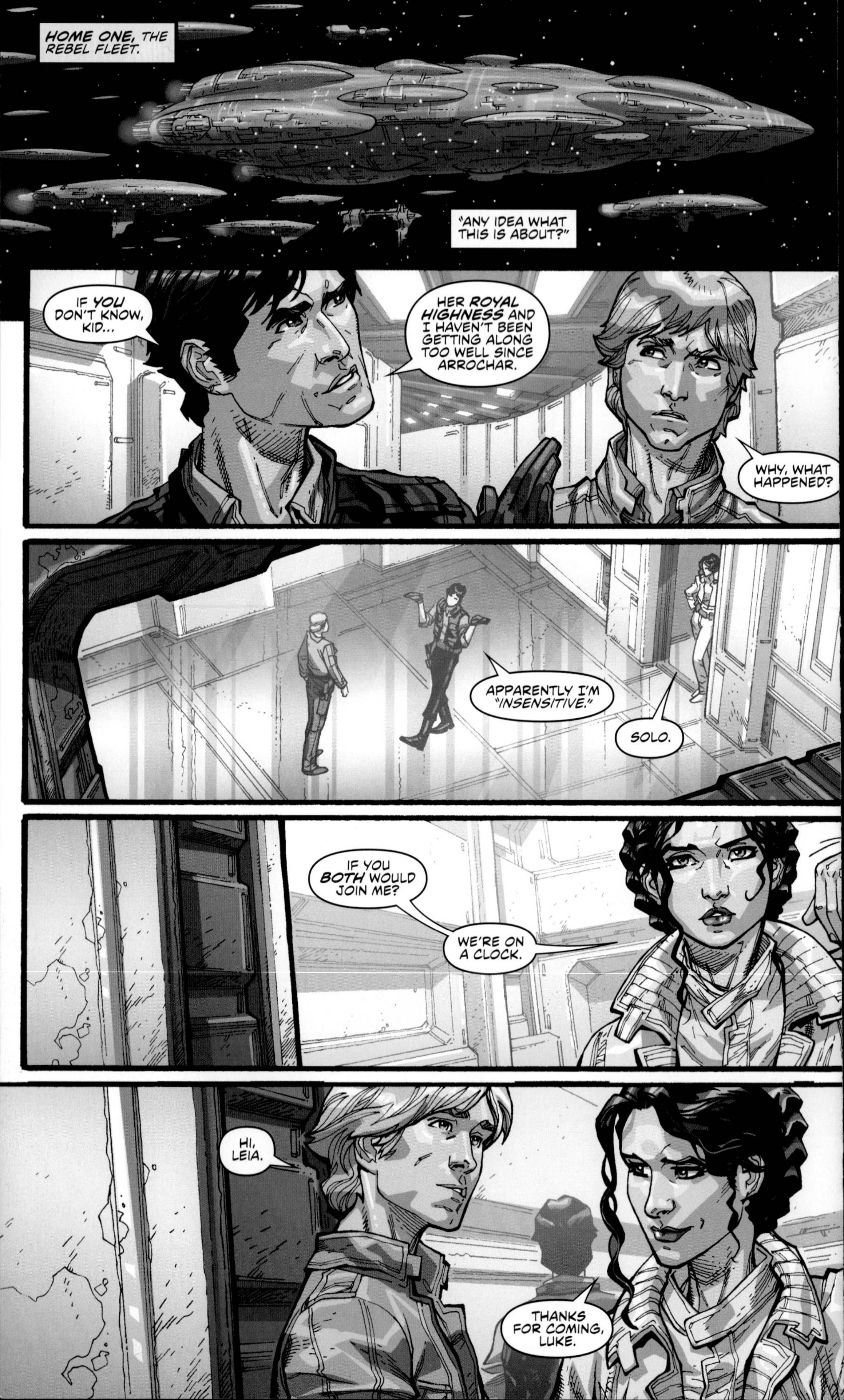
HOME ONE, THE REBEL FLEET.
"ANY IDEA WHAT THIS IS ABOUT?"
IF YOU DON'T KNOW, KID...
HER ROYAL HIGHNESS AND I HAVEN'T BEEN GETTING ALONG TOO WELL SINCE ARROCHAR.
WHY, WHAT HAPPENED?
APPARENTLY I'M "INSENSITIVE."
SOLO.
IF YOU BOTH WOULD JOIN ME?
WE'RE ON A CLOCK.
HI, LEIA.
THANKS FOR COMING, LUKE.

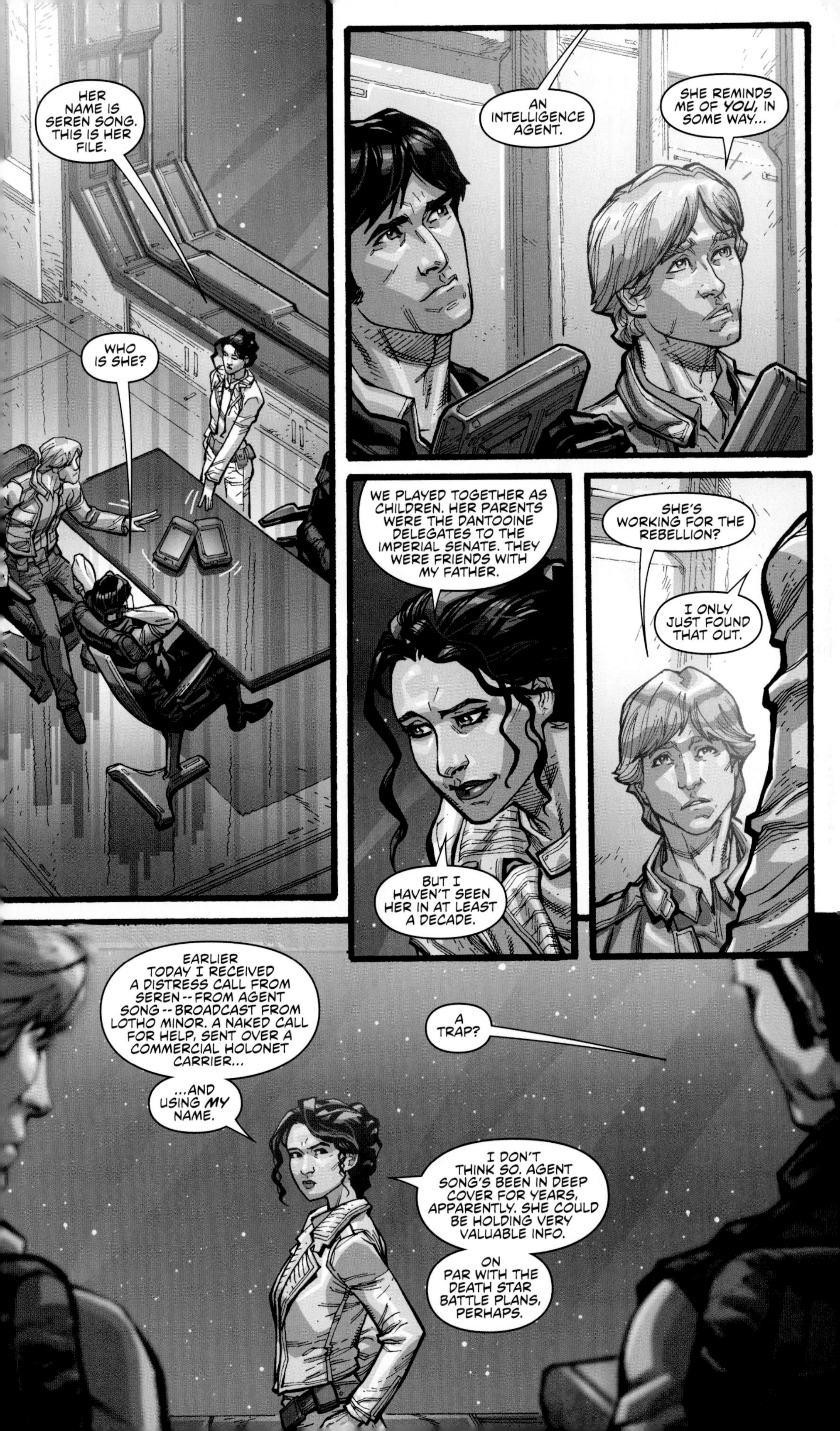
HER NAME IS SEREN SONG. THIS IS HER FILE.
WHO IS SHE?
AN INTELLIGENCE AGENT.
SHE REMINDS ME OF YOU, IN SOME WAY...
WE PLAYED TOGETHER AS CHILDREN. HER PARENTS WERE THE DANTOOINE DELEGATES TO THE IMPERIAL SENATE. THEY WERE FRIENDS WITH MY FATHER.
BUT I HAVEN'T SEEN HER IN AT LEAST A DECADE.
SHE'S WORKING FOR THE REBELLION?
I ONLY JUST FOUND THAT OUT.
EARLIER TODAY I RECEIVED A DISTRESS CALL FROM SEREN -- FROM AGENT SONG -- BROADCAST FROM LOTHO MINOR. A NAKED CALL FOR HELP, SENT OVER A COMMERCIAL HOLONET CARRIER...
...AND USING MY NAME.
A TRAP?
I DON'T THINK SO. AGENT SONG'S BEEN IN DEEP COVER FOR YEARS, APPARENTLY. SHE COULD BE HOLDING VERY VALUABLE INFO.
ON PAR WITH THE DEATH STAR BATTLE PLANS, PERHAPS.

NO ONE'S *THAT* LUCKY, SISTER.

...WE'VE HAD A BIT OF *BAD* LUCK RECENTLY. WE COULD USE SOME OF THE GOOD.

IN CASE YOU HADN'T NOTICED, HAN...

MON MOTHMA'S AUTHORIZED ME TO RESPOND TO THE CALL AND PULL SEREN OUT.

A RESCUE MISSION?

HOLD ON, HOLD ON. THE OLD LADY'S HAD THE *FALCON'S* REPAIRS REQUISITION ON HOLD FOR *WEEKS*, BECAUSE OF LACK OF MONEY AND MATERIALS. NO *WAY* IS SHE WASTING THE FLEET ON SOME WILD-GOOSE CHASE.

WELL, TODAY IS *YOUR* LUCKY DAY, CAPTAIN. YO[U] AUTHORIZATION TO PULL FROM TH[E] SHIP'S STORES A[S] MUCH SUPPLY A[S] YOU NEED FOR A TEN DAY MISSION...

...AND THE REPAIRS TO YOUR SHIP GOT UNDERWAY THIRTY MINUTES AGO.

I DON'T UNDERSTAND.

YOU'RE RIGHT, MON MOTHMA *WON'T* WASTE THE FLEET ON THIS. BUT SHE *WILL* WASTE ONE NON-OFFICIAL, HALF-JUNKED OLD SPICE FREIGHTER.

WE LEAVE IN TWO HOURS.

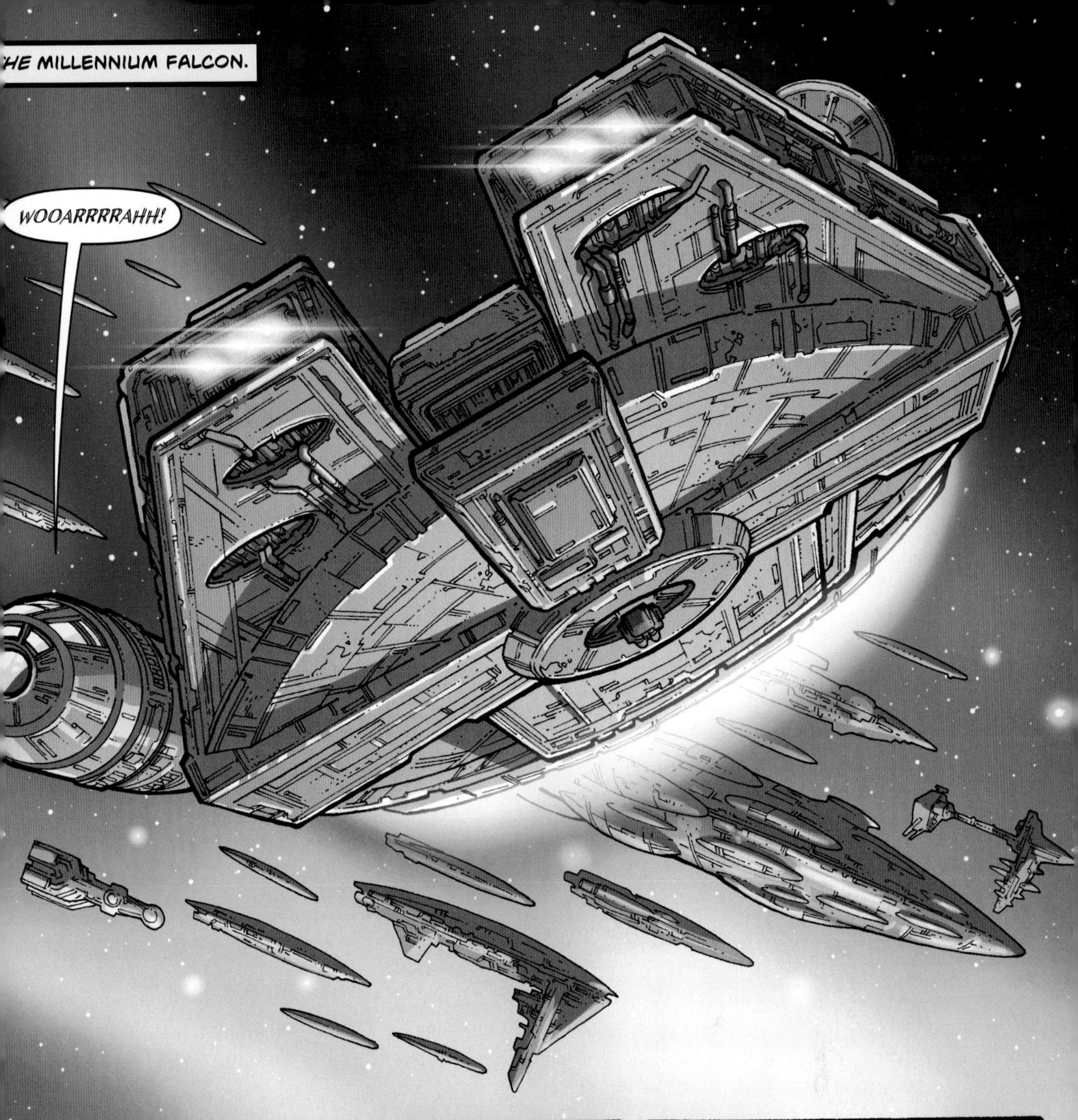
THE MILLENNIUM FALCON.
WOOARRRRRAHH!

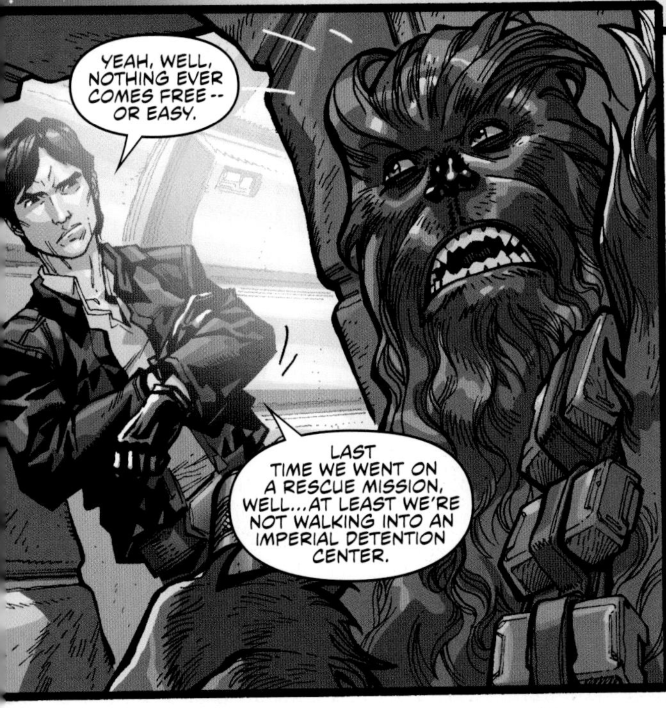
YEAH, WELL, NOTHING EVER COMES FREE -- OR EASY.
LAST TIME WE WENT ON A RESCUE MISSION, WELL...AT LEAST WE'RE NOT WALKING INTO AN IMPERIAL DETENTION CENTER.

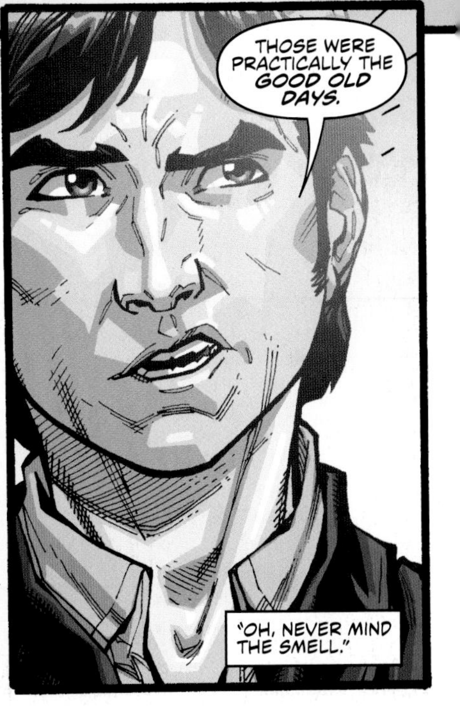
THOSE WERE PRACTICALLY THE GOOD OLD DAYS.
"OH, NEVER MIND THE SMELL."

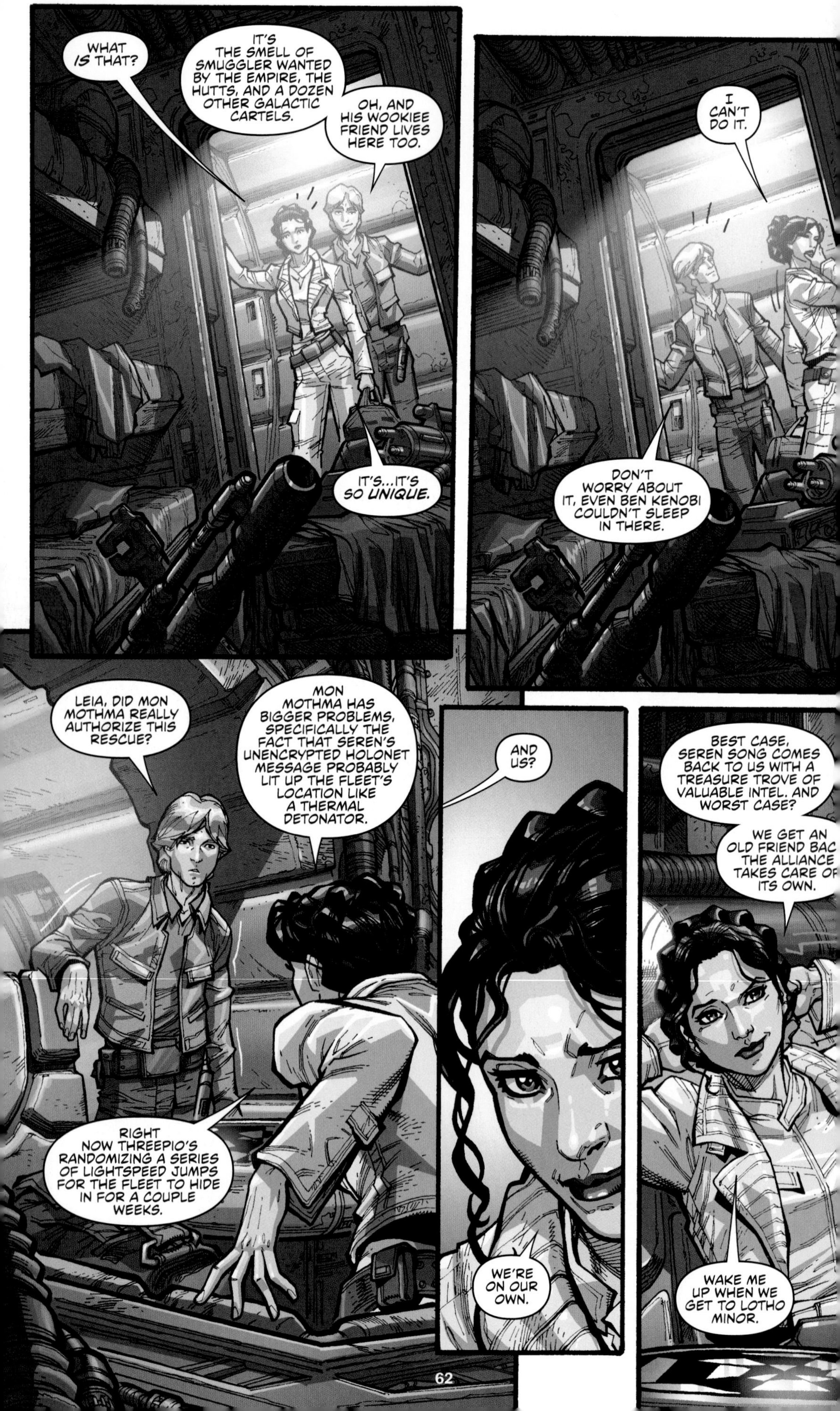
WHAT *IS* THAT?
IT'S THE SMELL OF SMUGGLER WANTED BY THE EMPIRE, THE HUTTS, AND A DOZEN OTHER GALACTIC CARTELS.
OH, AND HIS WOOKIEE FRIEND LIVES HERE TOO.
IT'S...IT'S SO ***UNIQUE***.
I CAN'T DO IT.
DON'T WORRY ABOUT IT, EVEN BEN KENOBI COULDN'T SLEEP IN THERE.
LEIA, DID MON MOTHMA REALLY AUTHORIZE THIS RESCUE?
MON MOTHMA HAS BIGGER PROBLEMS, SPECIFICALLY THE FACT THAT SEREN'S UNENCRYPTED HOLONET MESSAGE PROBABLY LIT UP THE FLEET'S LOCATION LIKE A THERMAL DETONATOR.
RIGHT NOW THREEPIO'S RANDOMIZING A SERIES OF LIGHTSPEED JUMPS FOR THE FLEET TO HIDE IN FOR A COUPLE WEEKS.
AND US?
WE'RE ON OUR OWN.
BEST CASE, SEREN SONG COMES BACK TO US WITH A TREASURE TROVE OF VALUABLE INTEL. AND WORST CASE?
WE GET AN OLD FRIEND BAC THE ALLIANCE TAKES CARE OF ITS OWN.
WAKE ME UP WHEN WE GET TO LOTHO MINOR.

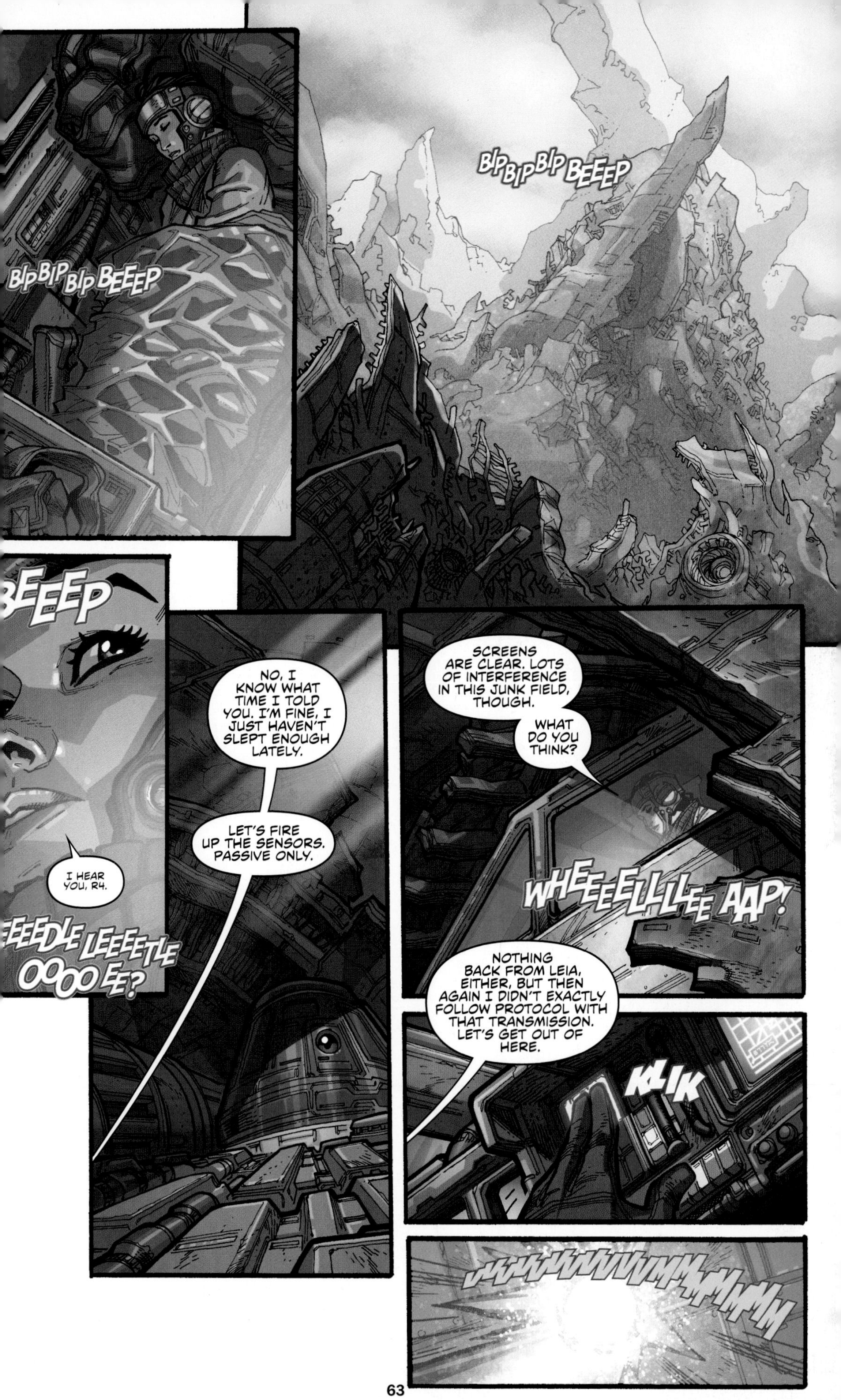
BIPBIPBIP BEEEP
BIPBIP BIP BEEEP
BEEEP
I HEAR YOU, R4.
EEEEDLE LEEEETLE OOOO EE?
NO, I KNOW WHAT TIME I TOLD YOU. I'M FINE, I JUST HAVEN'T SLEPT ENOUGH LATELY.
LET'S FIRE UP THE SENSORS. PASSIVE ONLY.
SCREENS ARE CLEAR. LOTS OF INTERFERENCE IN THIS JUNK FIELD, THOUGH.
WHAT DO YOU THINK?
WHEEEEELLLLEE AAP!
NOTHING BACK FROM LEIA, EITHER, BUT THEN AGAIN I DIDN'T EXACTLY FOLLOW PROTOCOL WITH THAT TRANSMISSION. LET'S GET OUT OF HERE.
KLIK
VVVVVVVVVVVVVVVVVMMMMMMMM

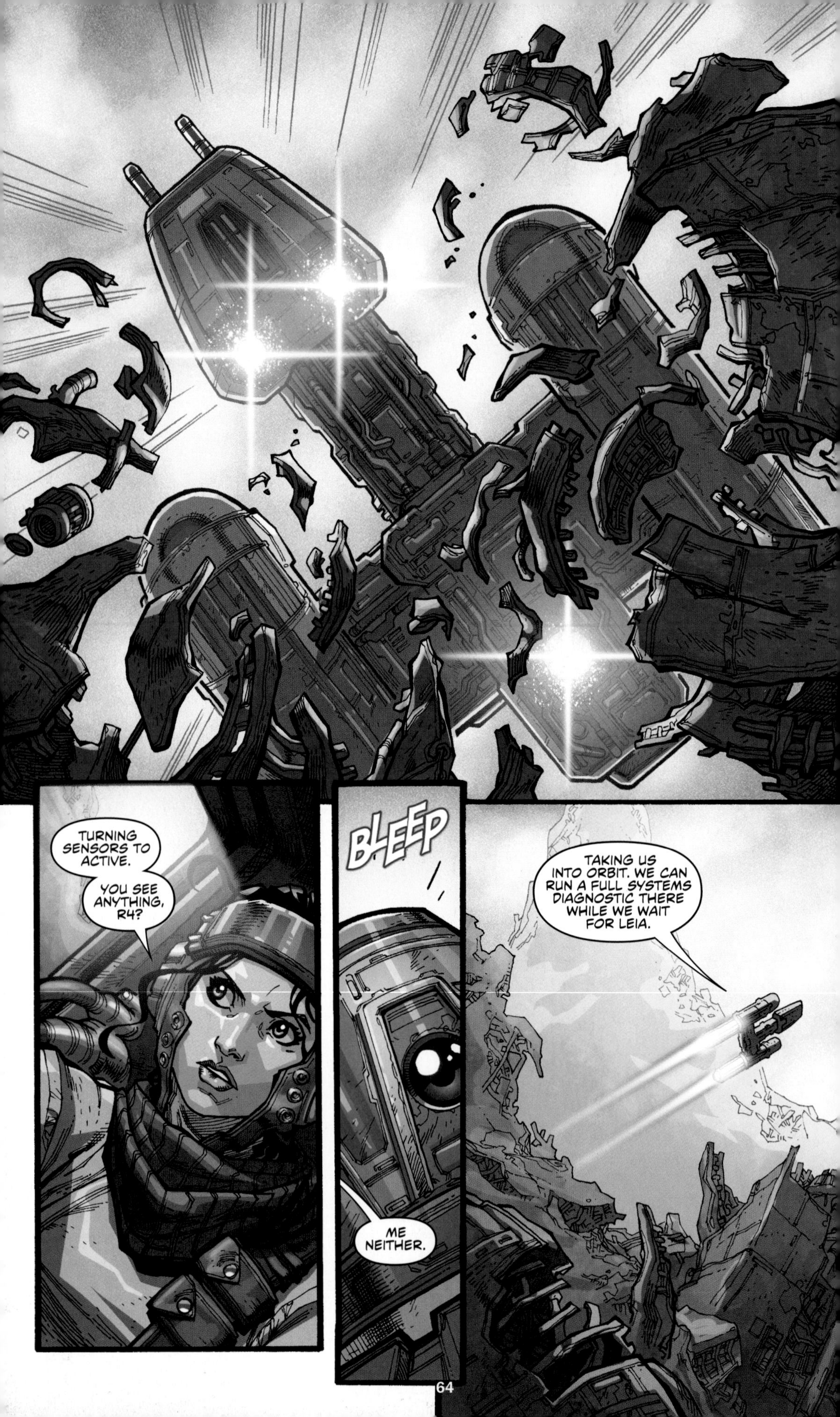
TURNING SENSORS TO ACTIVE.
YOU SEE ANYTHING, R4?
BLEEP
ME NEITHER.
TAKING US INTO ORBIT. WE CAN RUN A FULL SYSTEMS DIAGNOSTIC THERE WHILE WE WAIT FOR LEIA.

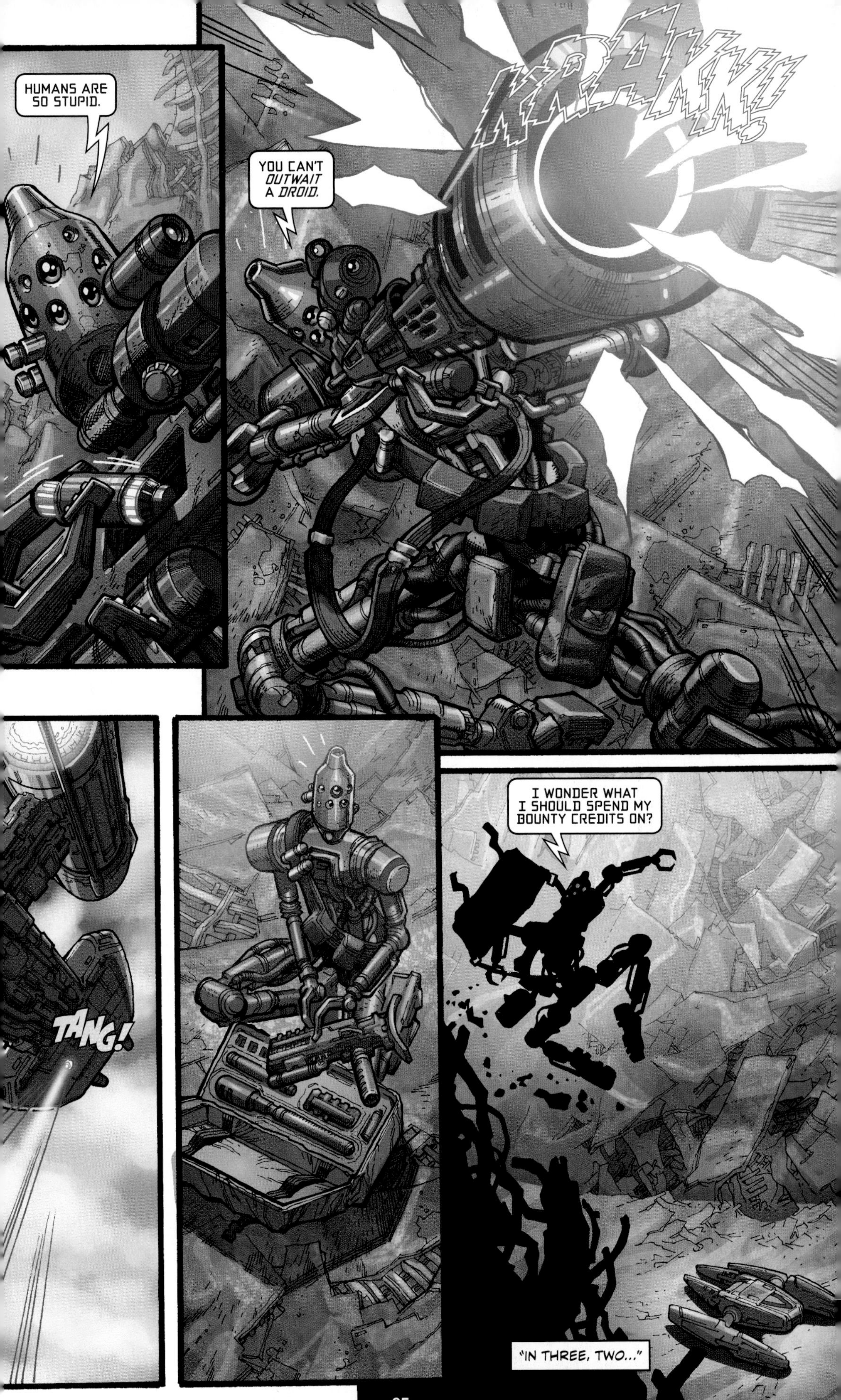
HUMANS ARE SO STUPID.
YOU CAN'T *OUTWAIT* A *DROID.*
KRAAK!
TANG!
I WONDER WHAT I SHOULD SPEND MY BOUNTY CREDITS ON?
"IN THREE, TWO..."

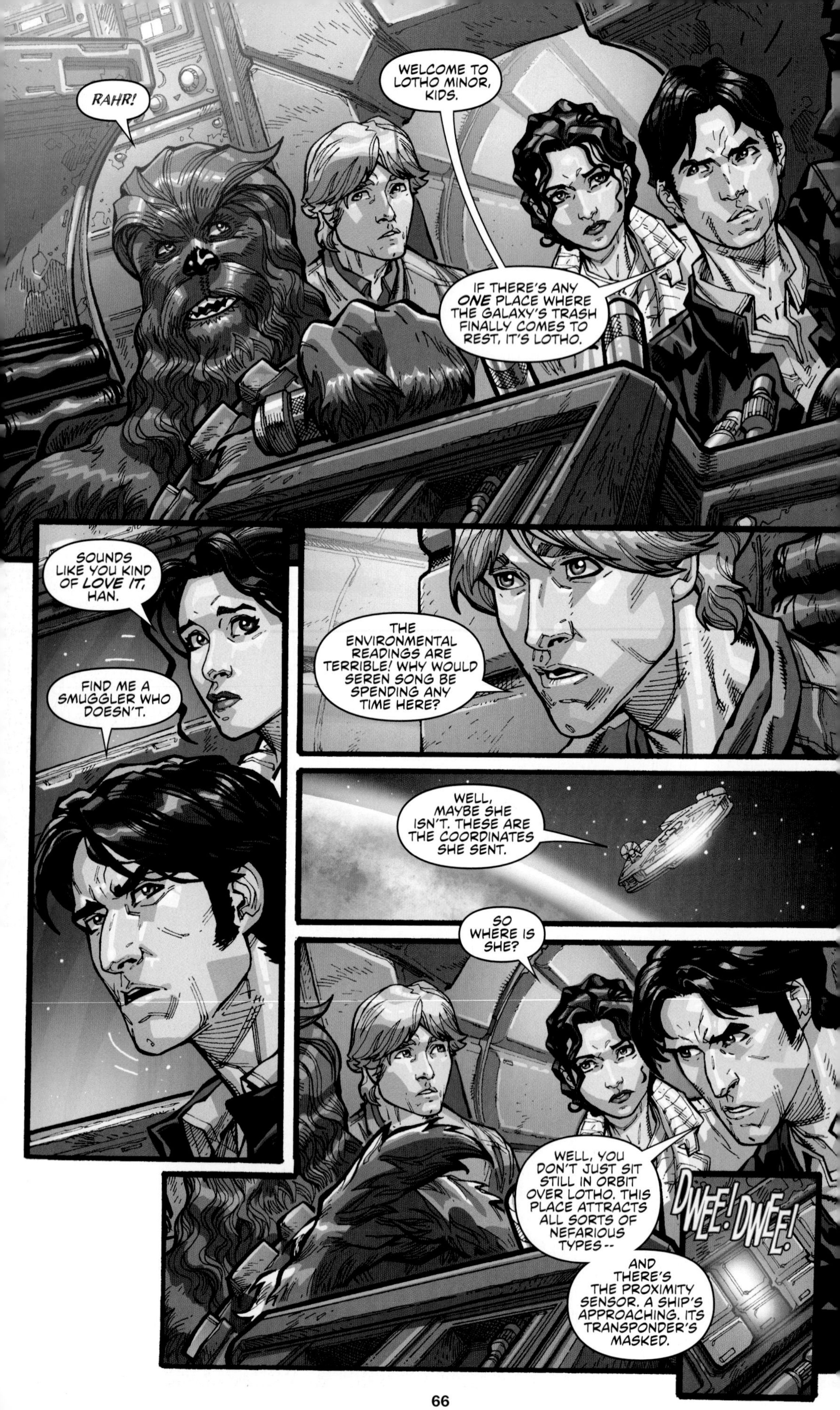
RAHR!
WELCOME TO LOTHO MINOR, KIDS.
IF THERE'S ANY *ONE* PLACE WHERE THE GALAXY'S TRASH FINALLY COMES TO REST, IT'S LOTHO.
SOUNDS LIKE YOU KIND OF *LOVE IT,* HAN.
FIND ME A SMUGGLER WHO DOESN'T.
THE ENVIRONMENTAL READINGS ARE TERRIBLE! WHY WOULD SEREN SONG BE SPENDING ANY TIME HERE?
WELL, MAYBE SHE ISN'T. THESE ARE THE COORDINATES SHE SENT.
SO WHERE IS SHE?
WELL, YOU DON'T JUST SIT STILL IN ORBIT OVER LOTHO. THIS PLACE ATTRACTS ALL SORTS OF NEFARIOUS TYPES--
DWEE! DWEE!
AND THERE'S THE PROXIMITY SENSOR. A SHIP'S APPROACHING. ITS TRANSPONDER'S MASKED.

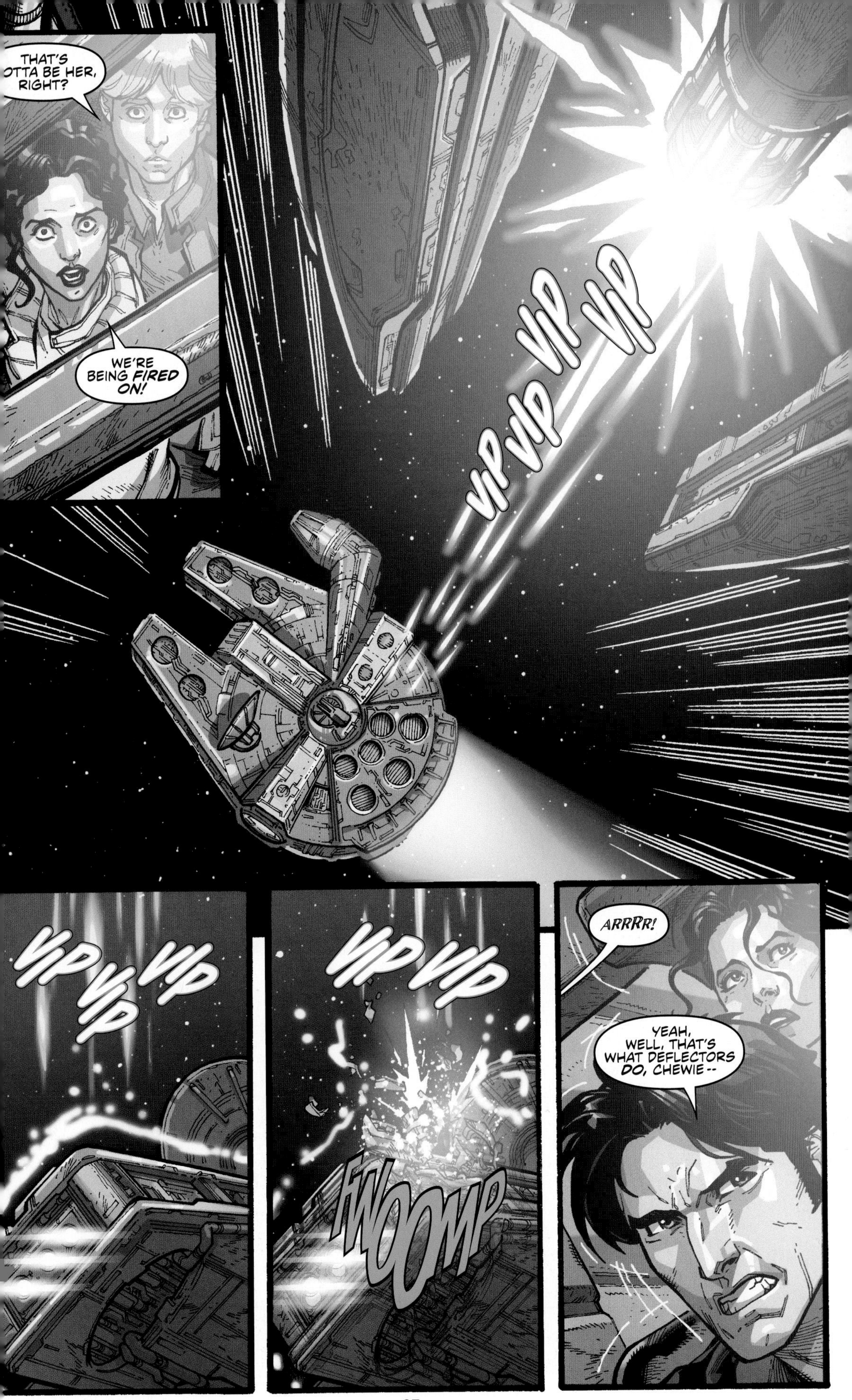
THAT'S OTTA BE HER, RIGHT?
WE'RE BEING FIRED ON!
VIP VIP VIP VIP
VIP VIP VIP
VIP VIP
FWOOMP
ARRRR!
YEAH, WELL, THAT'S WHAT DEFLECTORS DO, CHEWIE --

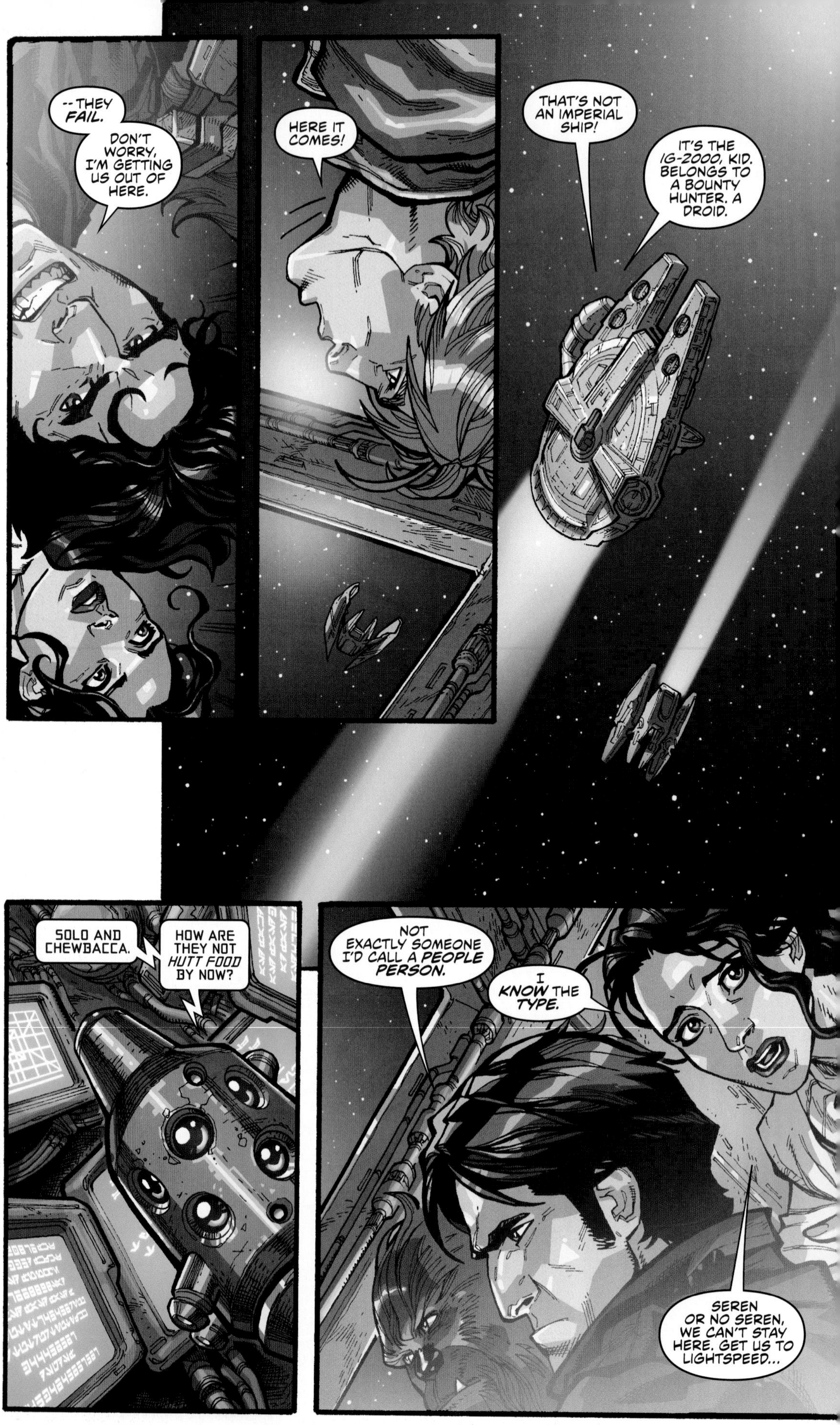
--THEY *FAIL.*
DON'T WORRY, I'M GETTING US OUT OF HERE.
HERE IT COMES!
THAT'S NOT AN IMPERIAL SHIP!
IT'S THE *IG-2000*, KID. BELONGS TO A BOUNTY HUNTER. A DROID.
SOLO AND CHEWBACCA.
HOW ARE THEY NOT *HUTT FOOD* BY NOW?
NOT EXACTLY SOMEONE I'D CALL A *PEOPLE PERSON.*
I *KNOW* THE *TYPE.*
SEREN OR NO SEREN, WE CAN'T STAY HERE. GET US TO LIGHTSPEED...

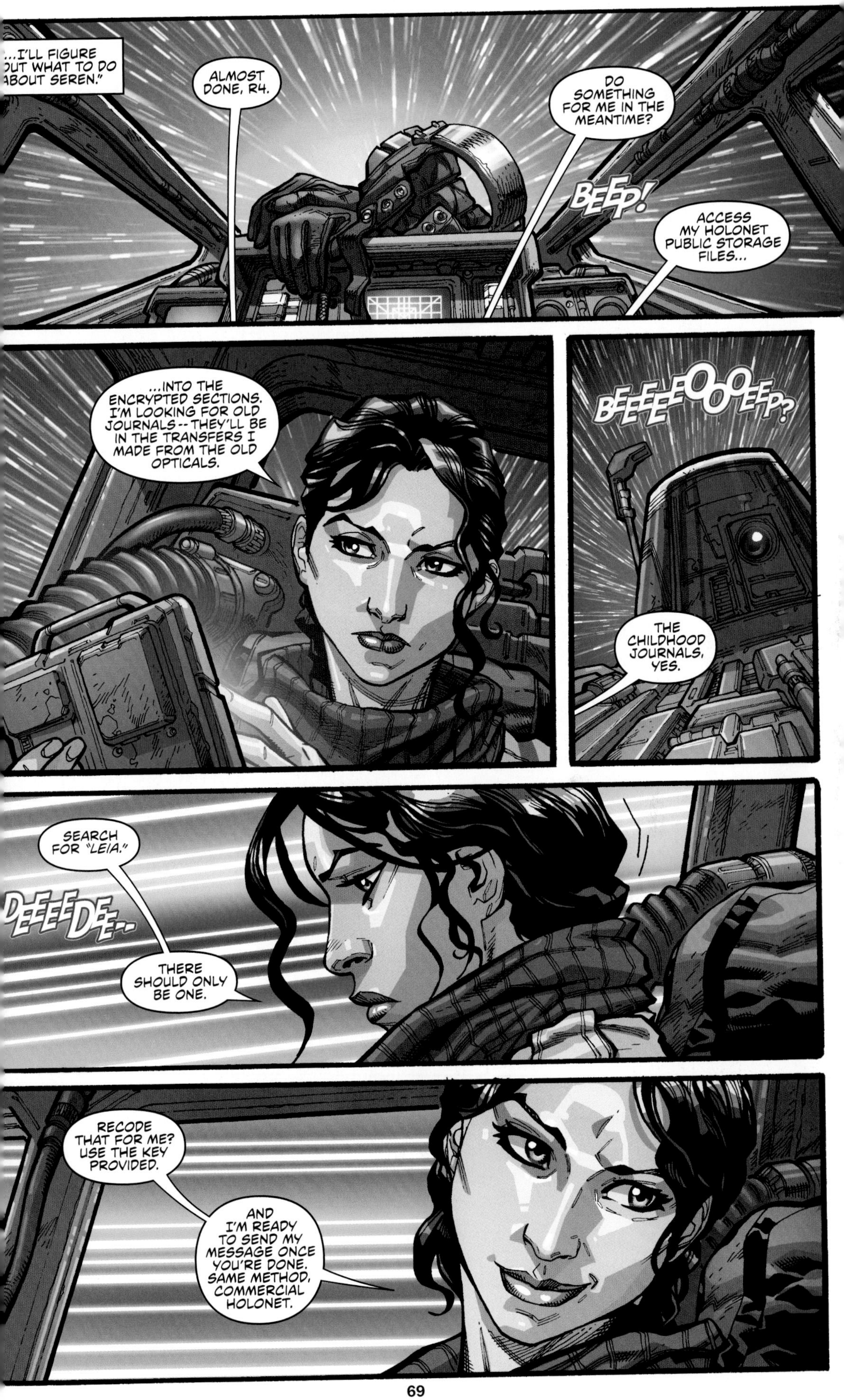
...I'LL FIGURE OUT WHAT TO DO ABOUT SEREN."
ALMOST DONE, R4.
DO SOMETHING FOR ME IN THE MEANTIME?
BEEP!
ACCESS MY HOLONET PUBLIC STORAGE FILES...
...INTO THE ENCRYPTED SECTIONS. I'M LOOKING FOR OLD JOURNALS--THEY'LL BE IN THE TRANSFERS I MADE FROM THE OLD OPTICALS.
BEEEEEOOOOEEP?
THE CHILDHOOD JOURNALS, YES.
SEARCH FOR "LEIA."
DEEEEDEE--
THERE SHOULD ONLY BE ONE.
RECODE THAT FOR ME? USE THE KEY PROVIDED.
AND I'M READY TO SEND MY MESSAGE ONCE YOU'RE DONE. SAME METHOD, COMMERCIAL HOLONET.

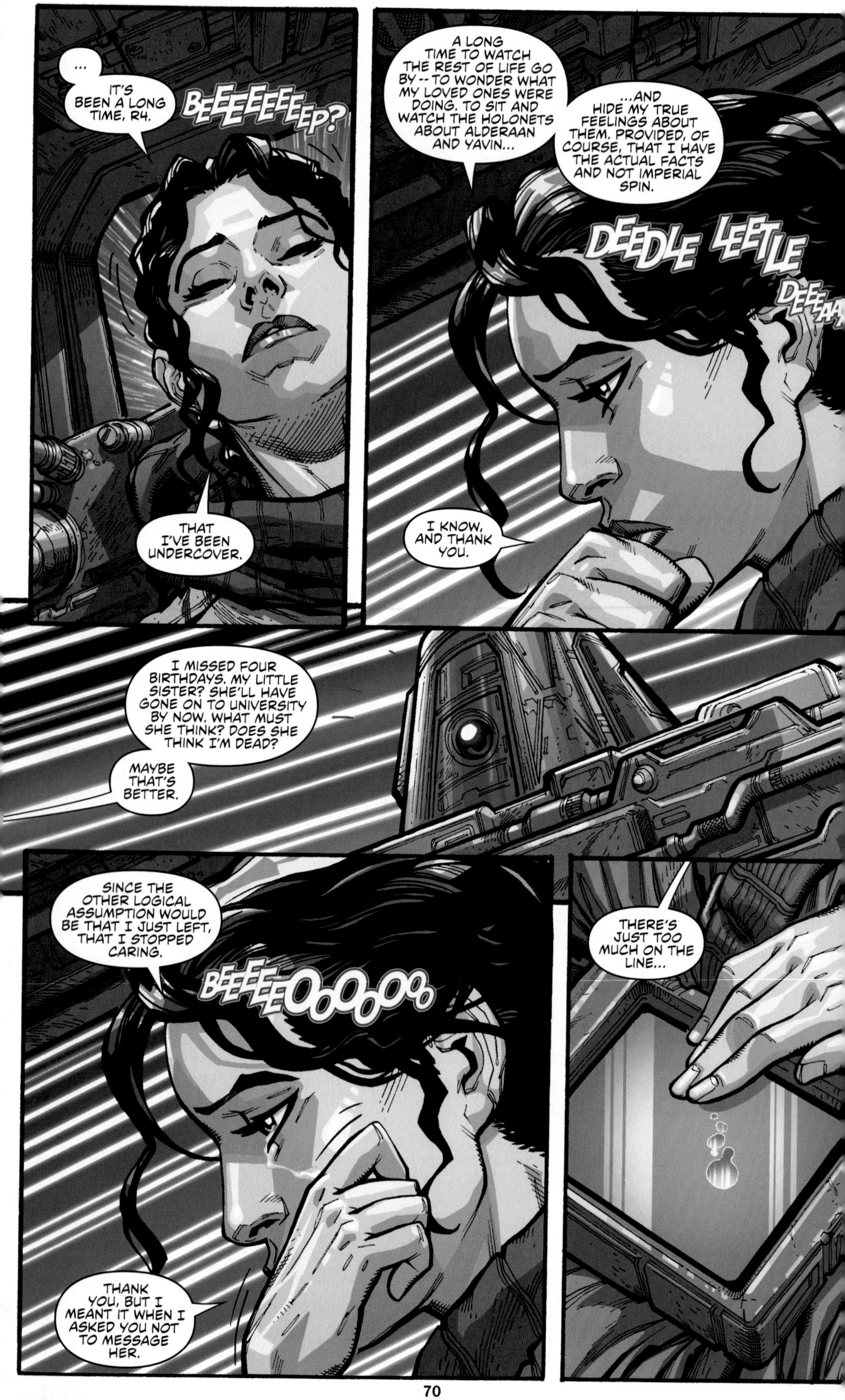

...
IT'S BEEN A LONG TIME, R4.
BEEEEEEEEEP?
THAT I'VE BEEN UNDERCOVER.
A LONG TIME TO WATCH THE REST OF LIFE GO BY -- TO WONDER WHAT MY LOVED ONES WERE DOING. TO SIT AND WATCH THE HOLONETS ABOUT ALDERAAN AND YAVIN...
...AND HIDE MY TRUE FEELINGS ABOUT THEM. PROVIDED, OF COURSE, THAT I HAVE THE ACTUAL FACTS AND NOT IMPERIAL SPIN.
DEEDLE LEETLE
I KNOW, AND THANK YOU.
I MISSED FOUR BIRTHDAYS. MY LITTLE SISTER? SHE'LL HAVE GONE ON TO UNIVERSITY BY NOW. WHAT MUST SHE THINK? DOES SHE THINK I'M DEAD?
MAYBE THAT'S BETTER.
SINCE THE OTHER LOGICAL ASSUMPTION WOULD BE THAT I JUST LEFT, THAT I STOPPED CARING.
BEEEEEOOOOOO
THANK YOU, BUT I MEANT IT WHEN I ASKED YOU NOT TO MESSAGE HER.
THERE'S JUST TOO MUCH ON THE LINE...

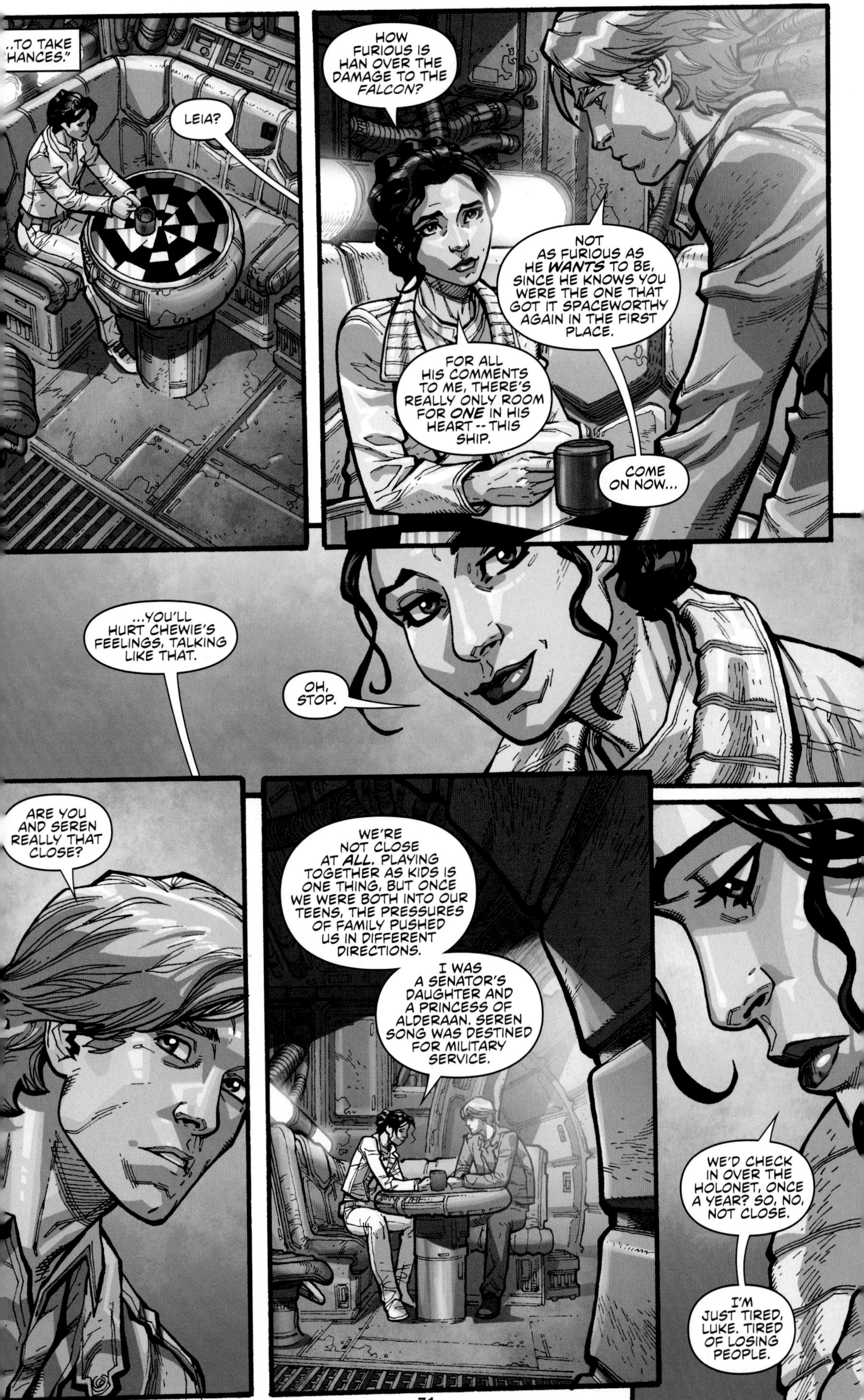
..TO TAKE HANCES."
LEIA?
HOW FURIOUS IS HAN OVER THE DAMAGE TO THE *FALCON*?
NOT AS FURIOUS AS HE ***WANTS*** TO BE, SINCE HE KNOWS YOU WERE THE ONE THAT GOT IT SPACEWORTHY AGAIN IN THE FIRST PLACE.
FOR ALL HIS COMMENTS TO ME, THERE'S REALLY ONLY ROOM FOR *ONE* IN HIS HEART -- THIS SHIP.
COME ON NOW...
...YOU'LL HURT CHEWIE'S FEELINGS, TALKING LIKE THAT.
OH, STOP.
ARE YOU AND SEREN REALLY THAT CLOSE?
WE'RE NOT CLOSE AT *ALL*. PLAYING TOGETHER AS KIDS IS ONE THING, BUT ONCE WE WERE BOTH INTO OUR TEENS, THE PRESSURES OF FAMILY PUSHED US IN DIFFERENT DIRECTIONS.
I WAS A SENATOR'S DAUGHTER AND A PRINCESS OF ALDERAAN. SEREN SONG WAS DESTINED FOR MILITARY SERVICE.
WE'D CHECK IN OVER THE HOLONET, ONCE A YEAR? SO, NO, NOT CLOSE.
I'M JUST TIRED, LUKE. TIRED OF LOSING PEOPLE.

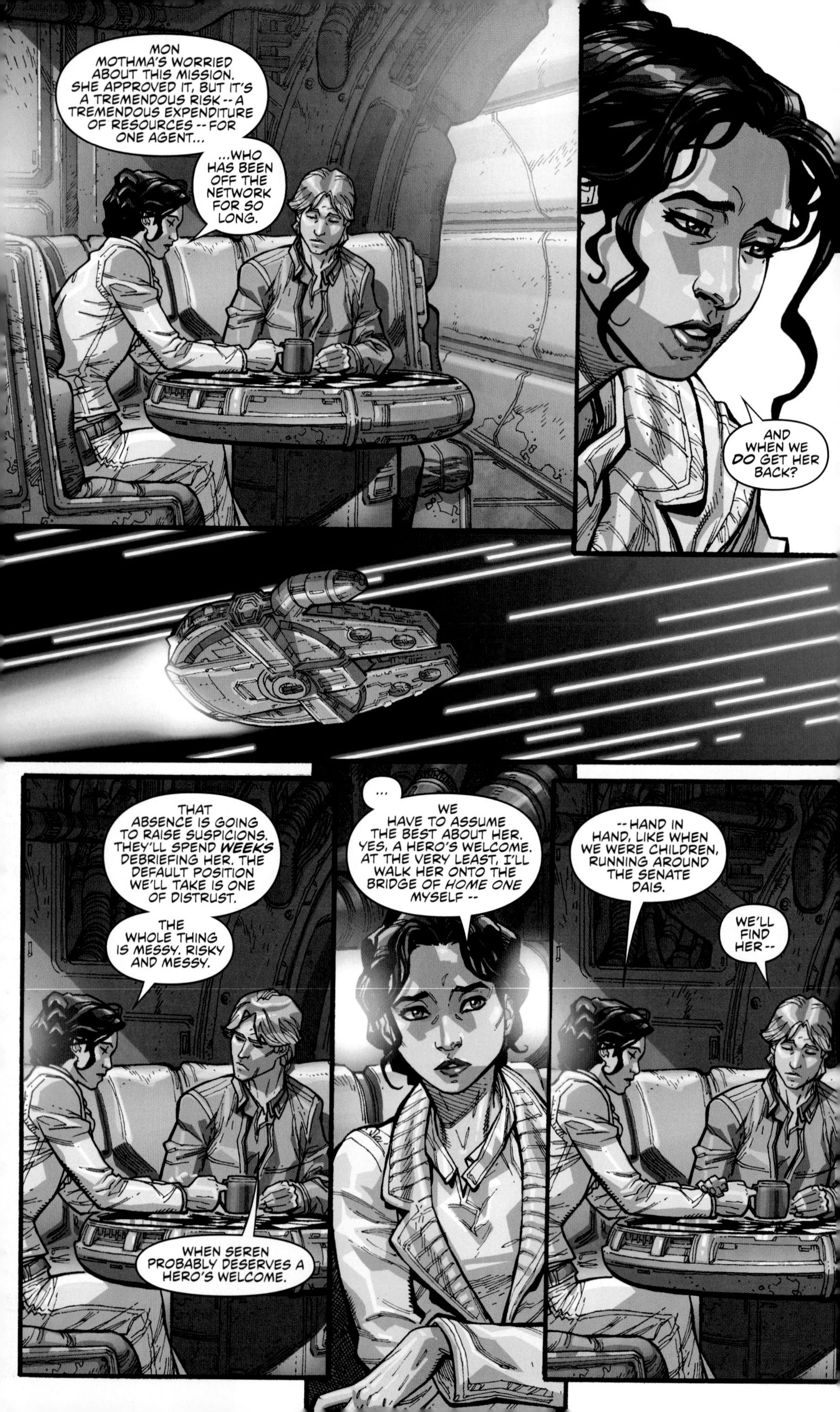
MON MOTHMA'S WORRIED ABOUT THIS MISSION. SHE APPROVED IT, BUT IT'S A TREMENDOUS RISK -- A TREMENDOUS EXPENDITURE OF RESOURCES -- FOR ONE AGENT...
...WHO HAS BEEN OFF THE NETWORK FOR SO LONG.
AND WHEN WE *DO* GET HER BACK?
THAT ABSENCE IS GOING TO RAISE SUSPICIONS. THEY'LL SPEND ***WEEKS*** DEBRIEFING HER. THE DEFAULT POSITION WE'LL TAKE IS ONE OF DISTRUST.
THE WHOLE THING IS MESSY. RISKY AND MESSY.
WHEN SEREN PROBABLY DESERVES A HERO'S WELCOME.
...
WE HAVE TO ASSUME THE BEST ABOUT HER. YES, A HERO'S WELCOME. AT THE VERY LEAST, I'LL WALK HER ONTO THE BRIDGE OF *HOME ONE* MYSELF --
-- HAND IN HAND, LIKE WHEN WE WERE CHILDREN, RUNNING AROUND THE SENATE DAIS.
WE'LL FIND HER --

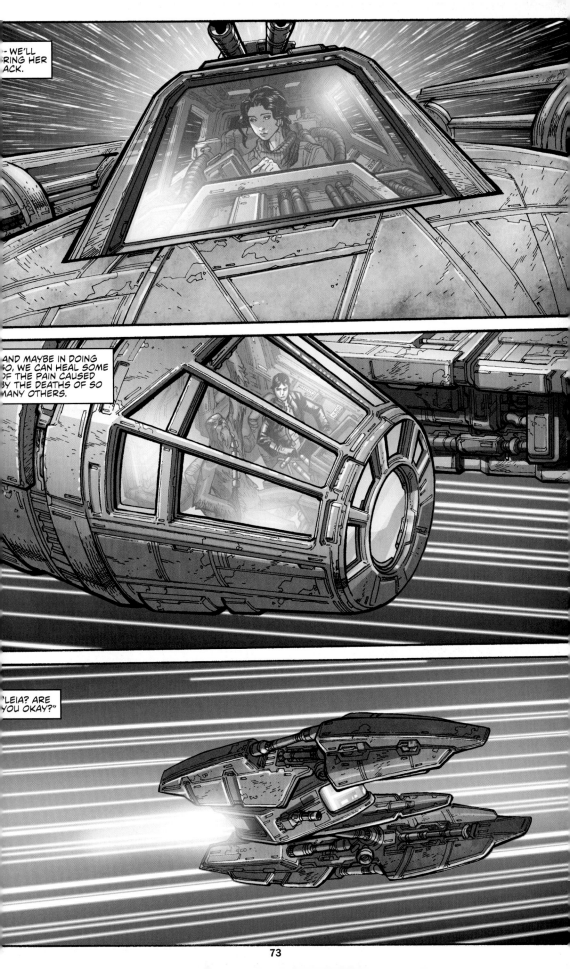

...WE'LL
RING HER
ACK.

AND MAYBE IN DOING
O, WE CAN HEAL SOME
F THE PAIN CAUSED
Y THE DEATHS OF SO
MANY OTHERS.

"LEIA? ARE
YOU OKAY?"

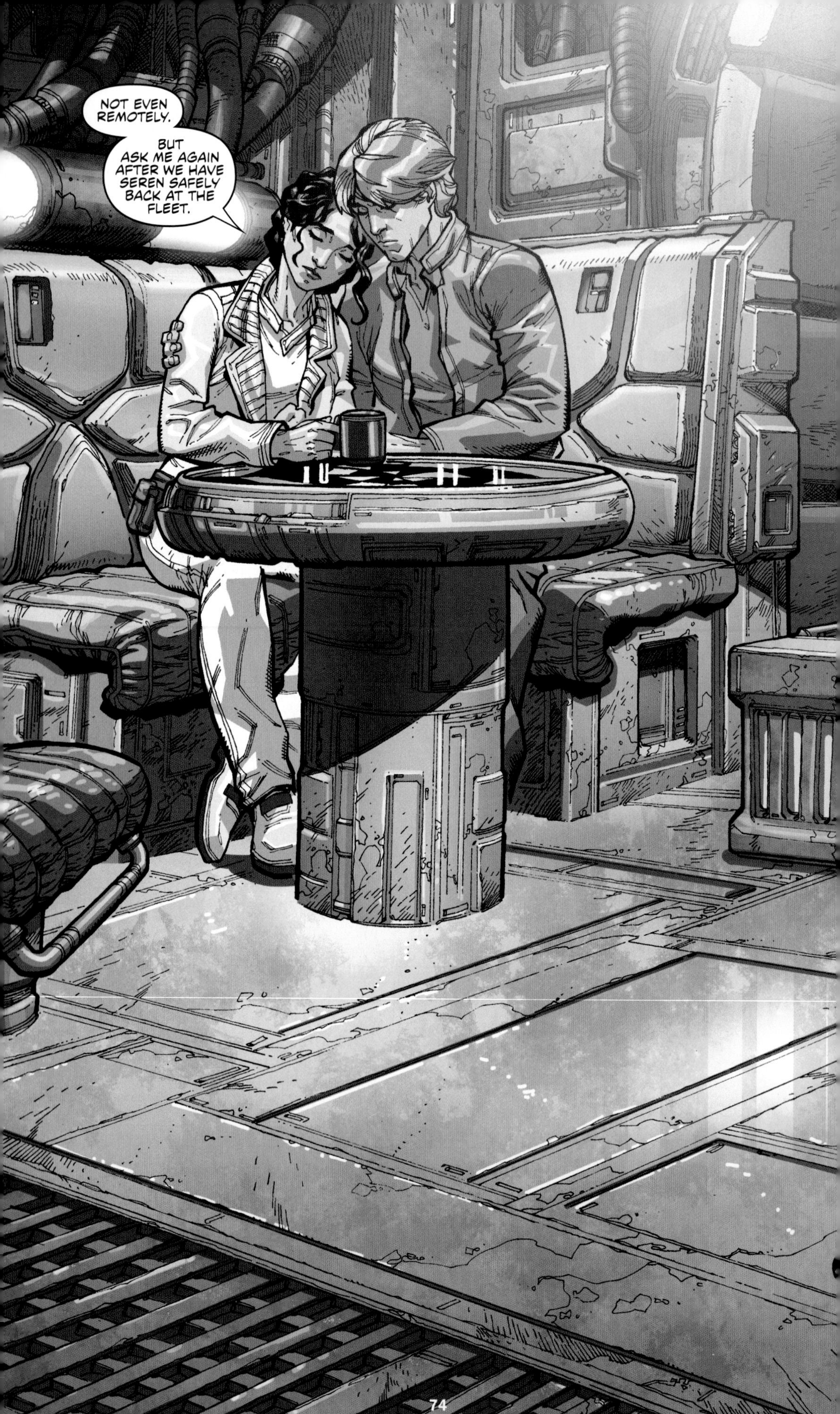
NOT EVEN REMOTELY.
BUT ASK ME AGAIN AFTER WE HAVE SEREN SAFELY BACK AT THE FLEET.

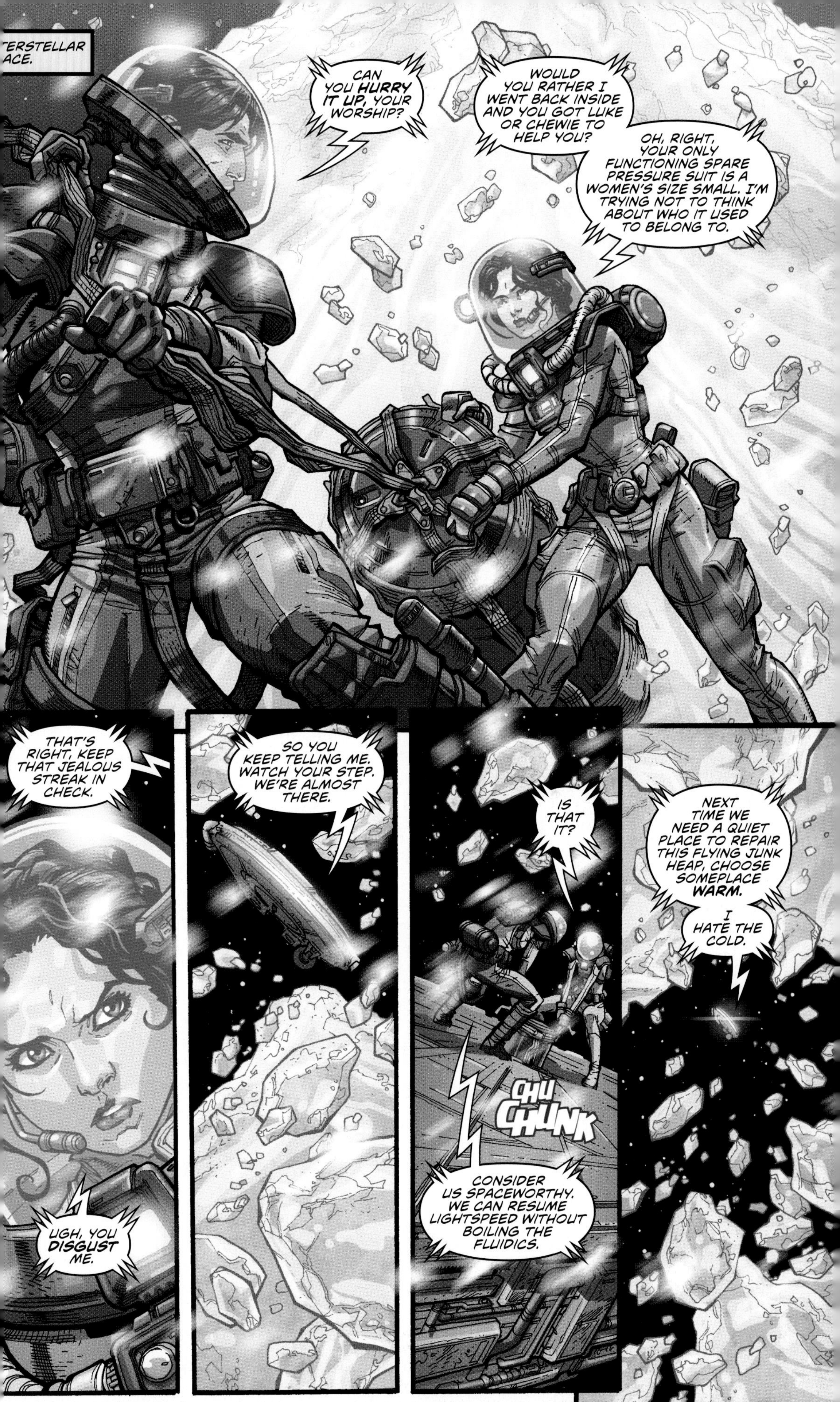

ERSTELLAR ACE.
CAN YOU HURRY IT UP, YOUR WORSHIP?
WOULD YOU RATHER I WENT BACK INSIDE AND YOU GOT LUKE OR CHEWIE TO HELP YOU?
OH, RIGHT, YOUR ONLY FUNCTIONING SPARE PRESSURE SUIT IS A WOMEN'S SIZE SMALL. I'M TRYING NOT TO THINK ABOUT WHO IT USED TO BELONG TO.
THAT'S RIGHT, KEEP THAT JEALOUS STREAK IN CHECK.
UGH, YOU DISGUST ME.
SO YOU KEEP TELLING ME. WATCH YOUR STEP. WE'RE ALMOST THERE.
IS THAT IT?
CHU CHUNK
CONSIDER US SPACEWORTHY. WE CAN RESUME LIGHTSPEED WITHOUT BOILING THE FLUIDICS.
NEXT TIME WE NEED A QUIET PLACE TO REPAIR THIS FLYING JUNK HEAP, CHOOSE SOMEPLACE WARM.
I HATE THE COLD.

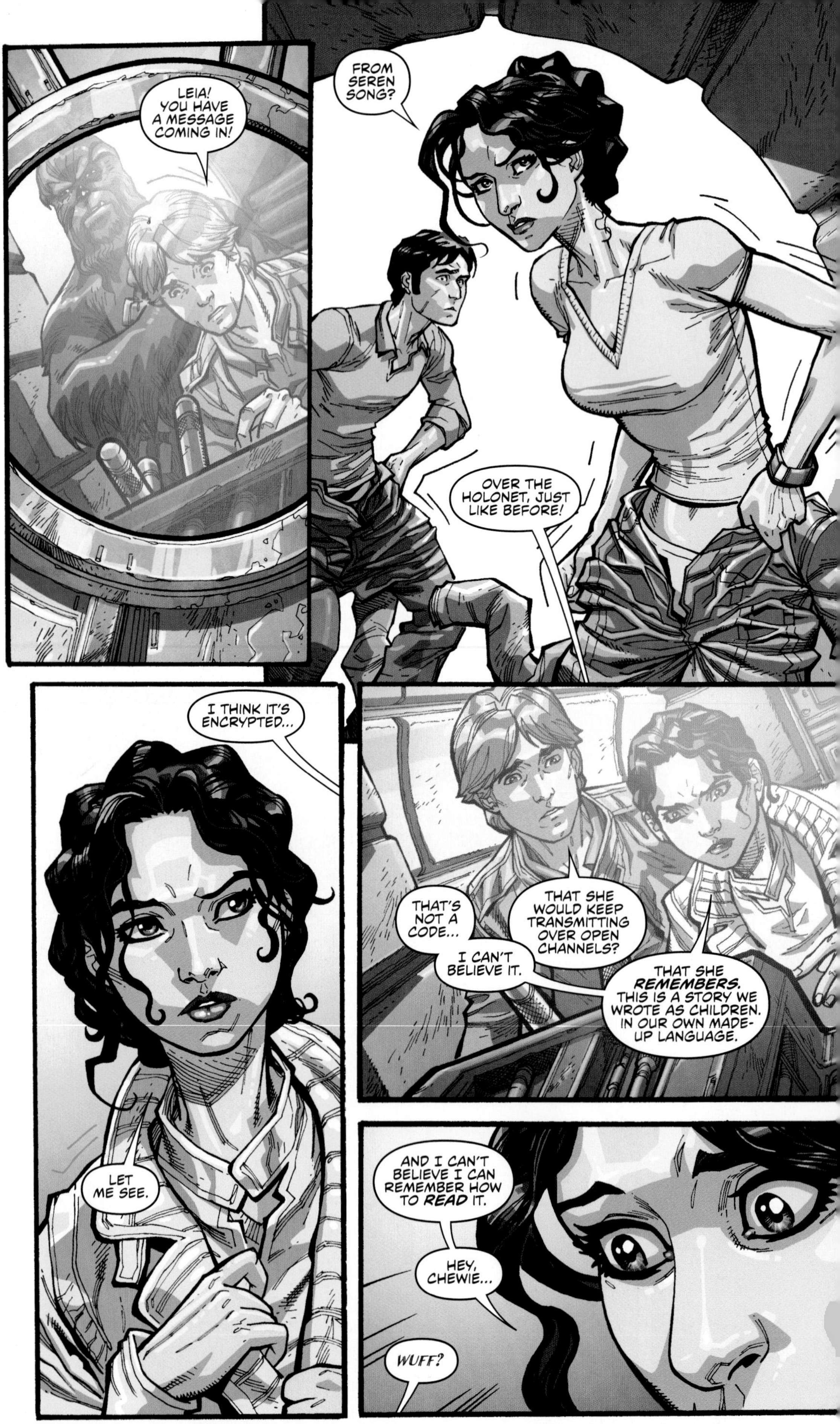
LEIA! YOU HAVE A MESSAGE COMING IN!
FROM SEREN SONG?
OVER THE HOLONET, JUST LIKE BEFORE!
I THINK IT'S ENCRYPTED...
LET ME SEE.
THAT'S NOT A CODE...
I CAN'T BELIEVE IT.
THAT SHE WOULD KEEP TRANSMITTING OVER OPEN CHANNELS?
THAT SHE *REMEMBERS.* THIS IS A STORY WE WROTE AS CHILDREN. IN OUR OWN MADE-UP LANGUAGE.
AND I CAN'T BELIEVE I CAN REMEMBER HOW TO *READ* IT.
HEY, CHEWIE...
WUFF?

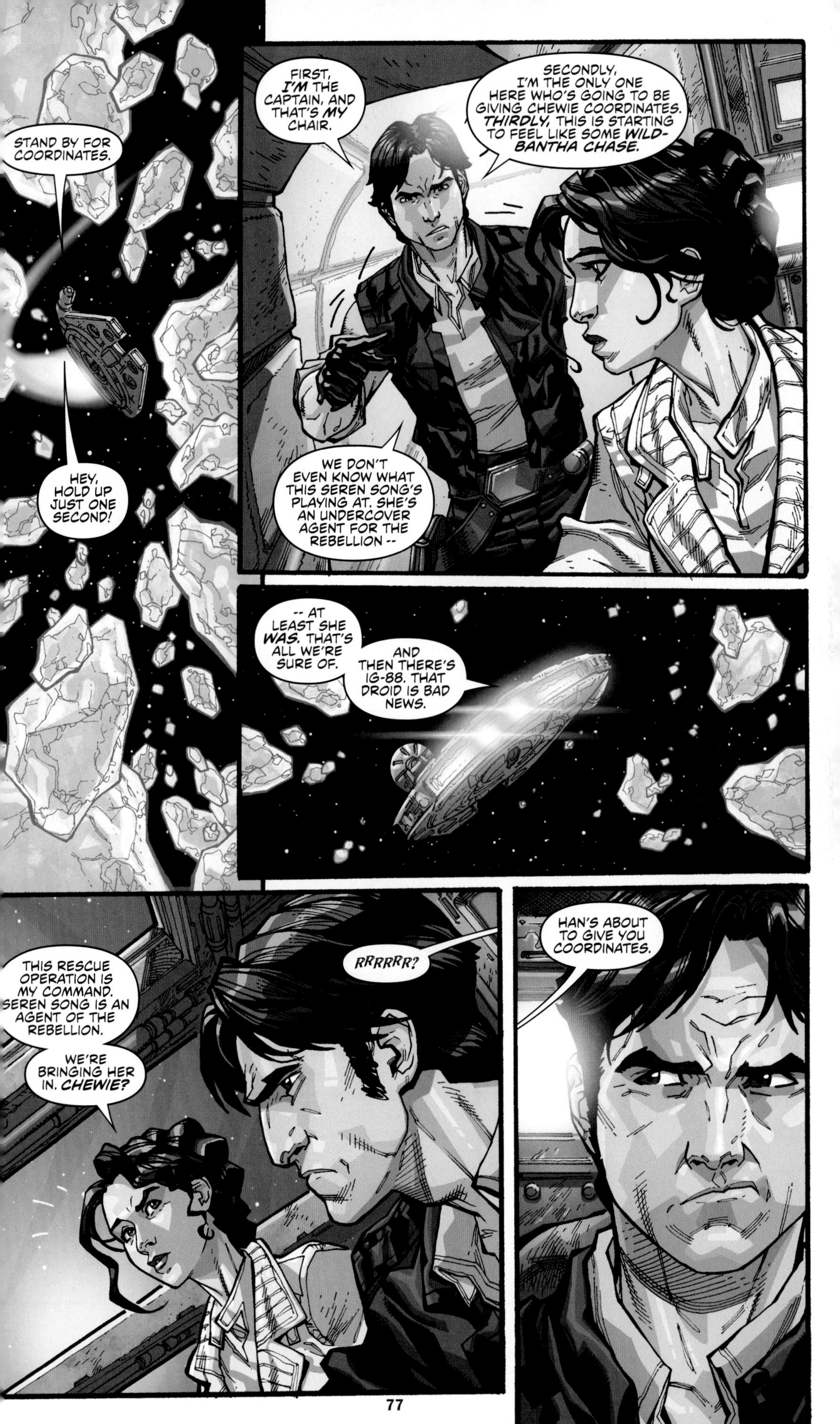
STAND BY FOR COORDINATES.
HEY, HOLD UP JUST ONE SECOND!
FIRST, I'M THE CAPTAIN, AND THAT'S MY CHAIR.
SECONDLY, I'M THE ONLY ONE HERE WHO'S GOING TO BE GIVING CHEWIE COORDINATES. THIRDLY, THIS IS STARTING TO FEEL LIKE SOME WILD-BANTHA CHASE.
WE DON'T EVEN KNOW WHAT THIS SEREN SONG'S PLAYING AT. SHE'S AN UNDERCOVER AGENT FOR THE REBELLION --
-- AT LEAST SHE WAS. THAT'S ALL WE'RE SURE OF.
AND THEN THERE'S IG-88. THAT DROID IS BAD NEWS.
THIS RESCUE OPERATION IS MY COMMAND. SEREN SONG IS AN AGENT OF THE REBELLION.
WE'RE BRINGING HER IN. CHEWIE?
RRRRRR?
HAN'S ABOUT TO GIVE YOU COORDINATES.

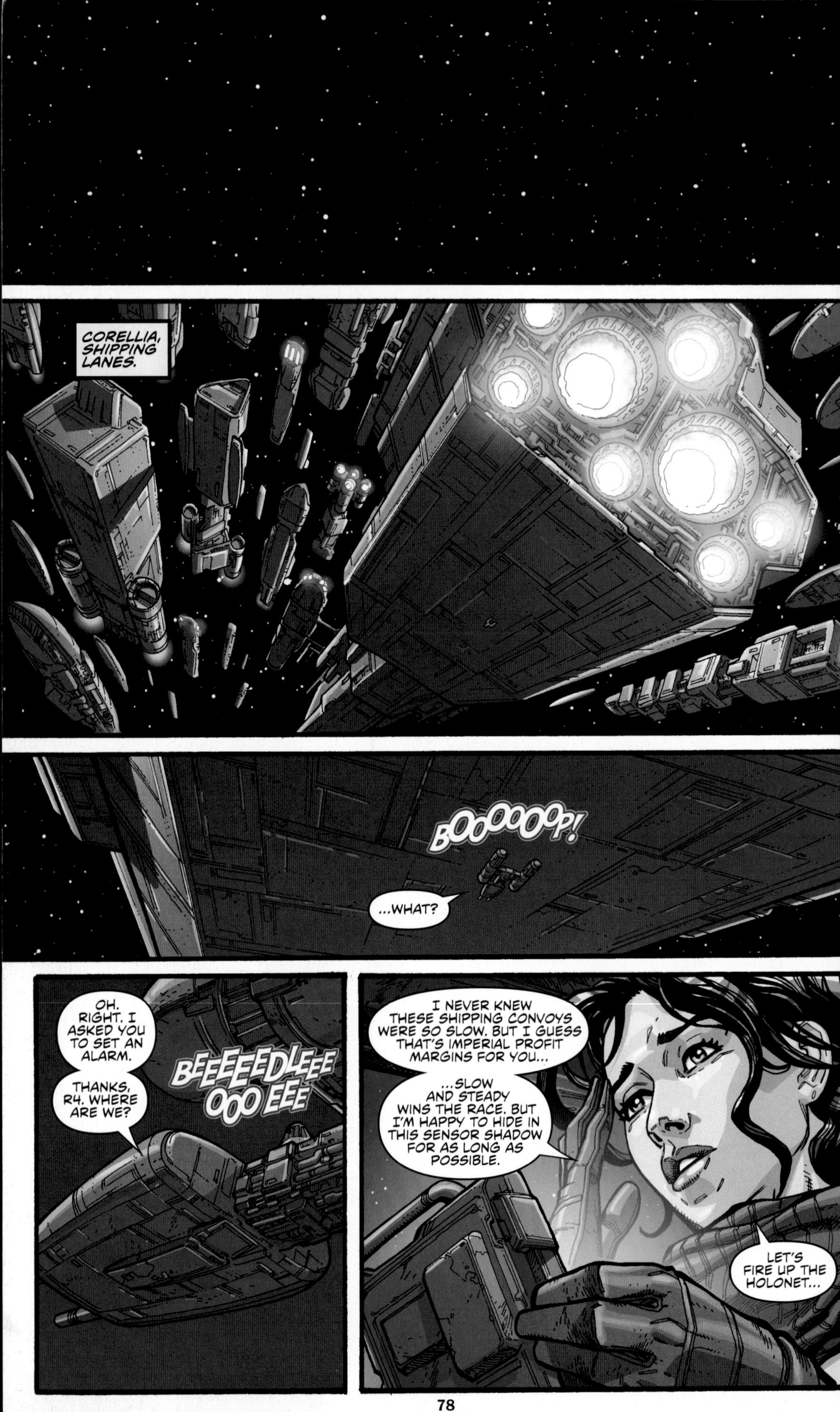
CORELLIA, SHIPPING LANES.
BOOOOOOP!
...WHAT?
OH. RIGHT. I ASKED YOU TO SET AN ALARM.
BEEEEEDLEEE OOO EEE
THANKS, R4. WHERE ARE WE?
I NEVER KNEW THESE SHIPPING CONVOYS WERE SO SLOW. BUT I GUESS THAT'S IMPERIAL PROFIT MARGINS FOR YOU...
...SLOW AND STEADY WINS THE RACE. BUT I'M HAPPY TO HIDE IN THIS SENSOR SHADOW FOR AS LONG AS POSSIBLE.
LET'S FIRE UP THE HOLONET...

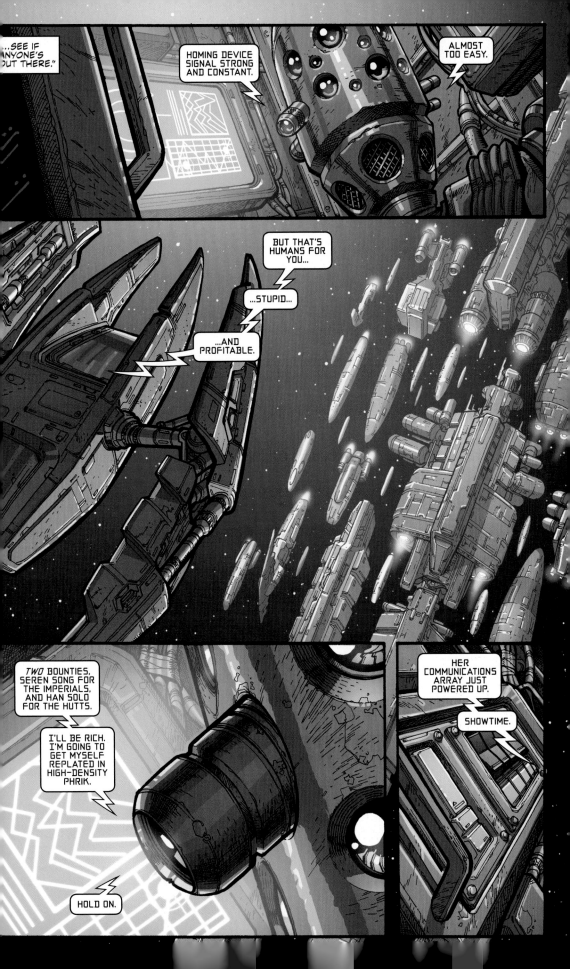

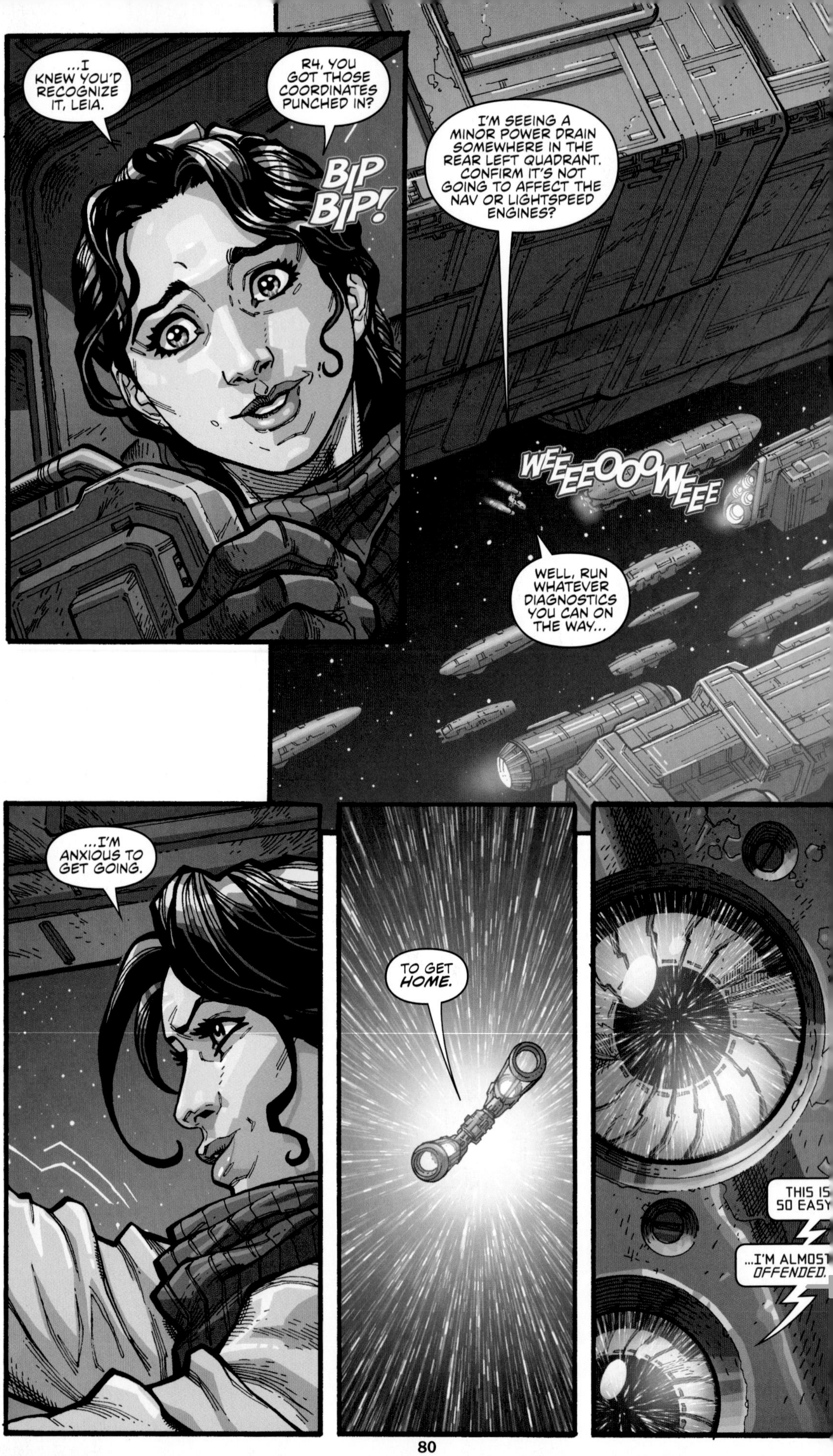
...I KNEW YOU'D RECOGNIZE IT, LEIA.
R4, YOU GOT THOSE COORDINATES PUNCHED IN?
BIP BIP!
I'M SEEING A MINOR POWER DRAIN SOMEWHERE IN THE REAR LEFT QUADRANT. CONFIRM IT'S NOT GOING TO AFFECT THE NAV OR LIGHTSPEED ENGINES?
WEEEEOOOWEEE
WELL, RUN WHATEVER DIAGNOSTICS YOU CAN ON THE WAY...
...I'M ANXIOUS TO GET GOING.
TO GET HOME.
THIS IS SO EASY
...I'M ALMOST OFFENDED.

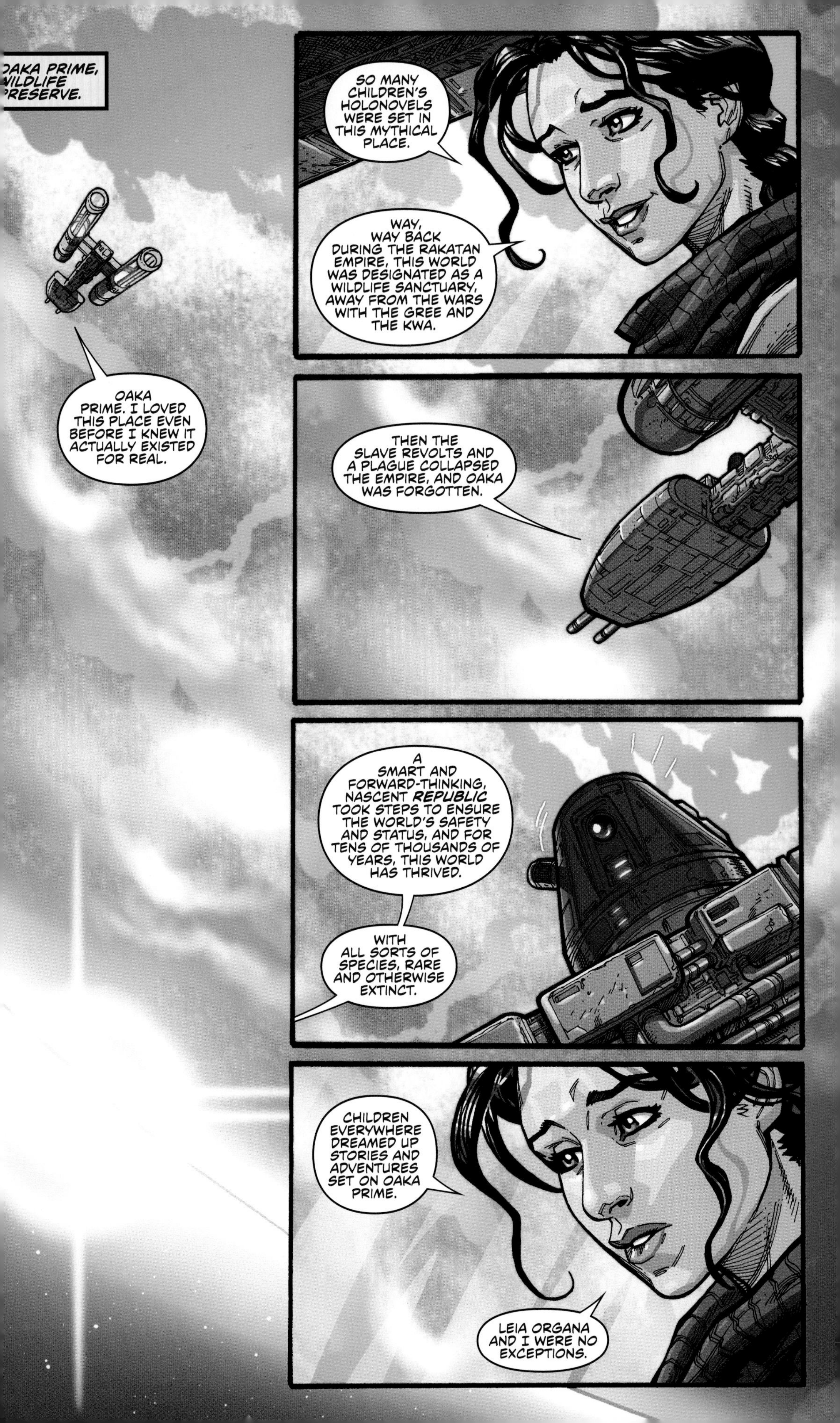
OAKA PRIME, WILDLIFE PRESERVE.
OAKA PRIME. I LOVED THIS PLACE EVEN BEFORE I KNEW IT ACTUALLY EXISTED FOR REAL.
SO MANY CHILDREN'S HOLONOVELS WERE SET IN THIS MYTHICAL PLACE.
WAY, WAY BACK DURING THE RAKATAN EMPIRE, THIS WORLD WAS DESIGNATED AS A WILDLIFE SANCTUARY, AWAY FROM THE WARS WITH THE GREE AND THE KWA.
THEN THE SLAVE REVOLTS AND A PLAGUE COLLAPSED THE EMPIRE, AND OAKA WAS FORGOTTEN.
A SMART AND FORWARD-THINKING, NASCENT REPUBLIC TOOK STEPS TO ENSURE THE WORLD'S SAFETY AND STATUS, AND FOR TENS OF THOUSANDS OF YEARS, THIS WORLD HAS THRIVED.
WITH ALL SORTS OF SPECIES, RARE AND OTHERWISE EXTINCT.
CHILDREN EVERYWHERE DREAMED UP STORIES AND ADVENTURES SET ON OAKA PRIME.
LEIA ORGANA AND I WERE NO EXCEPTIONS.

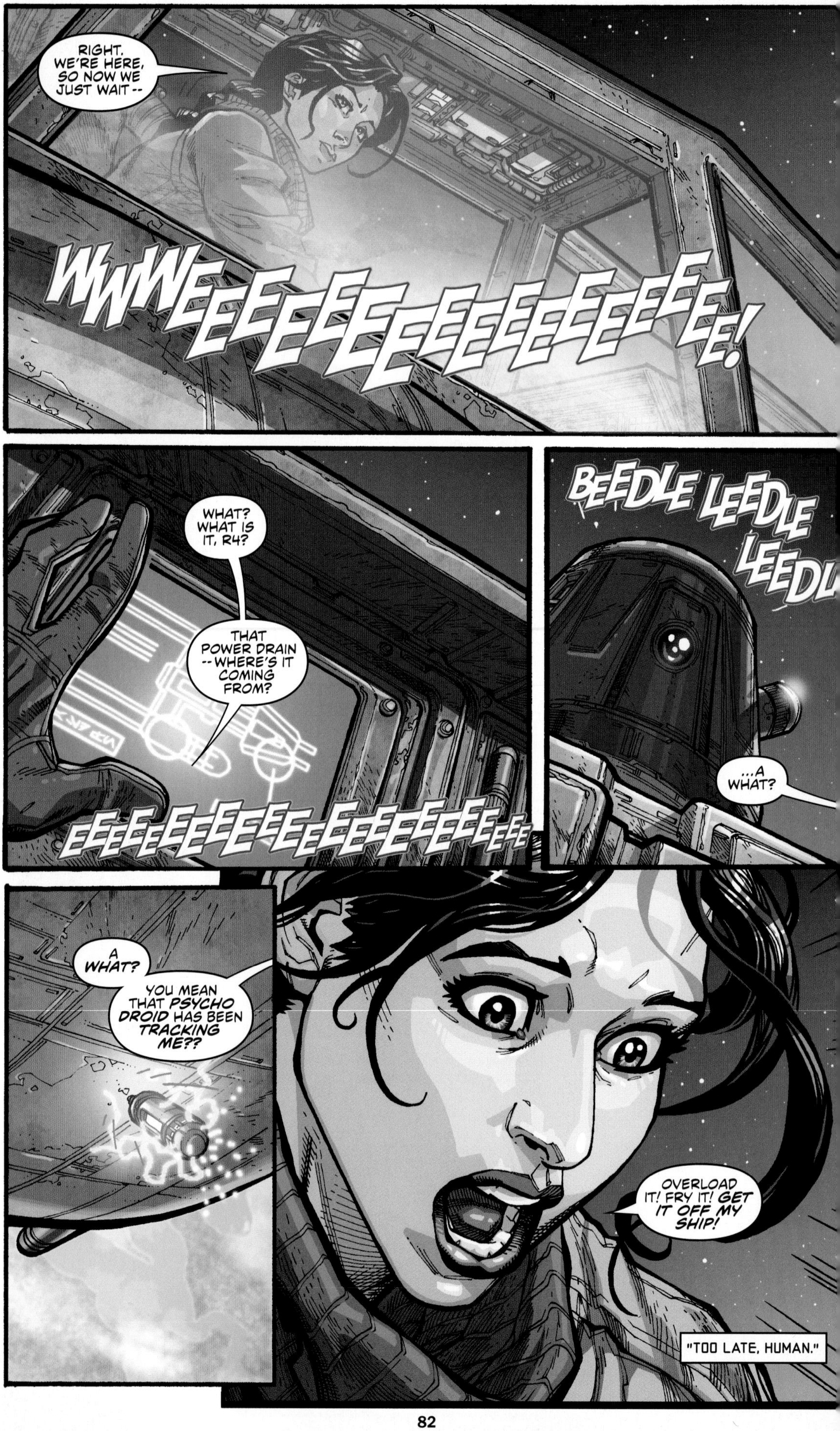
RIGHT. WE'RE HERE, SO NOW WE JUST WAIT --
WWWEEEEEEEEEEEEEEEEEEEE!
WHAT? WHAT IS IT, R4?
THAT POWER DRAIN --WHERE'S IT COMING FROM?
EEEEEEEEEEEEEEEEEEEEEEEEEEE
BEEDLE LEEDLE LEEDU
...A WHAT?
A WHAT?
YOU MEAN THAT PSYCHO DROID HAS BEEN TRACKING ME??
OVERLOAD IT! FRY IT! GET IT OFF MY SHIP!
"TOO LATE, HUMAN."

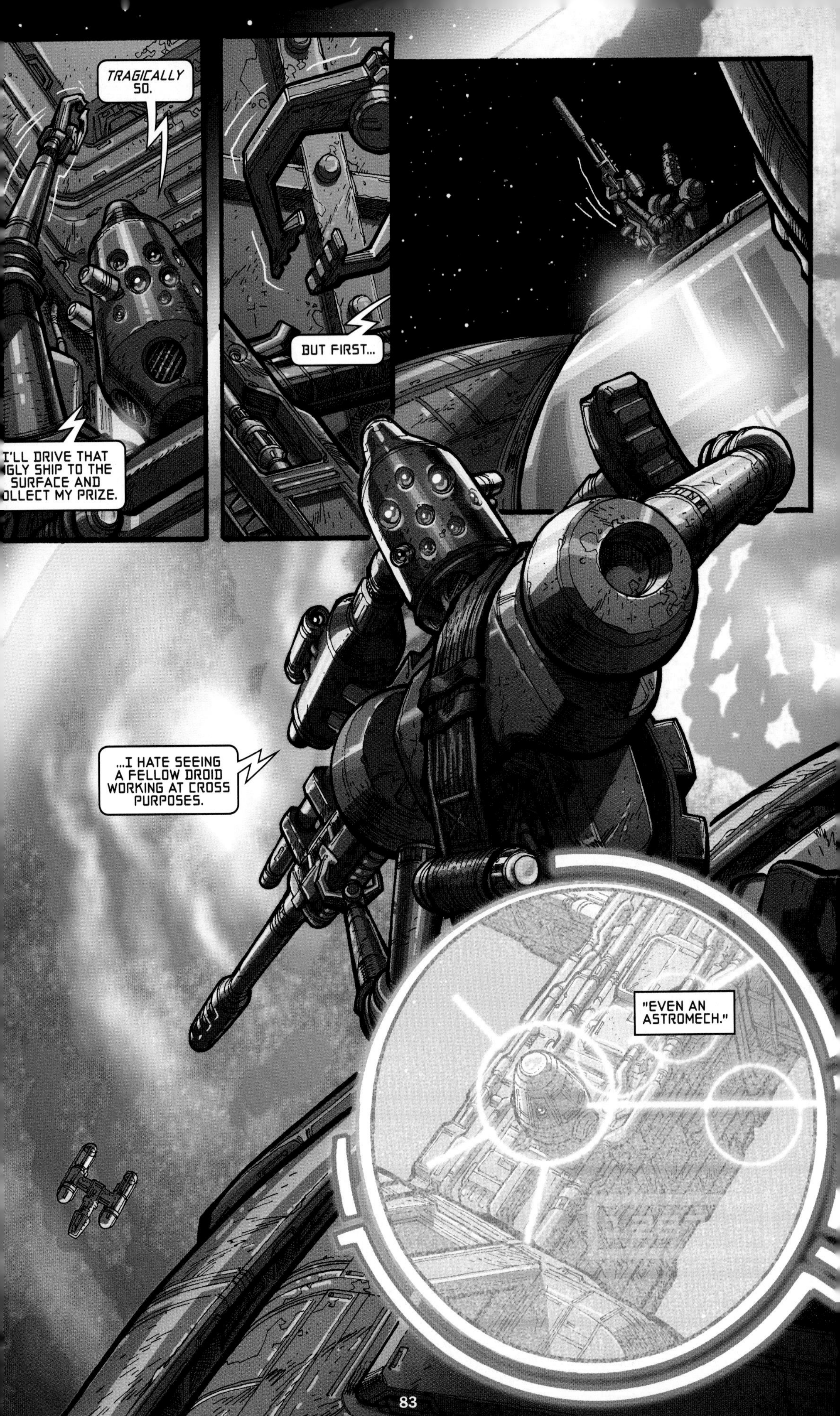
TRAGICALLY SO.
I'LL DRIVE THAT
GLY SHIP TO THE
SURFACE AND
OLLECT MY PRIZE.
BUT FIRST...
...I HATE SEEING A FELLOW DROID WORKING AT CROSS PURPOSES.
"EVEN AN ASTROMECH."

NEARLY THERE, YOUR LADYSHIP.

ARE YOU GOING TO TALK TO SEREN SONG LIKE THAT?

OR AM I JUST THE LUCKY ONE?

I'LL BE ON MY BEST BEHAVIOR.

RRRRRRRRUFFFF WUFFF!

YEAH, YEAH.

OAKA PRIME, HERE WE COME.

YOU NERVOUS?

IT JUST OCCURRED TO ME, AFTER WHAT HAPPENED TO ALDERAAN...

...I SHOULDN'T EXPECT MANY OPPORTUNITIES TO RECONNECT WITH CHILDHOOD FRIENDS.

THERE SHE IS!

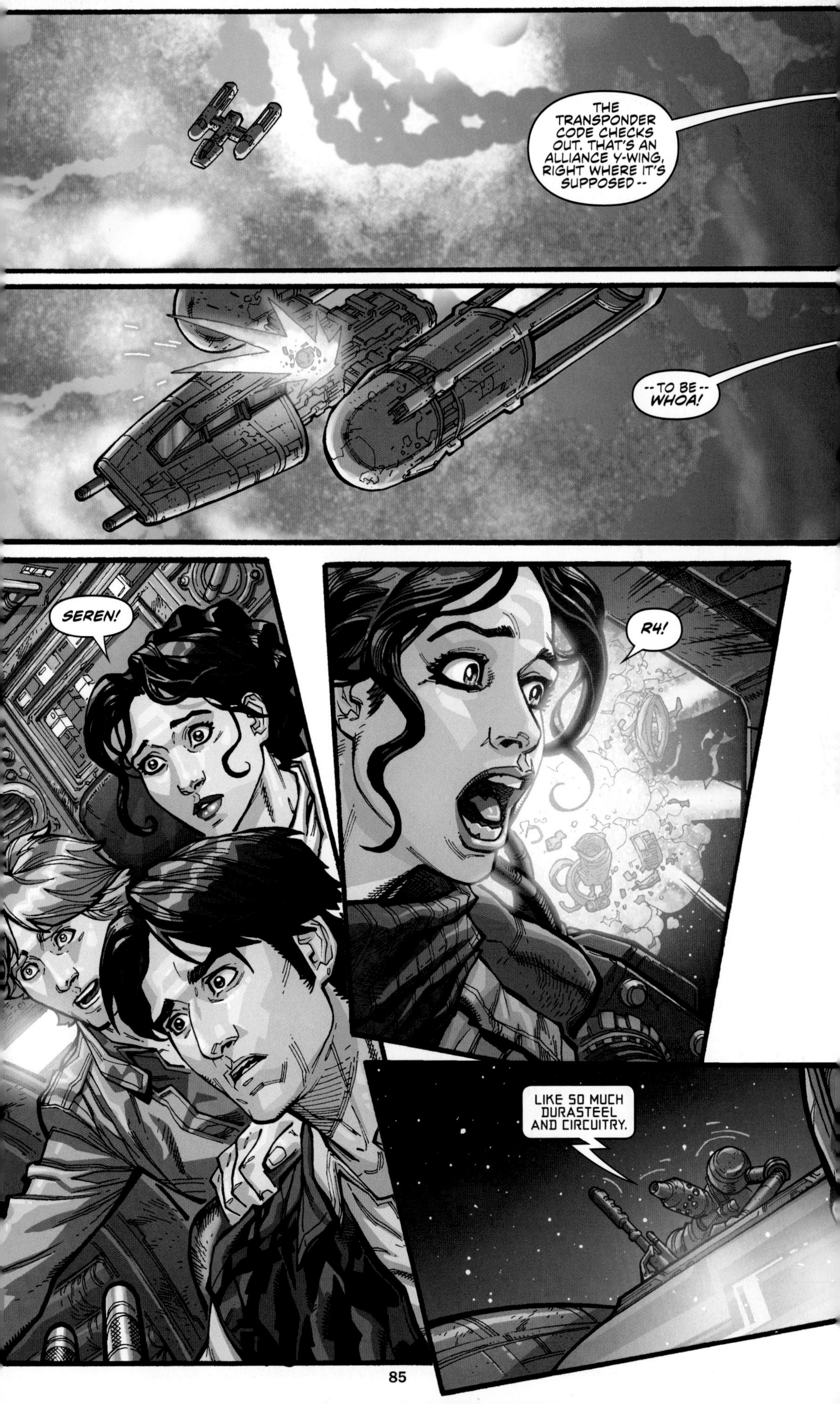
THE TRANSPONDER CODE CHECKS OUT. THAT'S AN ALLIANCE Y-WING, RIGHT WHERE IT'S SUPPOSED --
--TO BE-- WHOA!
SEREN!
R4!
LIKE SO MUCH DURASTEEL AND CIRCUITRY.

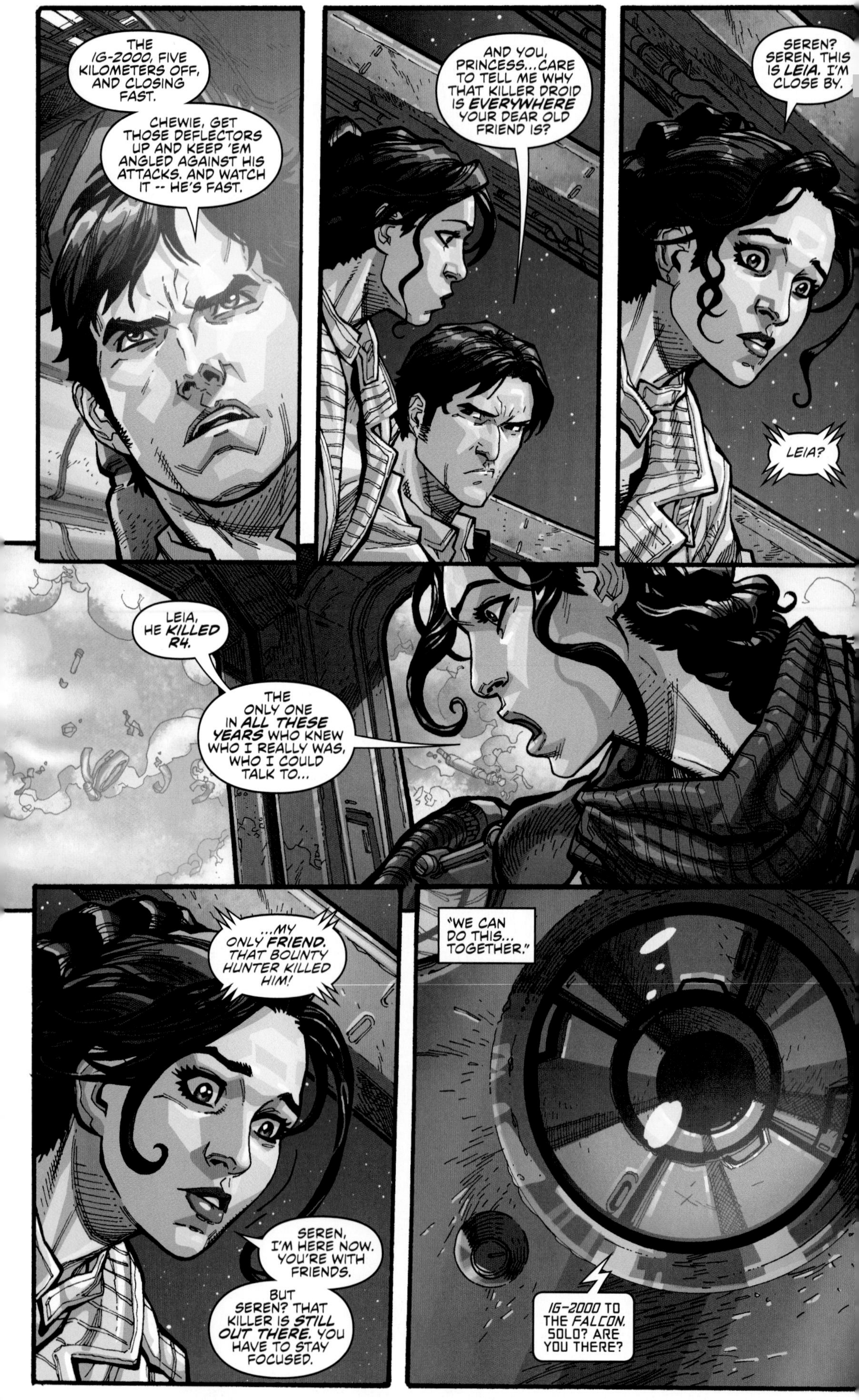
THE IG-2000, FIVE KILOMETERS OFF, AND CLOSING FAST.
CHEWIE, GET THOSE DEFLECTORS UP AND KEEP 'EM ANGLED AGAINST HIS ATTACKS. AND WATCH IT -- HE'S FAST.
AND YOU, PRINCESS... CARE TO TELL ME WHY THAT KILLER DROID IS EVERYWHERE YOUR DEAR OLD FRIEND IS?
SEREN? SEREN, THIS IS LEIA. I'M CLOSE BY.
LEIA?
LEIA, HE KILLED R4.
THE ONLY ONE IN ALL THESE YEARS WHO KNEW WHO I REALLY WAS, WHO I COULD TALK TO...
...MY ONLY FRIEND. THAT BOUNTY HUNTER KILLED HIM!
SEREN, I'M HERE NOW. YOU'RE WITH FRIENDS.
BUT SEREN? THAT KILLER IS STILL OUT THERE. YOU HAVE TO STAY FOCUSED.
"WE CAN DO THIS... TOGETHER."
IG-2000 TO THE FALCON. SOLO? ARE YOU THERE?

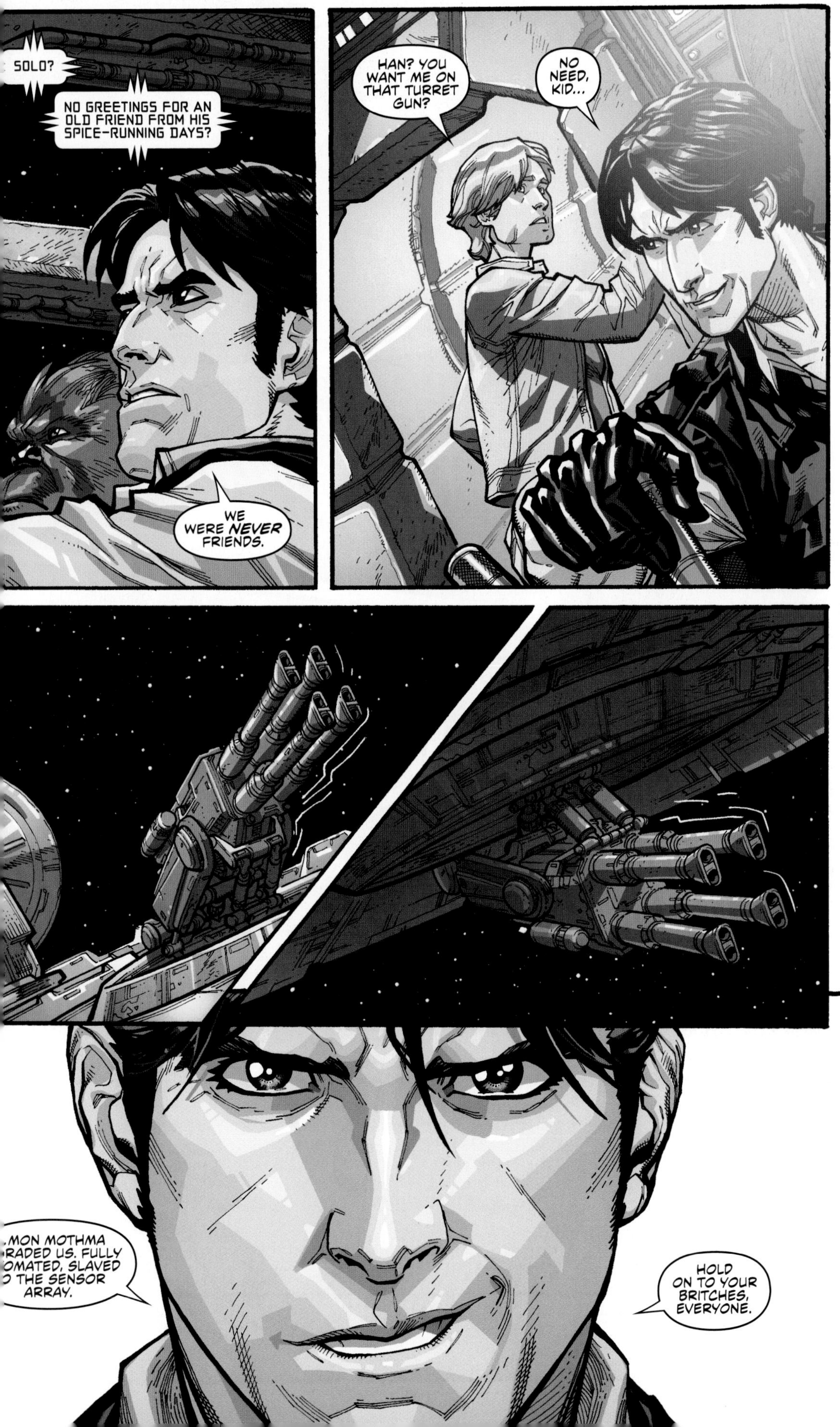
SOLO?
NO GREETINGS FOR AN OLD FRIEND FROM HIS SPICE-RUNNING DAYS?
WE WERE *NEVER* FRIENDS.
HAN? YOU WANT ME ON THAT TURRET GUN?
NO NEED, KID...
.MON MOTHMA RADED US. FULLY OMATED, SLAVED O THE SENSOR ARRAY.
HOLD ON TO YOUR BRITCHES, EVERYONE.

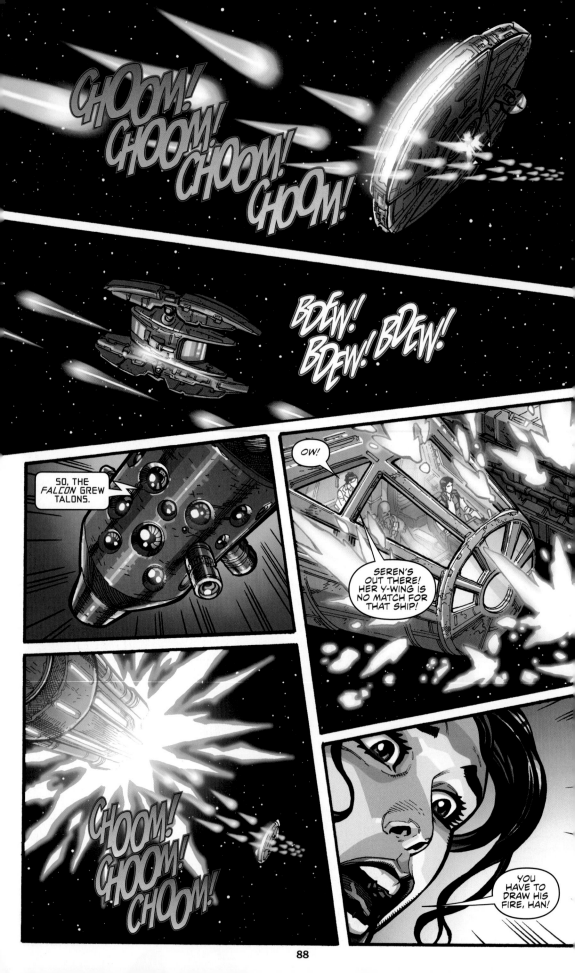

CHOOM! CHOOM! CHOOM! CHOOM!

BDEW! BDEW! BDEW!

SO, THE *FALCON* GREW TALONS.

OW!

SEREN'S OUT THERE! HER Y-WING IS NO MATCH FOR THAT SHIP!

CHOOM! CHOOM! CHOOM!

YOU HAVE TO DRAW HIS FIRE, HAN!

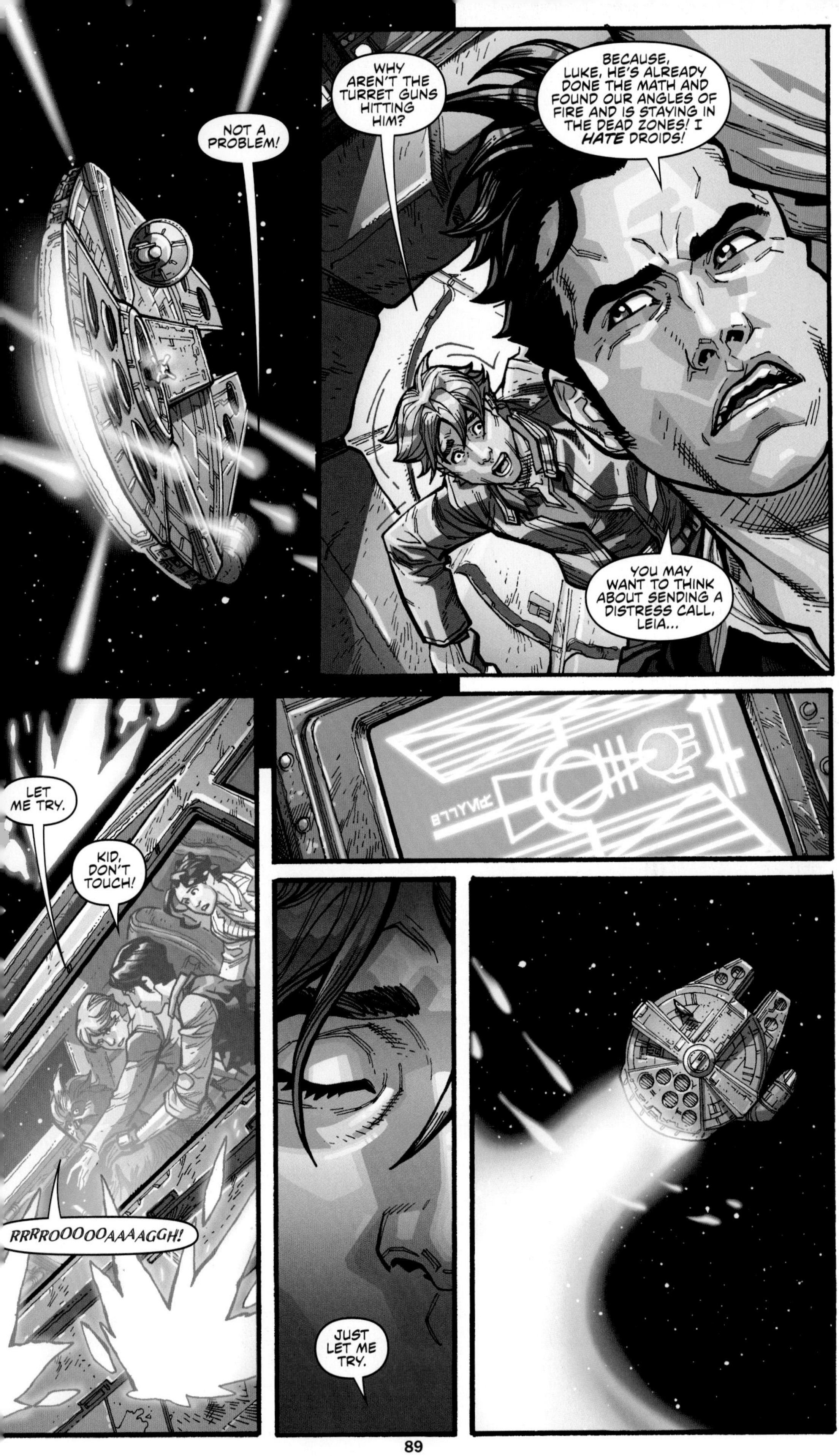
NOT A PROBLEM!
WHY AREN'T THE TURRET GUNS HITTING HIM?
BECAUSE, LUKE, HE'S ALREADY DONE THE MATH AND FOUND OUR ANGLES OF FIRE AND IS STAYING IN THE DEAD ZONES! I *HATE* DROIDS!
YOU MAY WANT TO THINK ABOUT SENDING A DISTRESS CALL, LEIA...
LET ME TRY.
KID, DON'T TOUCH!
RRRROOOOOAAAAGGH!
JUST LET ME TRY.

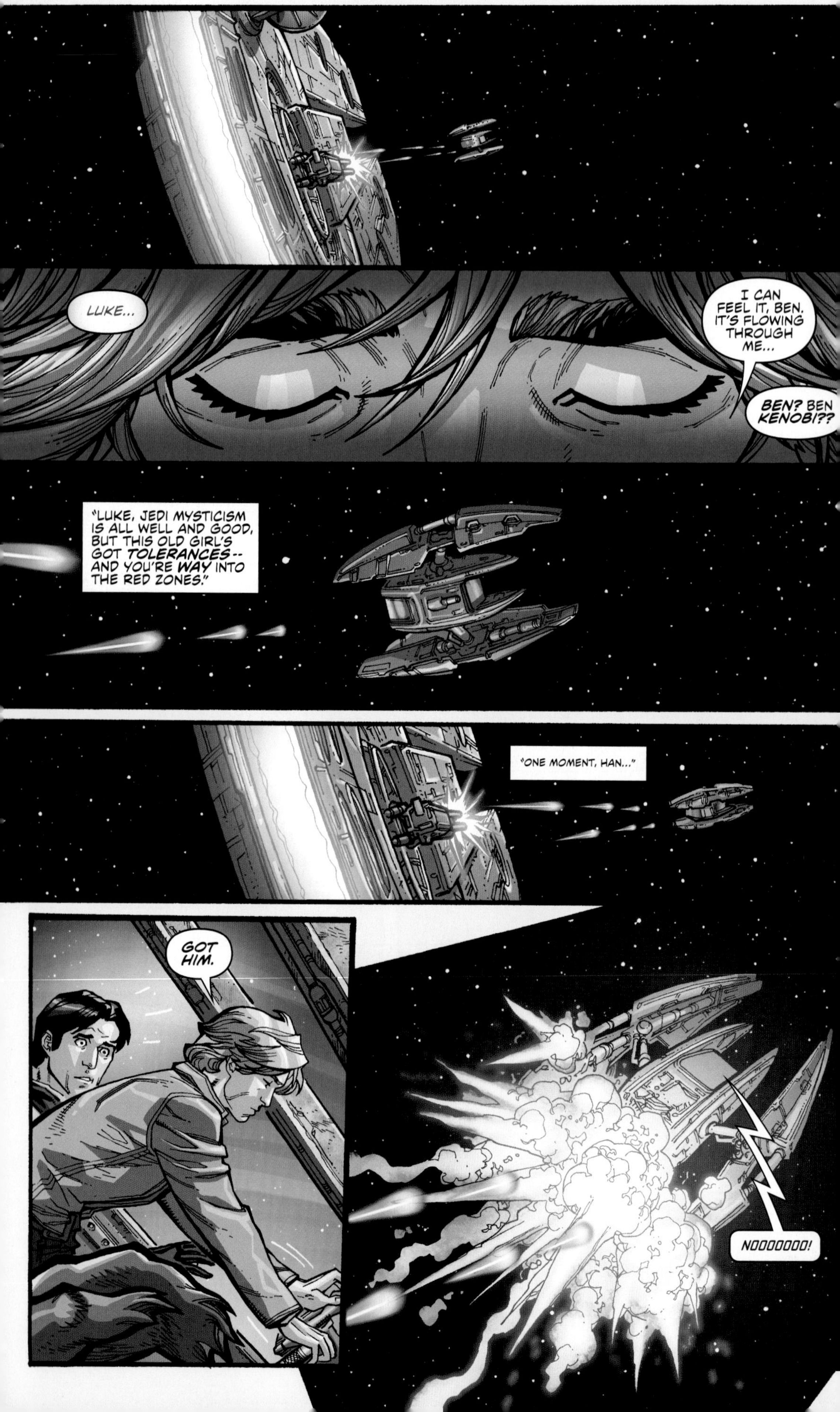
LUKE...
I CAN FEEL IT, BEN. IT'S FLOWING THROUGH ME...
BEN? BEN KENOBI??
"LUKE, JEDI MYSTICISM IS ALL WELL AND GOOD, BUT THIS OLD GIRL'S GOT TOLERANCES-- AND YOU'RE WAY INTO THE RED ZONES."
"ONE MOMENT, HAN..."
GOT HIM.
NOOOOOOO!

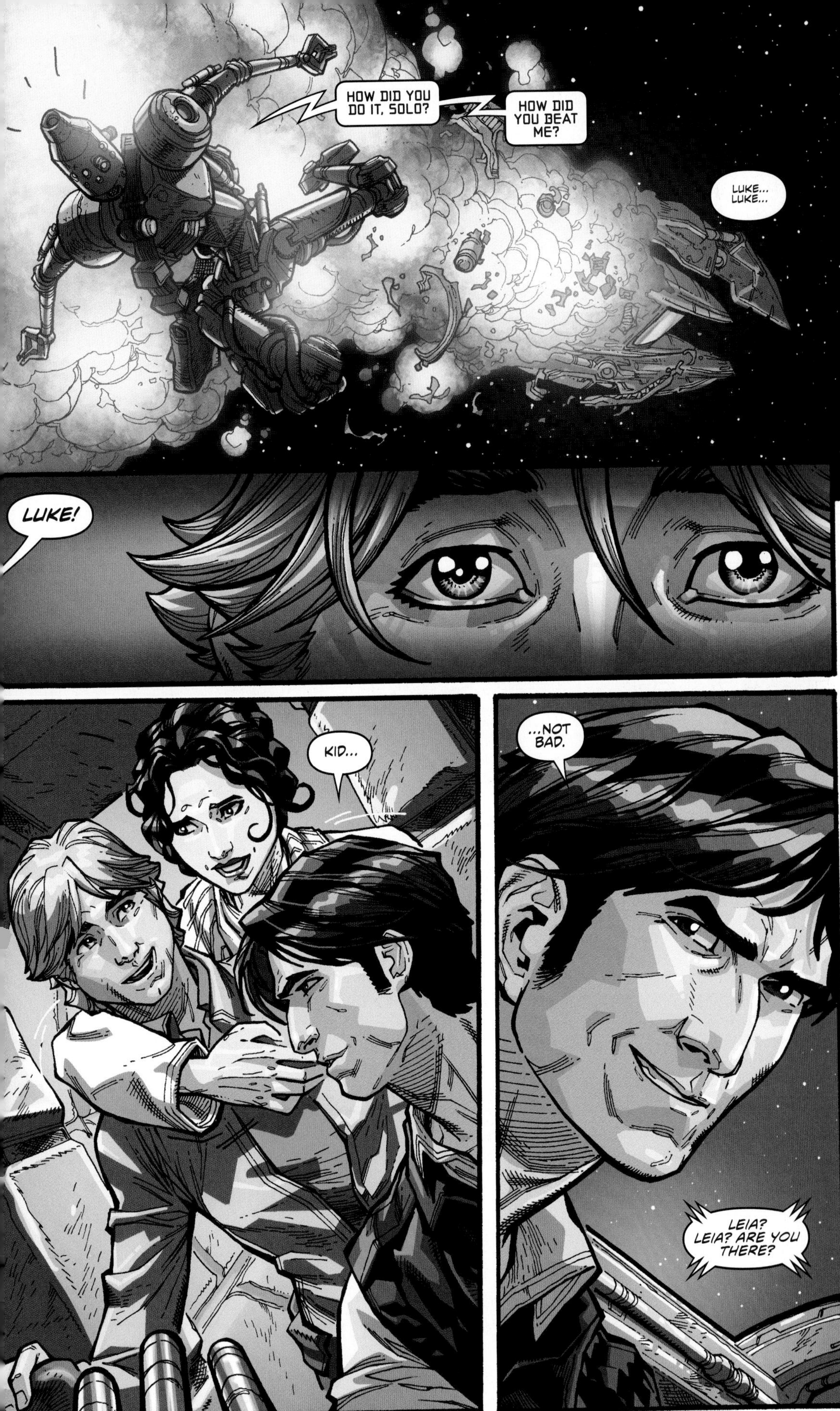
HOW DID YOU DO IT, SOLO?
HOW DID YOU BEAT ME?
LUKE... LUKE...
LUKE!
KID...
...NOT BAD.
LEIA? LEIA? ARE YOU THERE?

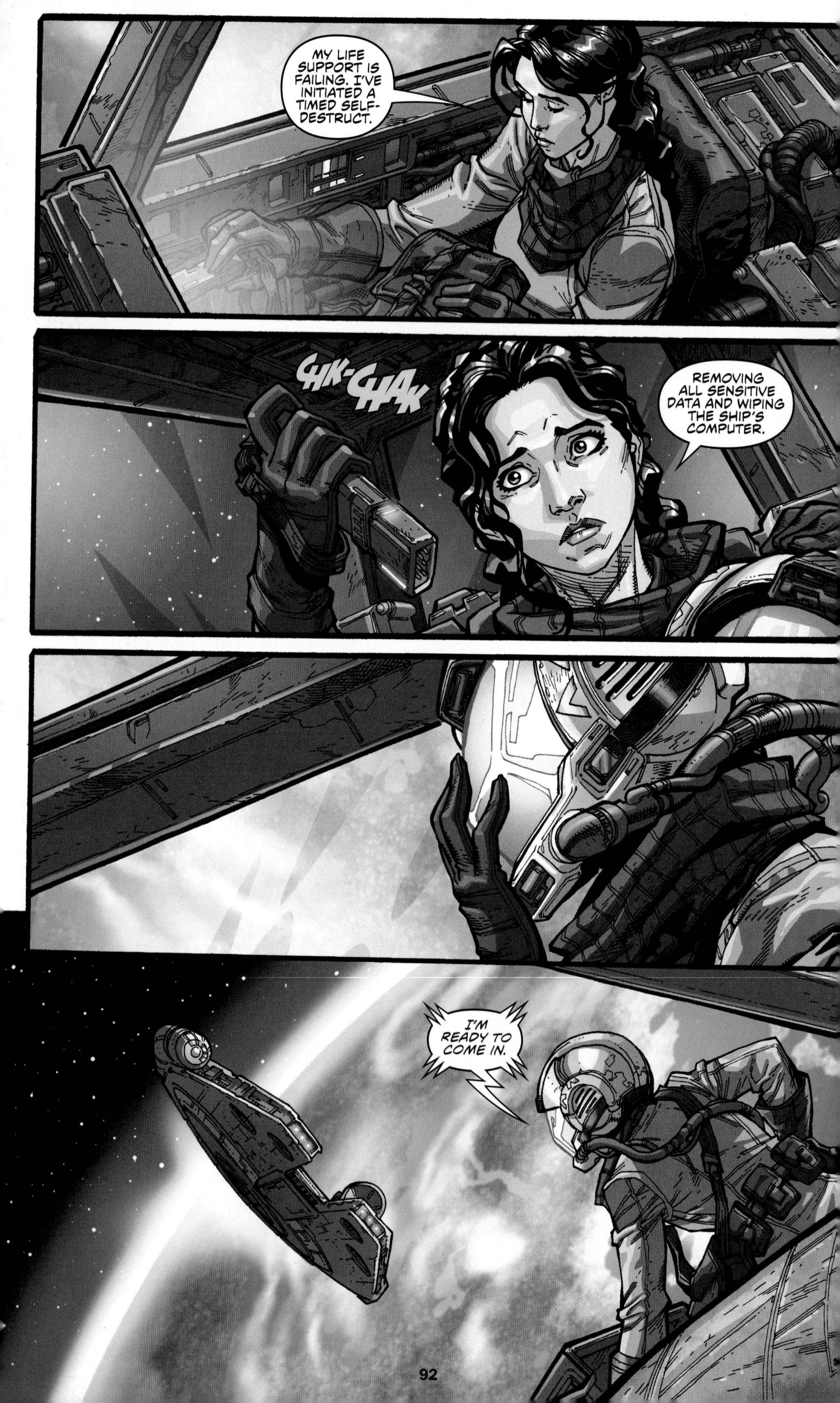
MY LIFE SUPPORT IS FAILING. I'VE INITIATED A TIMED SELF-DESTRUCT.
CHK-CHAK
REMOVING ALL SENSITIVE DATA AND WIPING THE SHIP'S COMPUTER.
I'M READY TO COME IN.

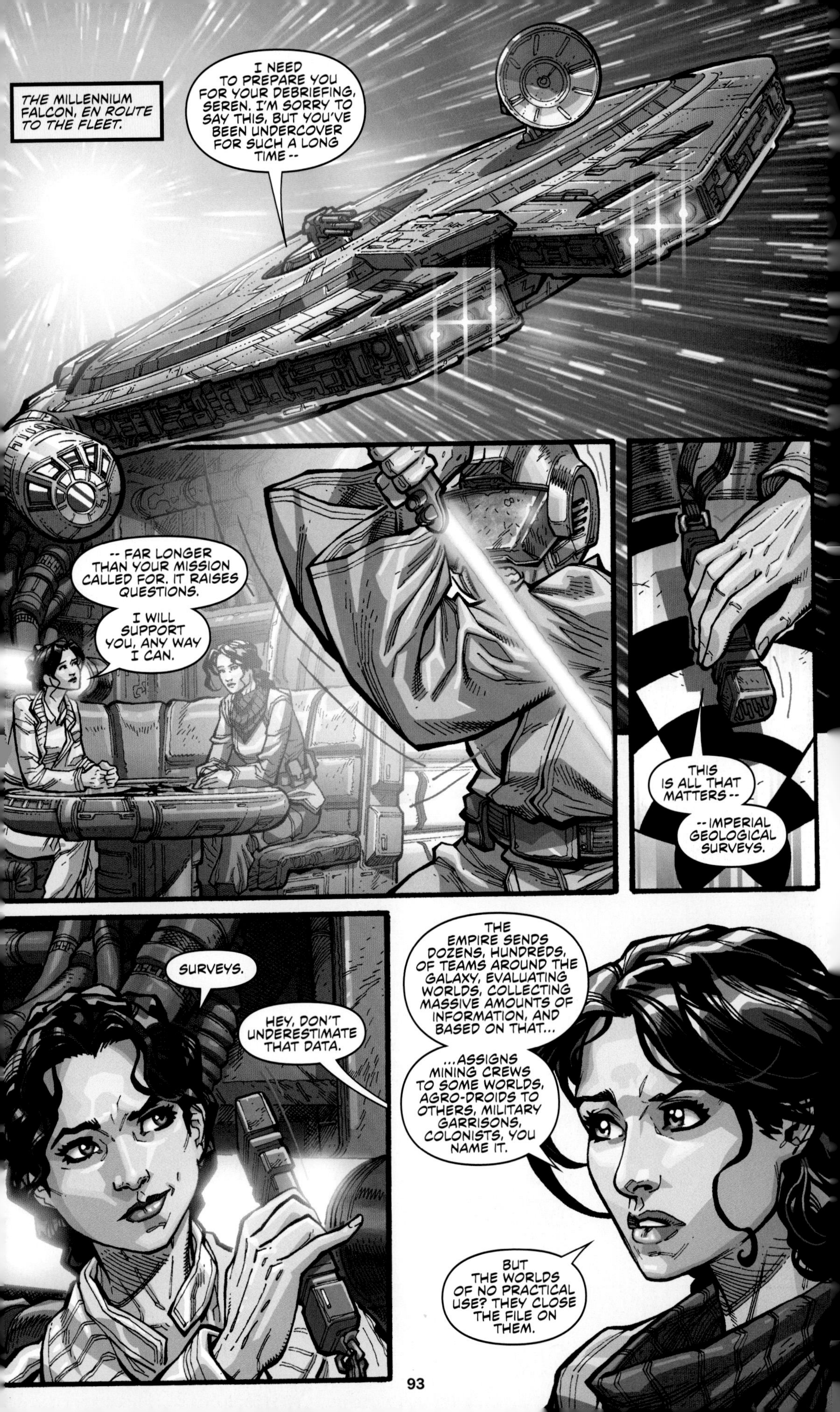

THE MILLENNIUM FALCON, EN ROUTE TO THE FLEET.
I NEED TO PREPARE YOU FOR YOUR DEBRIEFING, SEREN. I'M SORRY TO SAY THIS, BUT YOU'VE BEEN UNDERCOVER FOR SUCH A LONG TIME --
-- FAR LONGER THAN YOUR MISSION CALLED FOR. IT RAISES QUESTIONS.
I WILL SUPPORT YOU, ANY WAY I CAN.
THIS IS ALL THAT MATTERS --
-- IMPERIAL GEOLOGICAL SURVEYS.
SURVEYS.
HEY, DON'T UNDERESTIMATE THAT DATA.
THE EMPIRE SENDS DOZENS, HUNDREDS, OF TEAMS AROUND THE GALAXY, EVALUATING WORLDS, COLLECTING MASSIVE AMOUNTS OF INFORMATION, AND BASED ON THAT...
...ASSIGNS MINING CREWS TO SOME WORLDS, AGRO-DROIDS TO OTHERS, MILITARY GARRISONS, COLONISTS, YOU NAME IT.
BUT THE WORLDS OF NO PRACTICAL USE? THEY CLOSE THE FILE ON THEM.

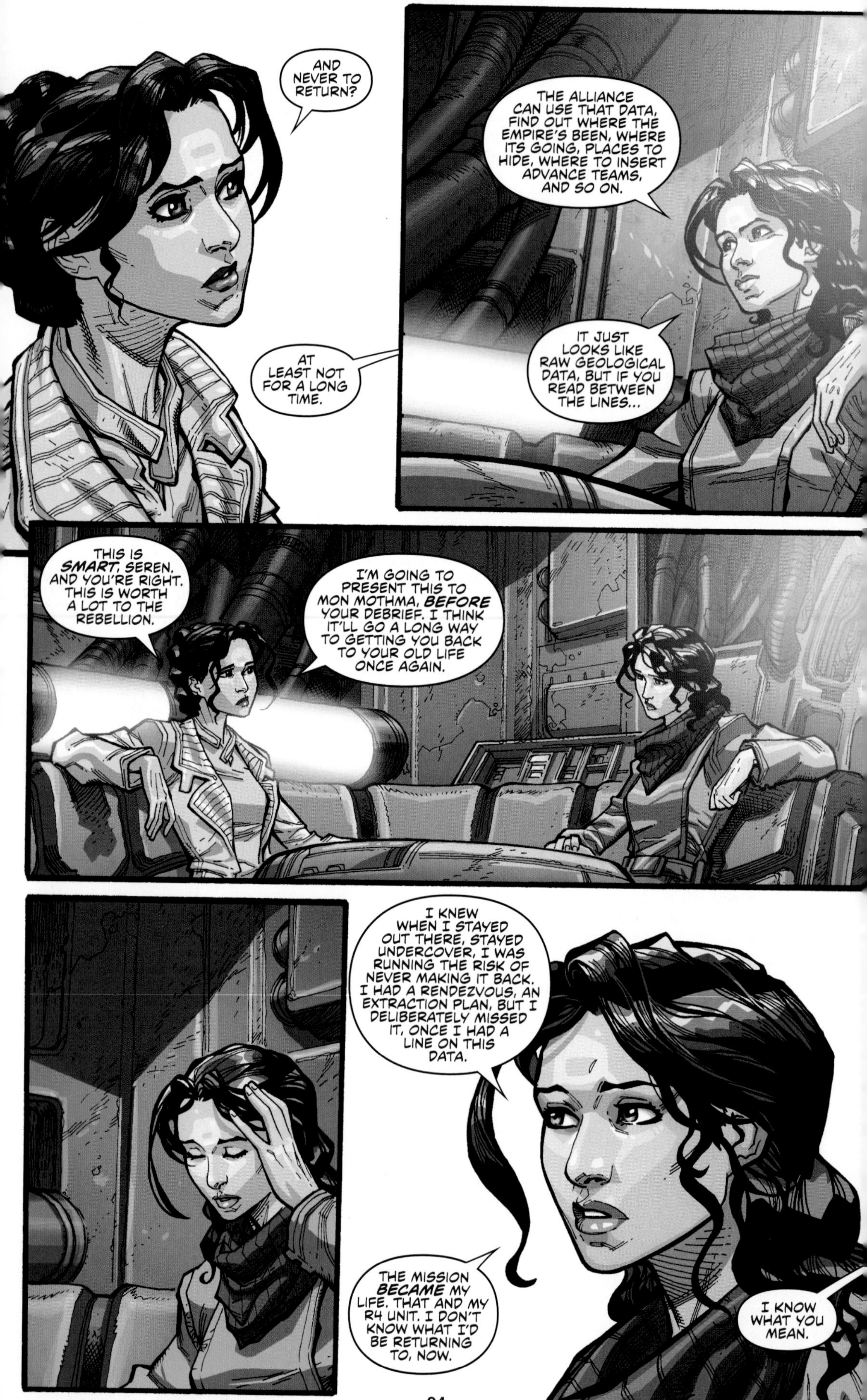

AND NEVER TO RETURN?
AT LEAST NOT FOR A LONG TIME.
THE ALLIANCE CAN USE THAT DATA, FIND OUT WHERE THE EMPIRE'S BEEN, WHERE ITS GOING, PLACES TO HIDE, WHERE TO INSERT ADVANCE TEAMS, AND SO ON.
IT JUST LOOKS LIKE RAW GEOLOGICAL DATA, BUT IF YOU READ BETWEEN THE LINES...
THIS IS *SMART*, SEREN. AND YOU'RE RIGHT. THIS IS WORTH A LOT TO THE REBELLION.
I'M GOING TO PRESENT THIS TO MON MOTHMA, *BEFORE* YOUR DEBRIEF. I THINK IT'LL GO A LONG WAY TO GETTING YOU BACK TO YOUR OLD LIFE ONCE AGAIN.
I KNEW WHEN I STAYED OUT THERE, STAYED UNDERCOVER, I WAS RUNNING THE RISK OF NEVER MAKING IT BACK. I HAD A RENDEZVOUS, AN EXTRACTION PLAN, BUT I DELIBERATELY MISSED IT, ONCE I HAD A LINE ON THIS DATA.
THE MISSION *BECAME* MY LIFE. THAT AND MY R4 UNIT. I DON'T KNOW WHAT I'D BE RETURNING TO, NOW.
I KNOW WHAT YOU MEAN.

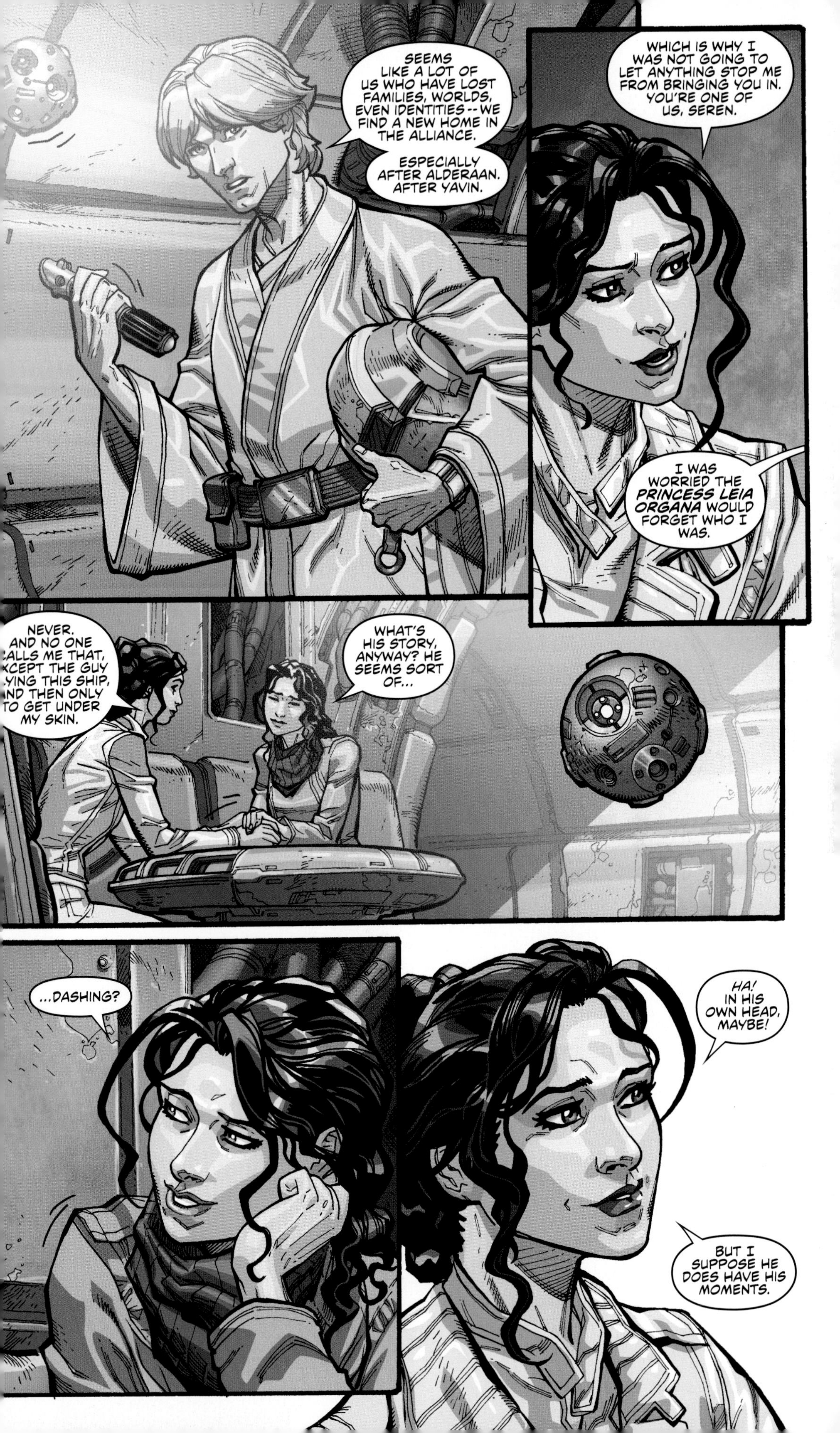
SEEMS LIKE A LOT OF US WHO HAVE LOST FAMILIES, WORLDS, EVEN IDENTITIES -- WE FIND A NEW HOME IN THE ALLIANCE.
ESPECIALLY AFTER ALDERAAN. AFTER YAVIN.
WHICH IS WHY I WAS NOT GOING TO LET ANYTHING STOP ME FROM BRINGING YOU IN. YOU'RE ONE OF US, SEREN.
I WAS WORRIED THE PRINCESS LEIA ORGANA WOULD FORGET WHO I WAS.
NEVER. AND NO ONE CALLS ME THAT, EXCEPT THE GUY FLYING THIS SHIP, AND THEN ONLY TO GET UNDER MY SKIN.
WHAT'S HIS STORY, ANYWAY? HE SEEMS SORT OF...
...DASHING?
HA! IN HIS OWN HEAD, MAYBE!
BUT I SUPPOSE HE DOES HAVE HIS MOMENTS.

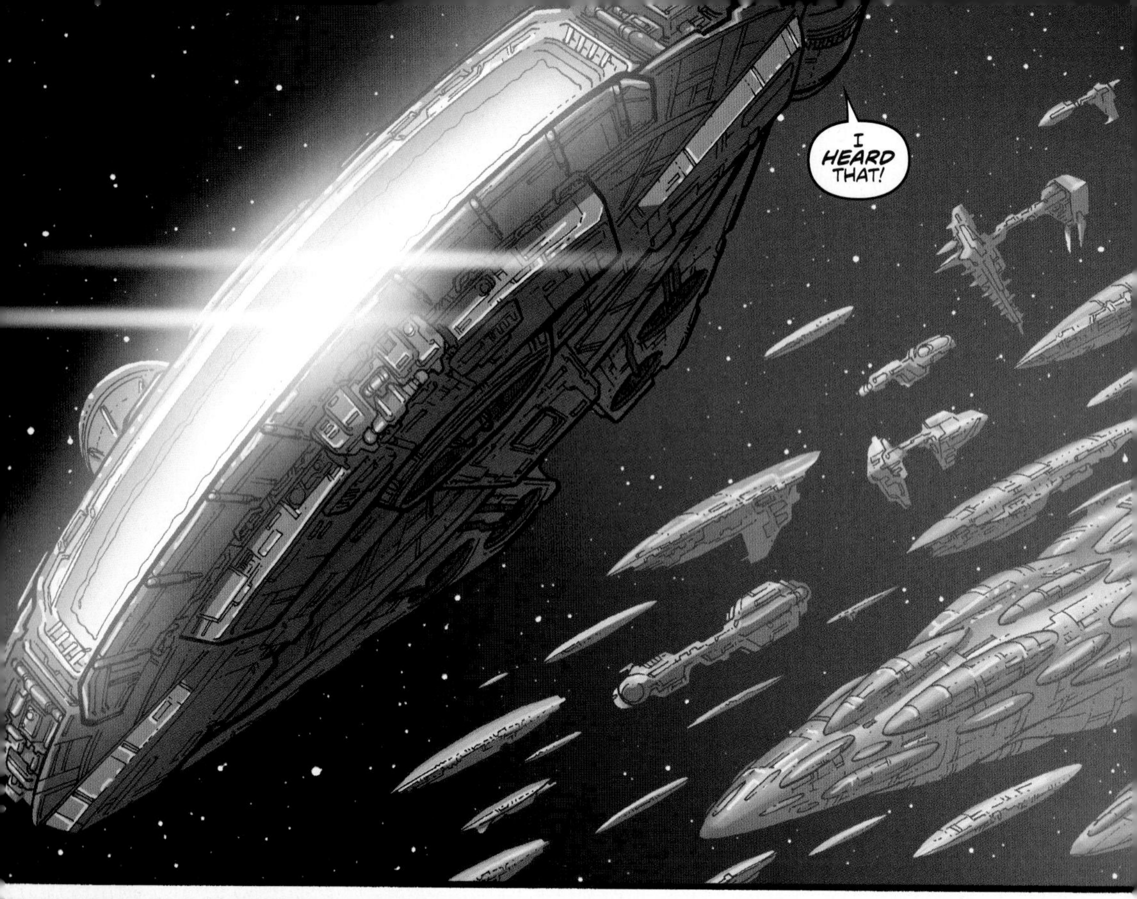
I HEARD THAT!

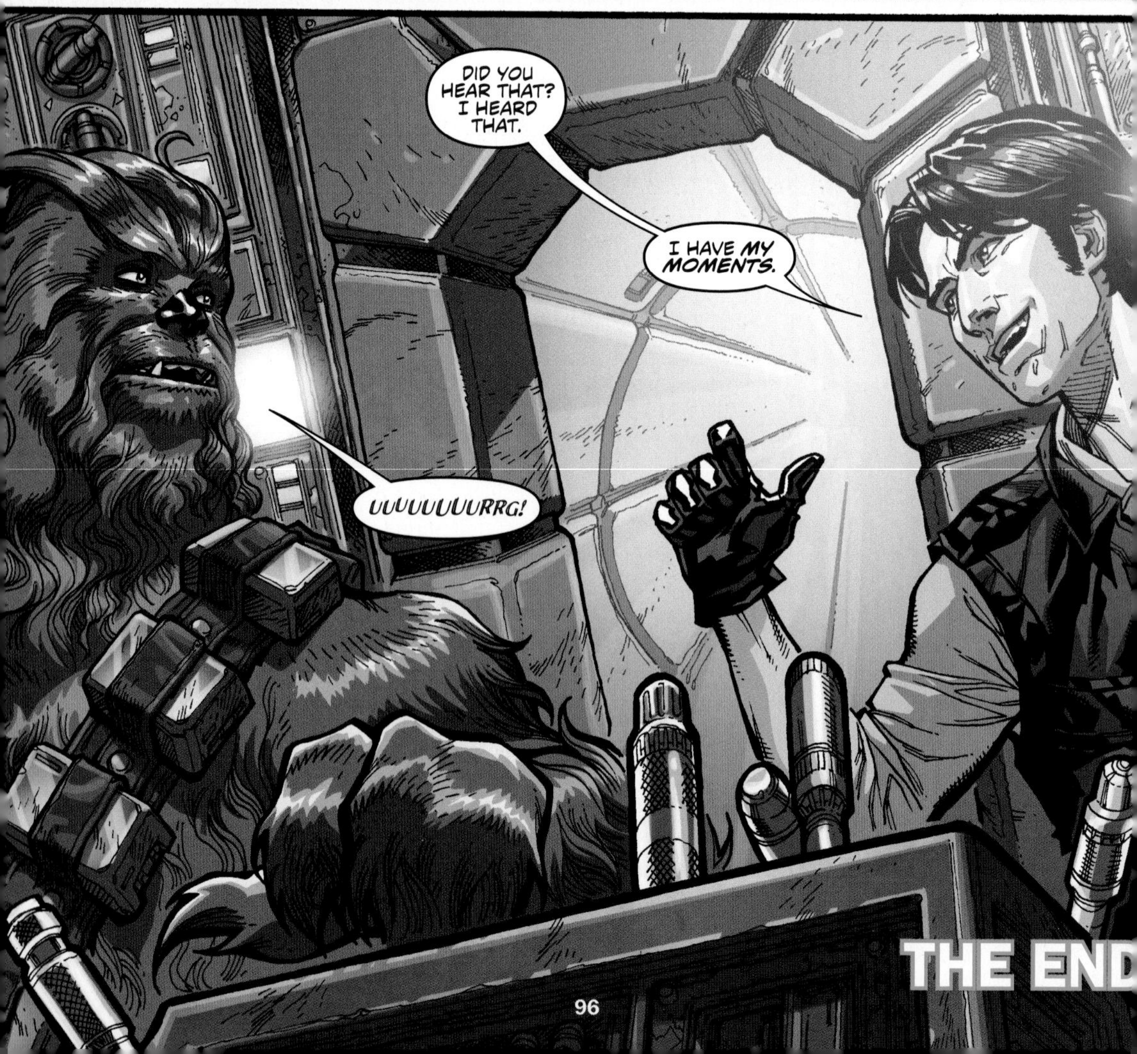
DID YOU HEAR THAT? I HEARD THAT.
I HAVE MY MOMENTS.
UUUUUUURRG!
THE END

HAN SOLO AND CHEWBACCA IN
"THE ART OF THE *BAD* DEAL"

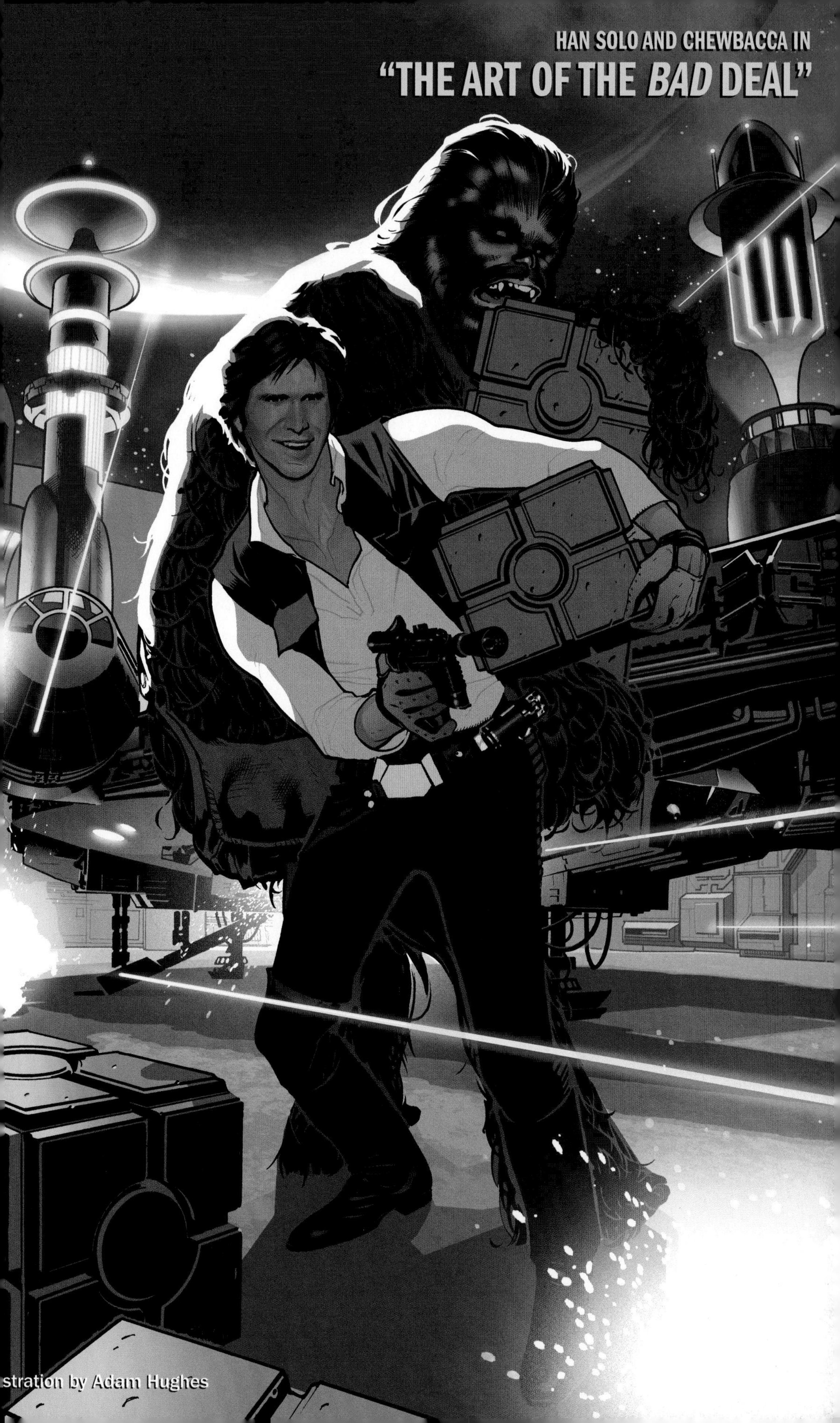

stration by Adam Hughes

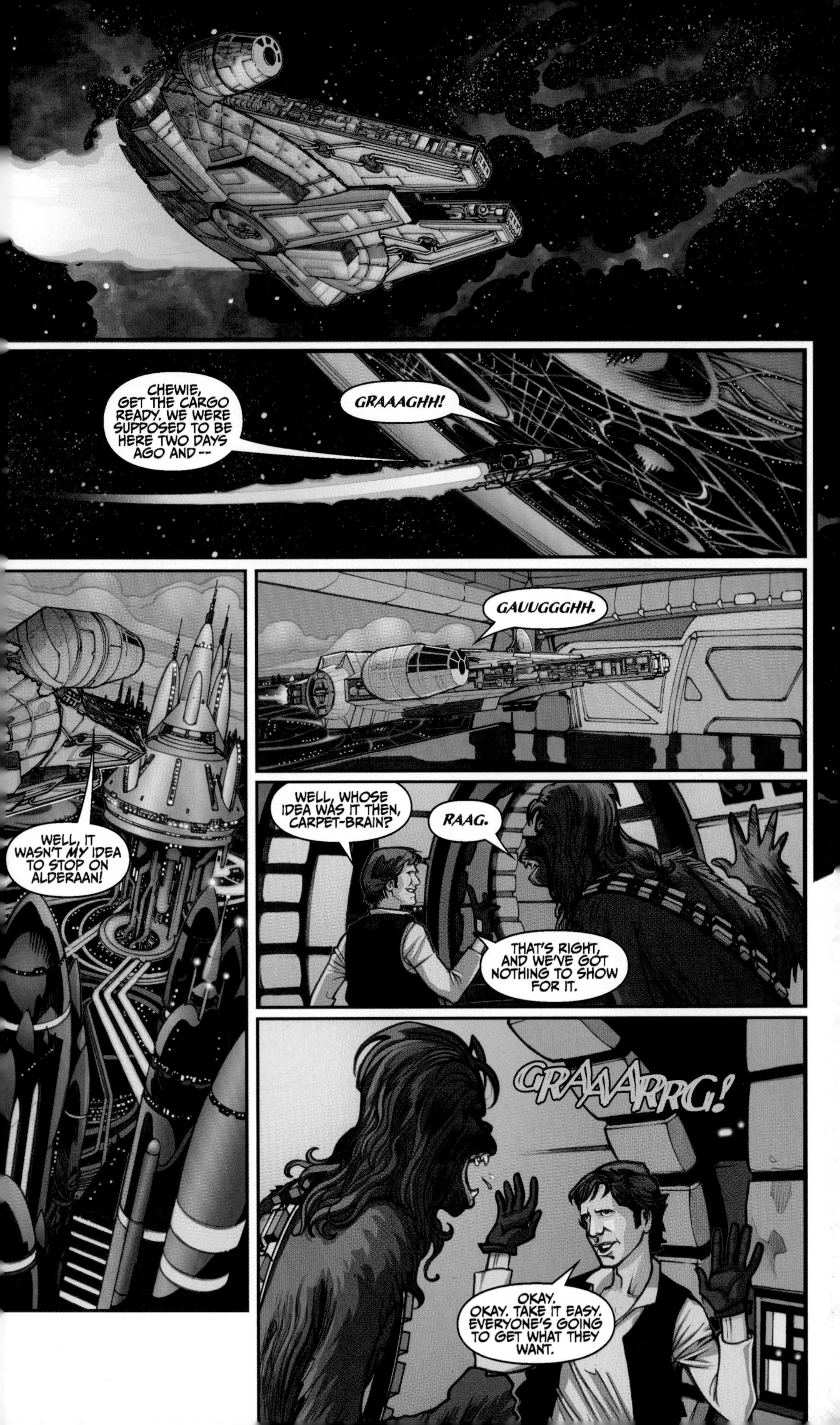
CHEWIE, GET THE CARGO READY. WE WERE SUPPOSED TO BE HERE TWO DAYS AGO AND --
GRAAAGHH!
WELL, IT WASN'T MY IDEA TO STOP ON ALDERAAN!
GAUUGGGHH.
WELL, WHOSE IDEA WAS IT THEN, CARPET-BRAIN?
RAAG.
THAT'S RIGHT, AND WE'VE GOT NOTHING TO SHOW FOR IT.
GRAAARRG!
OKAY. OKAY. TAKE IT EASY. EVERYONE'S GOING TO GET WHAT THEY WANT.

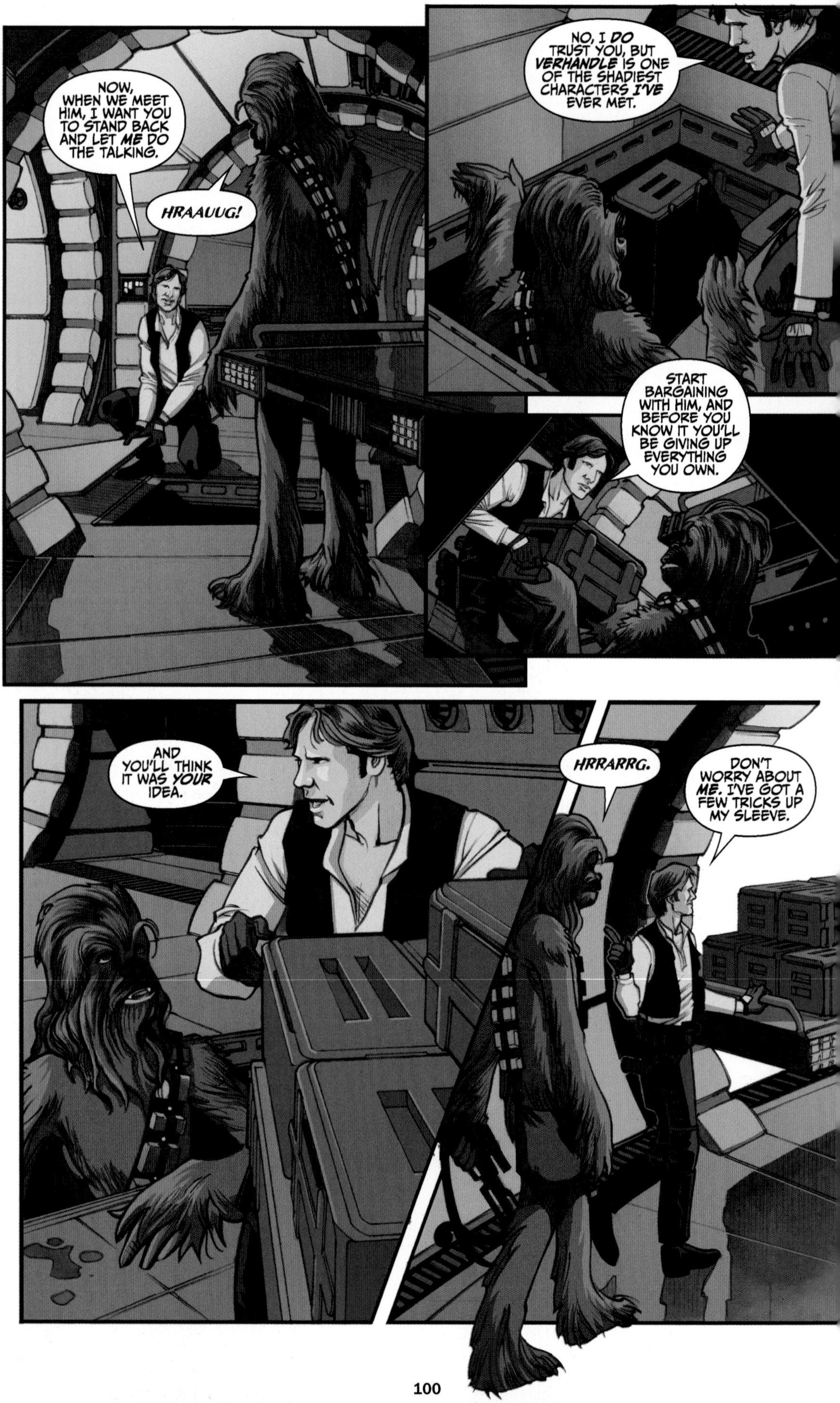
NOW, WHEN WE MEET HIM, I WANT YOU TO STAND BACK AND LET ME DO THE TALKING.
HRAAUUG!
NO, I DO TRUST YOU, BUT VERHANDLE IS ONE OF THE SHADIEST CHARACTERS I'VE EVER MET.
START BARGAINING WITH HIM, AND BEFORE YOU KNOW IT YOU'LL BE GIVING UP EVERYTHING YOU OWN.
AND YOU'LL THINK IT WAS YOUR IDEA.
HRRARRG.
DON'T WORRY ABOUT ME. I'VE GOT A FEW TRICKS UP MY SLEEVE.

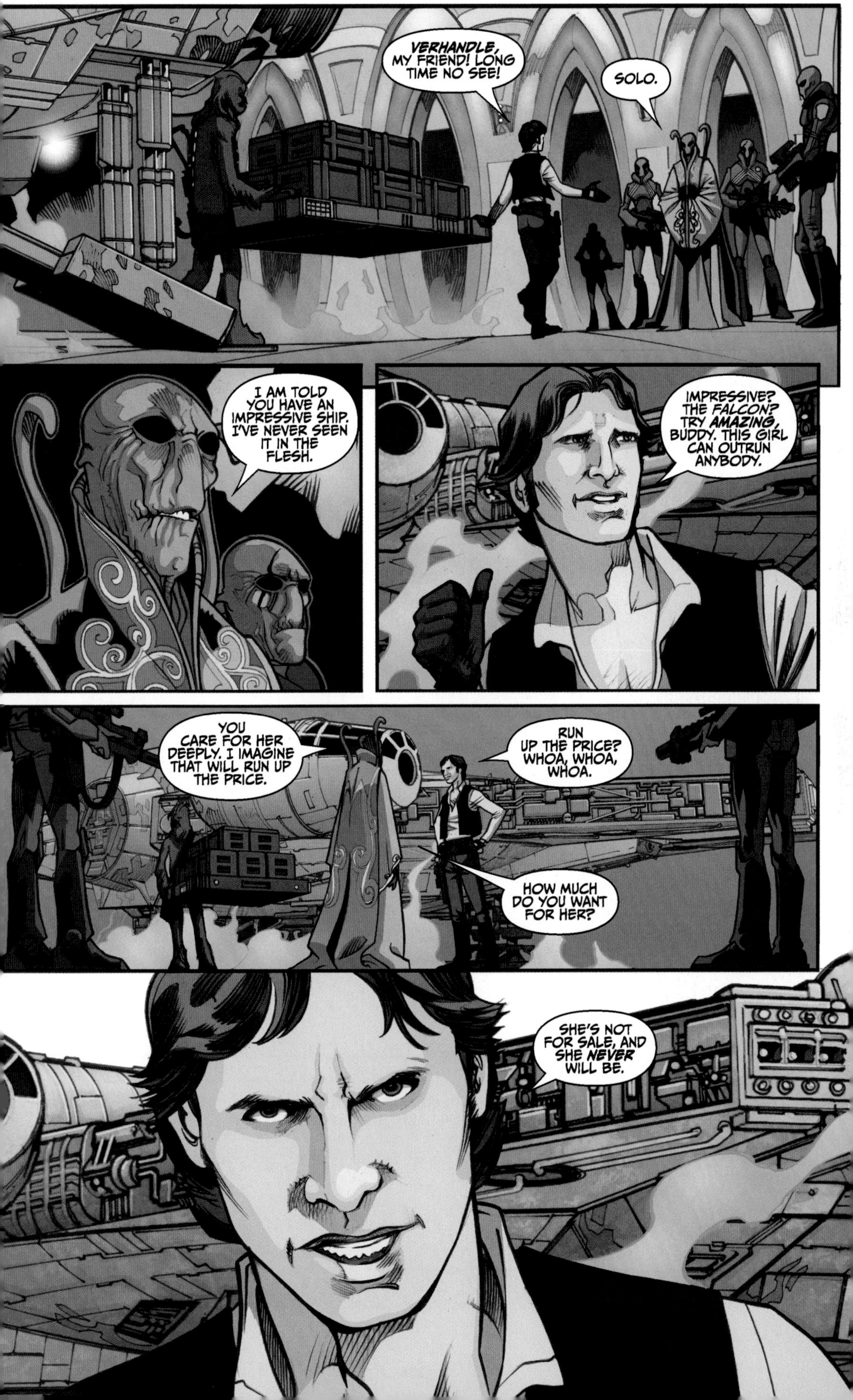
VERHANDLE, MY FRIEND! LONG TIME NO SEE!
SOLO.
I AM TOLD YOU HAVE AN IMPRESSIVE SHIP. I'VE NEVER SEEN IT IN THE FLESH.
IMPRESSIVE? THE FALCON? TRY AMAZING, BUDDY. THIS GIRL CAN OUTRUN ANYBODY.
YOU CARE FOR HER DEEPLY. I IMAGINE THAT WILL RUN UP THE PRICE.
RUN UP THE PRICE? WHOA, WHOA, WHOA.
HOW MUCH DO YOU WANT FOR HER?
SHE'S NOT FOR SALE, AND SHE NEVER WILL BE.

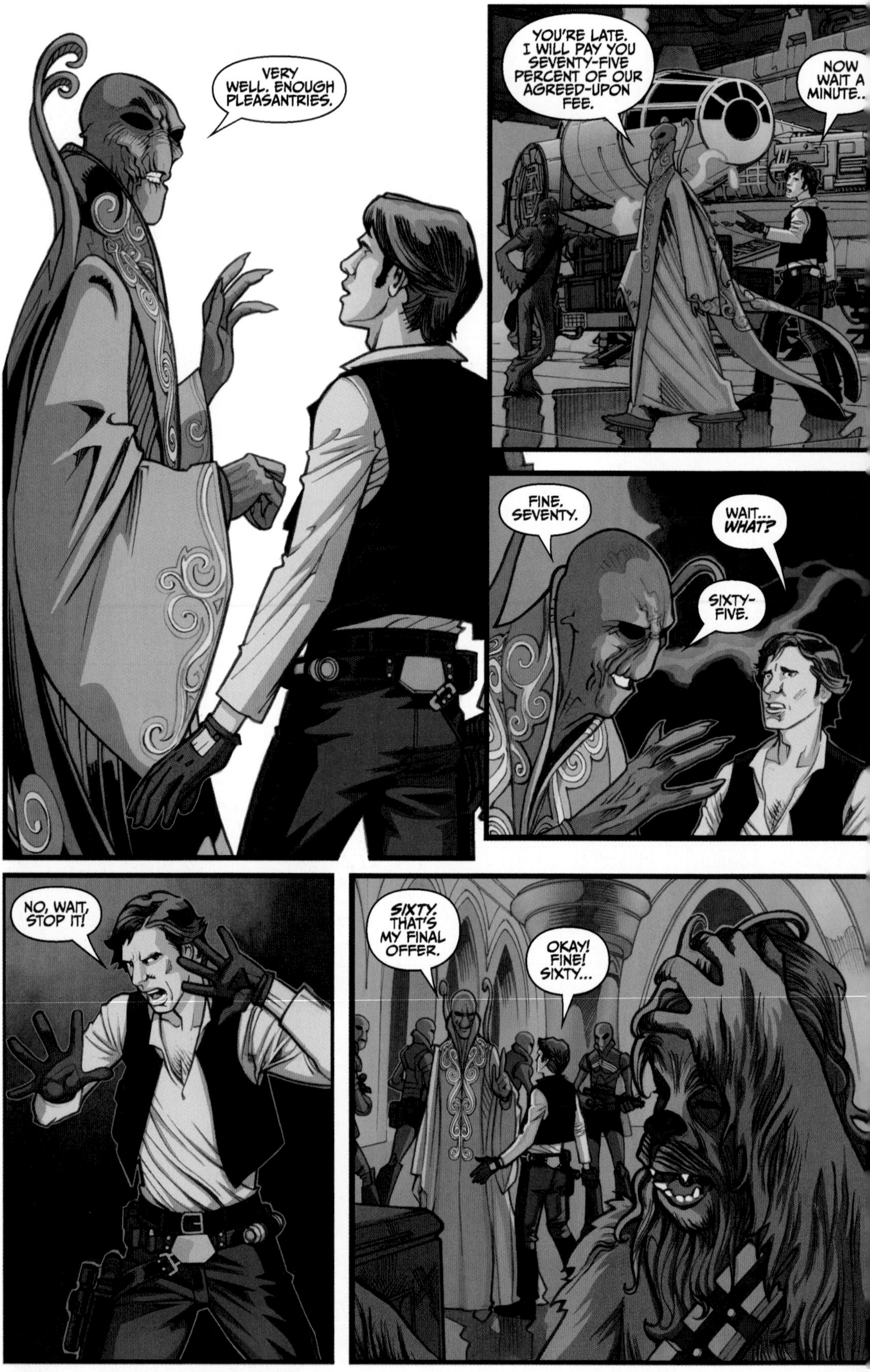

VERY WELL. ENOUGH PLEASANTRIES.
YOU'RE LATE. I WILL PAY YOU SEVENTY-FIVE PERCENT OF OUR AGREED-UPON FEE.
NOW WAIT A MINUTE...
FINE. SEVENTY.
WAIT... *WHAT?*
SIXTY-FIVE.
NO, WAIT, STOP IT!
SIXTY. THAT'S MY FINAL OFFER.
OKAY! FINE! SIXTY...

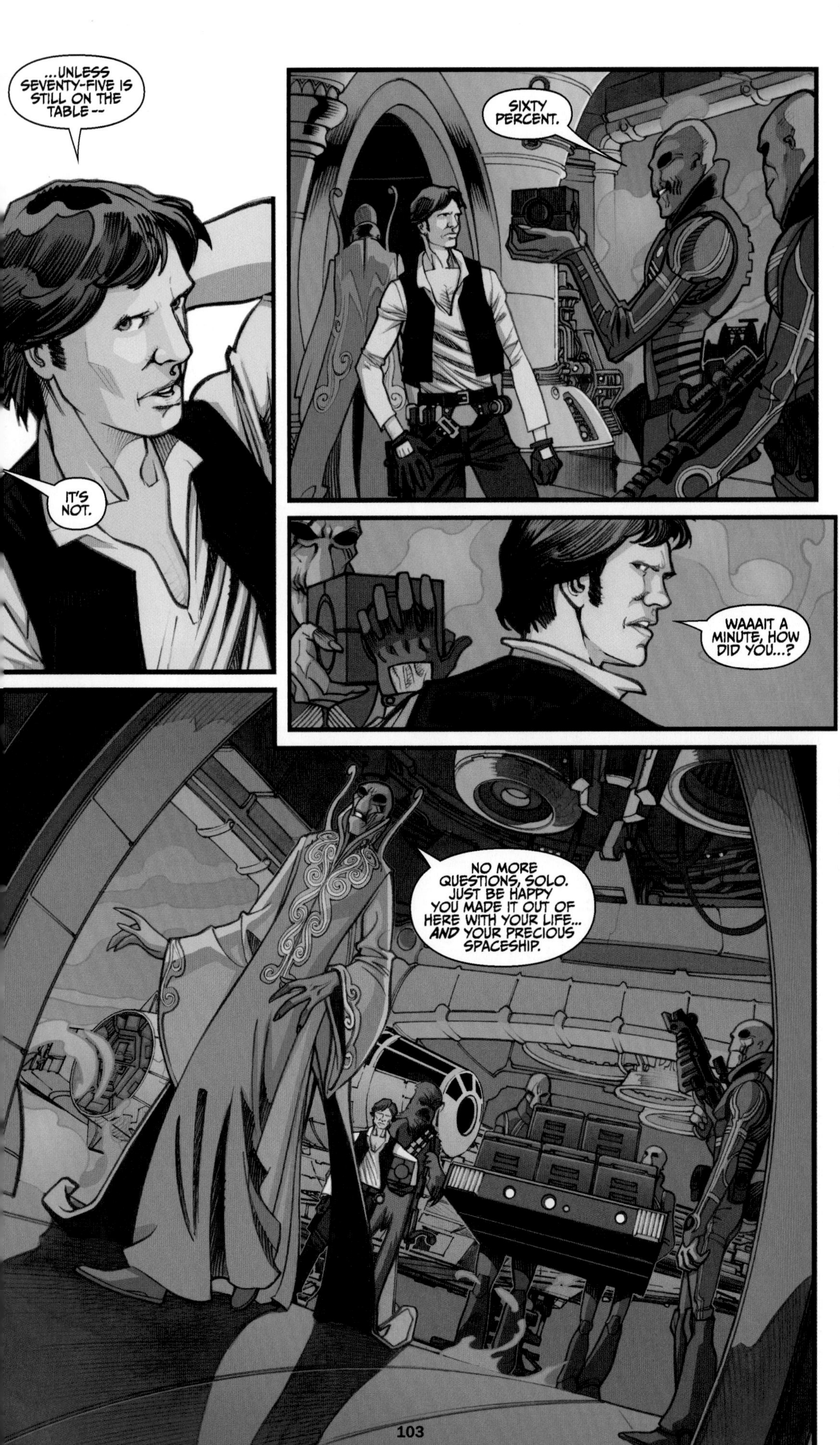
...UNLESS SEVENTY-FIVE IS STILL ON THE TABLE --
SIXTY PERCENT.
IT'S NOT.
WAAAIT A MINUTE, HOW DID YOU...?
NO MORE QUESTIONS, SOLO. JUST BE HAPPY YOU MADE IT OUT OF HERE WITH YOUR LIFE... *AND* YOUR PRECIOUS SPACESHIP.

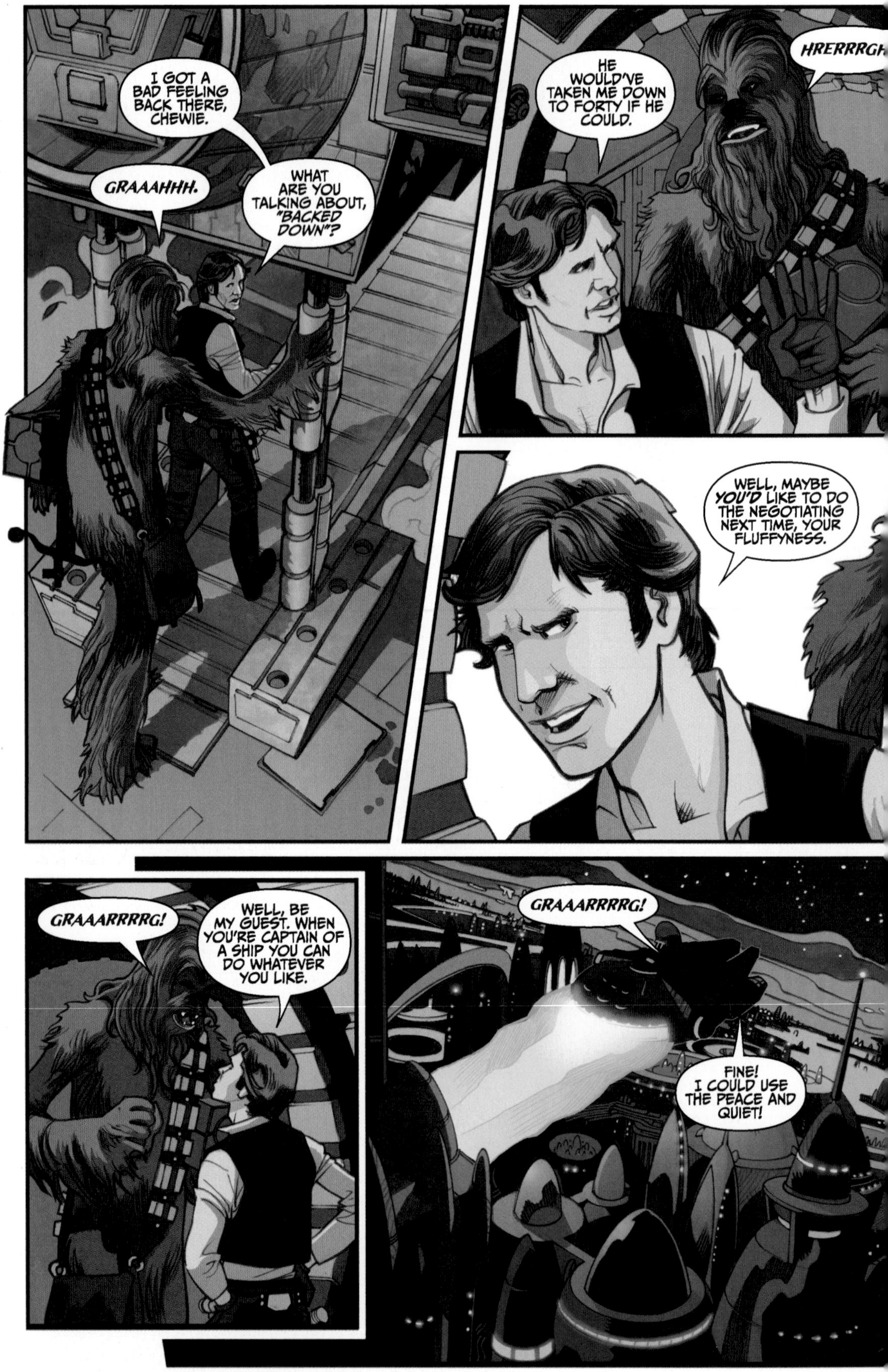
I GOT A BAD FEELING BACK THERE, CHEWIE.
GRAAAHHH.
WHAT ARE YOU TALKING ABOUT, "BACKED DOWN"?
HE WOULD'VE TAKEN ME DOWN TO FORTY IF HE COULD.
HRERRRGH
WELL, MAYBE YOU'D LIKE TO DO THE NEGOTIATING NEXT TIME, YOUR FLUFFYNESS.
GRAAARRRRG!
WELL, BE MY GUEST. WHEN YOU'RE CAPTAIN OF A SHIP YOU CAN DO WHATEVER YOU LIKE.
GRAAARRRRG!
FINE! I COULD USE THE PEACE AND QUIET!

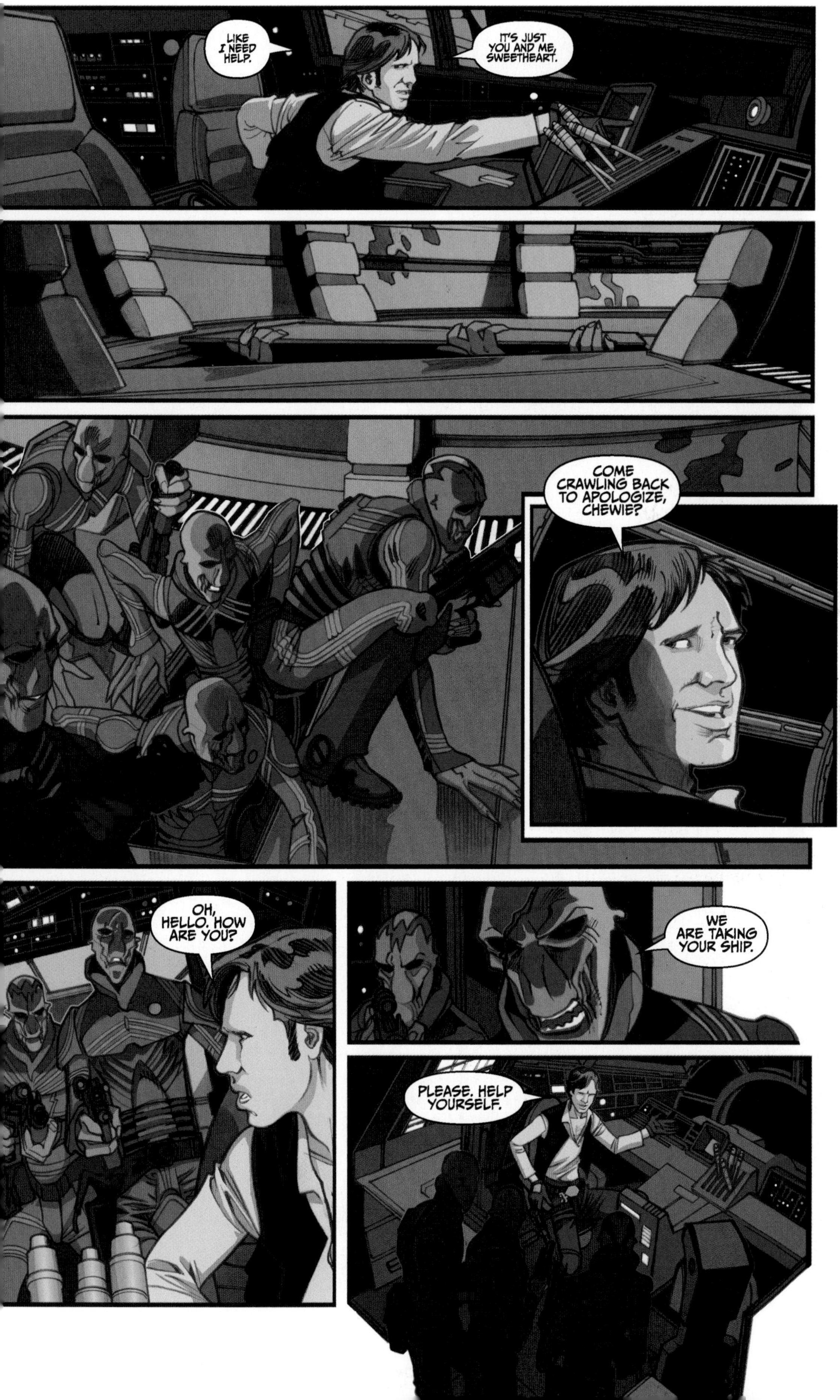
LIKE I NEED HELP.
IT'S JUST YOU AND ME, SWEETHEART.
COME CRAWLING BACK TO APOLOGIZE, CHEWIE?
OH, HELLO. HOW ARE YOU?
WE ARE TAKING YOUR SHIP.
PLEASE. HELP YOURSELF.

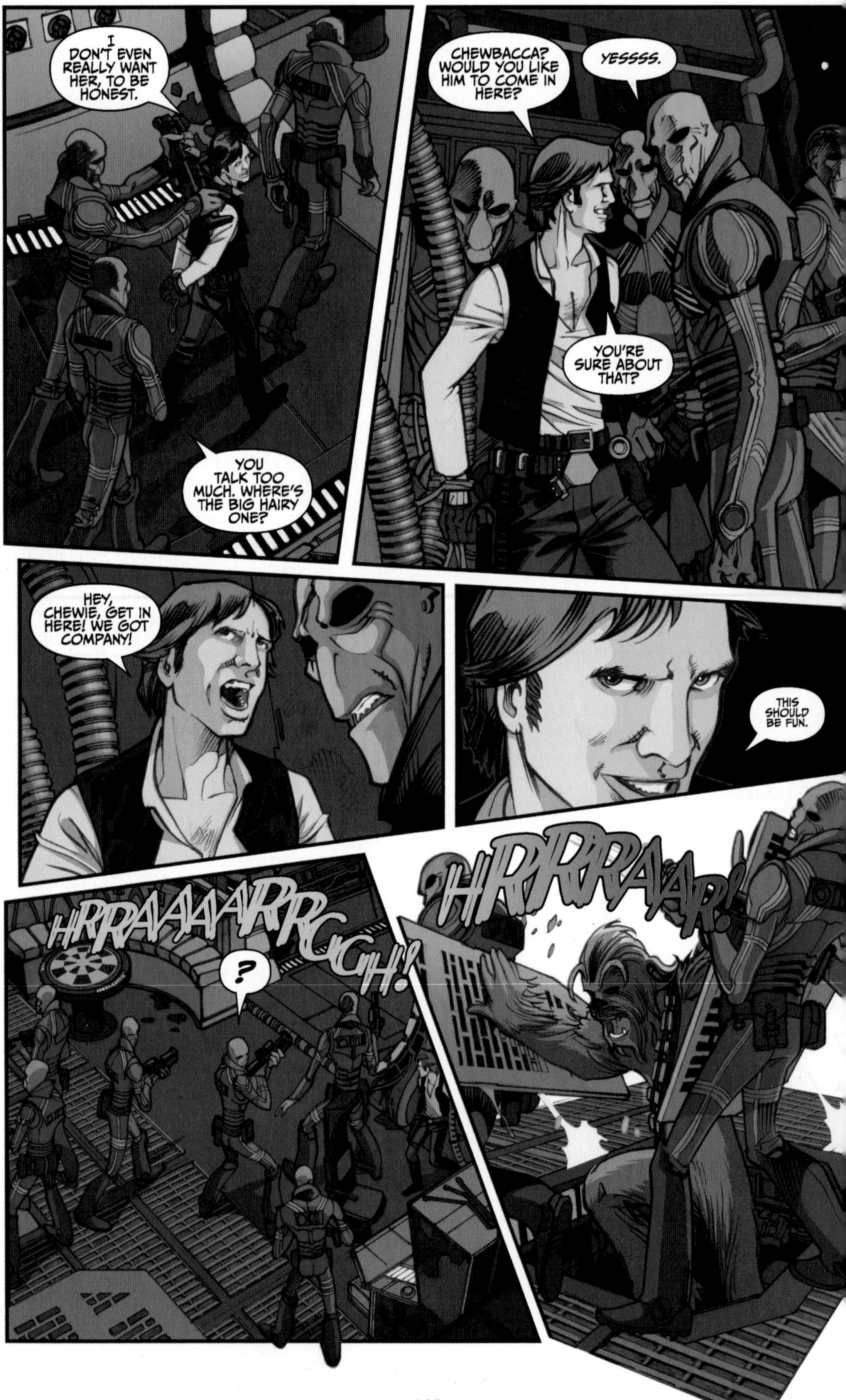
I DON'T EVEN REALLY WANT HER, TO BE HONEST.
YOU TALK TOO MUCH. WHERE'S THE BIG HAIRY ONE?
CHEWBACCA? WOULD YOU LIKE HIM TO COME IN HERE?
YESSSS.
YOU'RE SURE ABOUT THAT?
HEY, CHEWIE, GET IN HERE! WE GOT COMPANY!
THIS SHOULD BE FUN.
HRRAAAARRGGH!
?
HRRRAAR!

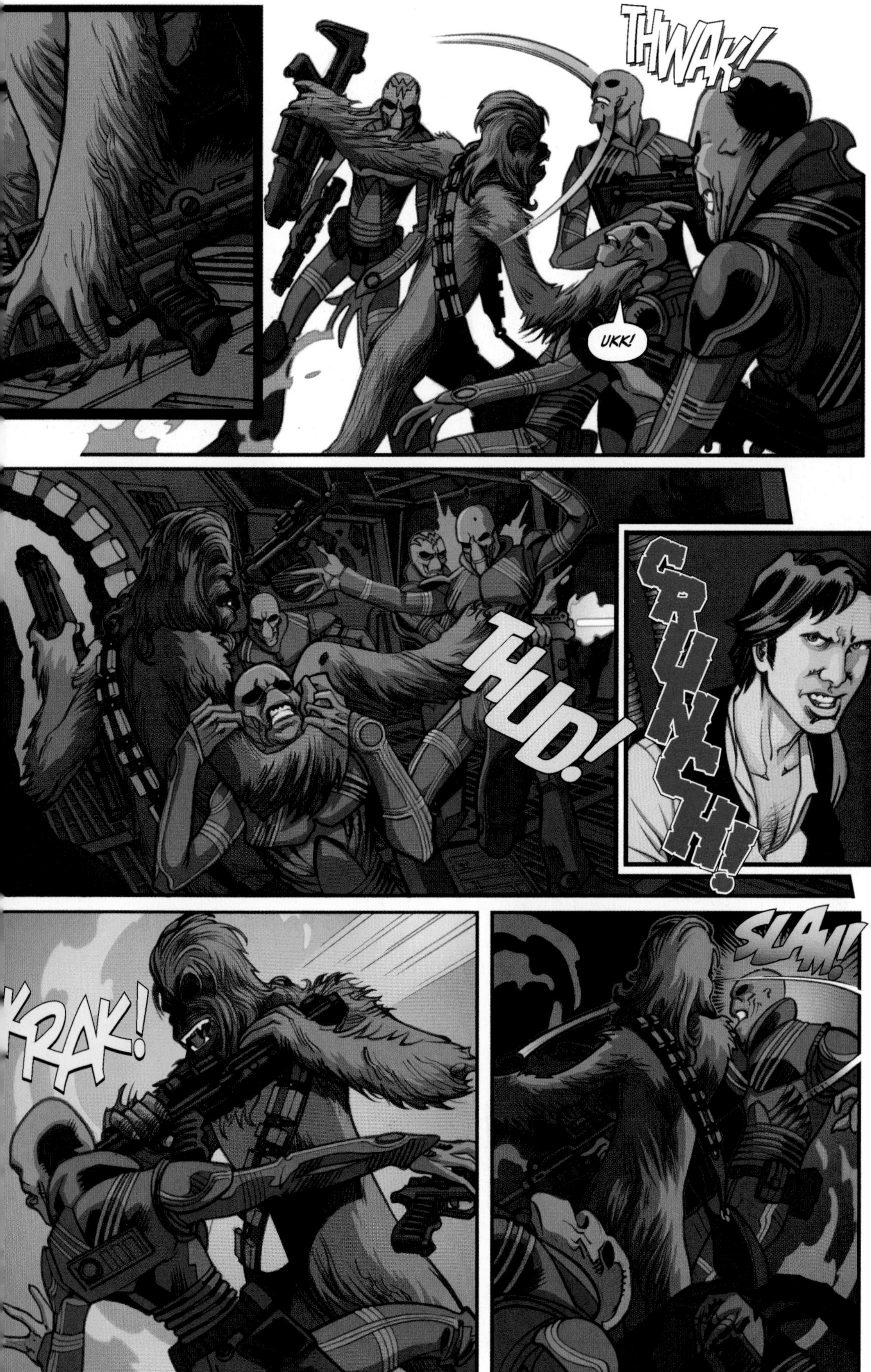
THWAK!
UKK!
THUD!
CRUNCH!
KRAK!
SLAM!

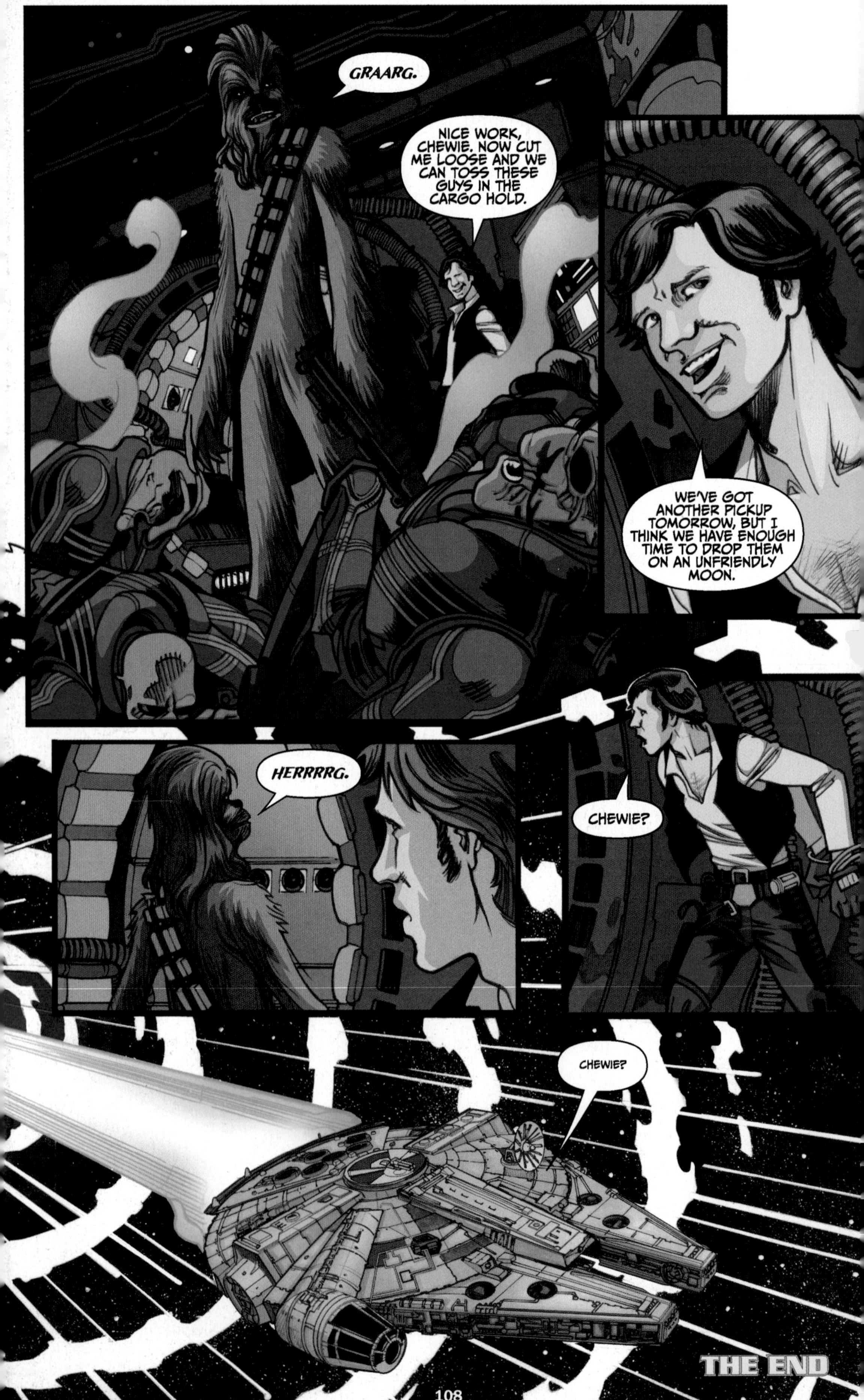

GRAARG.
NICE WORK, CHEWIE. NOW CUT ME LOOSE AND WE CAN TOSS THESE GUYS IN THE CARGO HOLD.
WE'VE GOT ANOTHER PICKUP TOMORROW, BUT I THINK WE HAVE ENOUGH TIME TO DROP THEM ON AN UNFRIENDLY MOON.
HERRRRG.
CHEWIE?
CHEWIE?
THE END

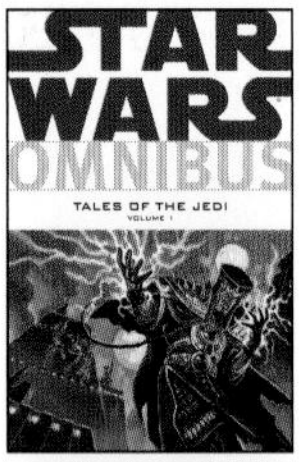
STAR
WARS
OMNIBUS
TALES OF THE JEDI
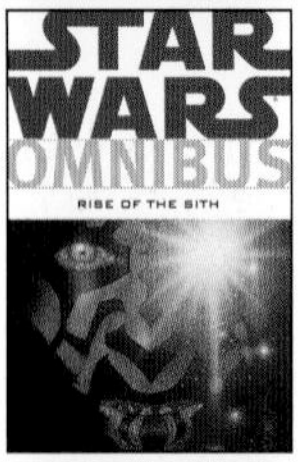
STAR
WARS
OMNIBUS
RISE OF THE SITH
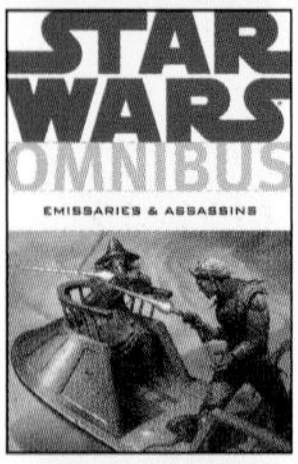
STAR
WARS
OMNIBUS
EMISSARIES & ASSASSINS
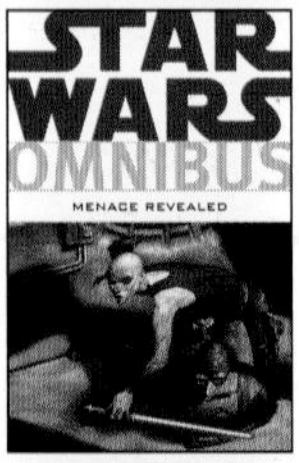
STAR
WARS
OMNIBUS
MENACE REVEALED
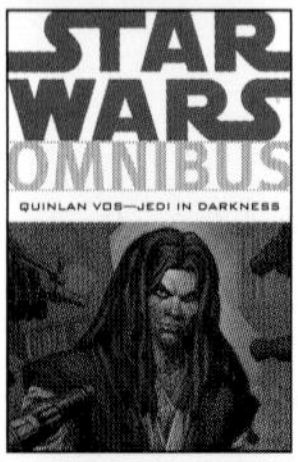
STAR
WARS
OMNIBUS
QUINLAN VOS—JEDI IN DARKNESS
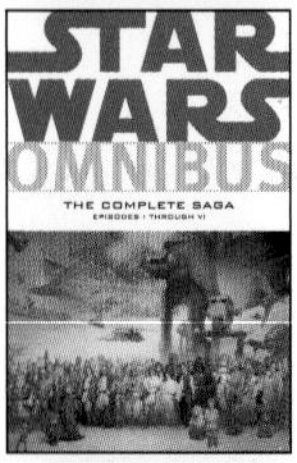
STAR
WARS
OMNIBUS
THE COMPLETE SAGA
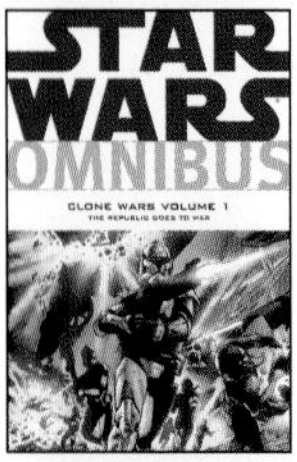
STAR
WARS
OMNIBUS
CLONE WARS VOLUME 1
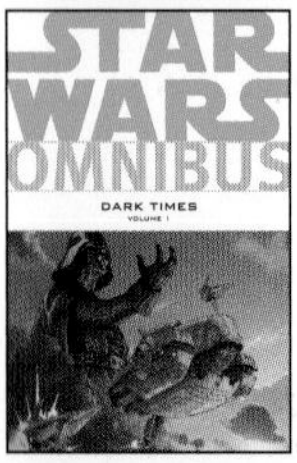
STAR
WARS
OMNIBUS
DARK TIMES

STAR WARS OMNIBUS COLLECTIONS

STAR WARS: TALES OF THE JEDI

Including the *Tales of the Jedi* stories "The Golden Age of the Sith," "The Freedon Nadd Uprising," and "Knights of the Old Republic," these huge omnibus editions are the ultimate introduction to the ancient history of the *Star Wars* universe!

Volume 1: ISBN 978-1-59307-830-0 | $24.99 **Volume 2: ISBN 978-1-59307-911-6 | $24.99**

STAR WARS: KNIGHTS OF THE OLD REPUBLIC

Padawan Zayne Carrick is suddenly a fugitive framed for the murder of his fellow Jedi-in-training. Little does the galaxy know, Zayne's own Masters are behind the massacre and dead set on recovering him before he can reveal the truth.

Volume 1: ISBN 978-1-61655-206-0 | $24.99 **Volume 3: ISBN 978-1-61655-227-5 | $24.99**
Volume 2: ISBN 978-1-61655-213-8 | $24.99

STAR WARS: RISE OF THE SITH

These thrilling tales illustrate the events leading up to *Episode I: The Phantom Menace*, when the Jedi Knights preserved peace and justice . . . as well as prevented the return of the Sith.

ISBN 978-1-59582-228-4 | $24.99

STAR WARS: EMISSARIES AND ASSASSINS

Discover more stories featuring Anakin Skywalker, Amidala, Obi-Wan, and Qui-Gon set during the time of *Episode I: The Phantom Menace*!

ISBN 978-1-59582-229-1 | $24.99

STAR WARS: MENACE REVEALED

Included here are one-shot adventures, short story arcs, specialty issues, and early *Dark Horse Extra* comic strips! All of these tales take place after *Episode I: The Phantom Menace*, and lead up to *Episode II: Attack of the Clones*.

ISBN 978-1-59582-273-4 | $24.99

STAR WARS: QUINLAN VOS—JEDI IN DARKNESS

From his first appearance as a mind-wiped amnesiac to his triumphant passage to the rank of Jedi Master, few Jedi had more brushes with the powers of the dark side and the evil of the underworld than Quinlan Vos.

ISBN 978-1-59582-555-1 | $24.99

STAR WARS: THE COMPLETE SAGA—EPISODES I THROUGH VI

The comics adaptations of the complete *Star Wars* film saga—in one volume! From the first fateful encounter with Darth Maul to Luke Skywalker's victory over the Sith and Darth Vader's redemption, it's all here.

ISBN 978-1-59582-832-3 | $24.99

STAR WARS: CLONE WARS

The Jedi Knights who were once protectors of the peace must become generals, leading the clone armies of the Republic to war! These stories follow *Attack of the Clones* and feature Jedi heroes Obi-Wan Kenobi, Anakin Skywalker, Mace Windu, and Quinlan Vos.

Volume 1: The Republic Goes to War ISBN 978-1-59582-927-6 | $24.99
Volume 2: The Enemy on All Sides ISBN 978-1-59582-958-0 | $24.99
Volume 3: The Republic Falls ISBN 978-1-59582-980-1 | $24.99

STAR WARS: DARK TIMES

The struggles of the Jedi intertwine with those of others now living in fear, including the diverse crew of a smuggling ship, the *Uhumele*, and a Nosaurian whose troubles begin when the Clone Wars end.

Volume 1: ISBN 978-1-61655-251-0 | $24.99 **Volume 2: ISBN 978-1-61655-252-7 | $24.99**

AVAILABLE AT YOUR LOCAL COMICS SHOP OR BOOKSTORE!

To find a comics shop in your area, call 1-888-266-4226

For more information or to order direct: • On the web: DarkHorse.com • E-mail: mailorder@darkhorse.com
• Phone: 1-800-862-0052 Mon.–Fri. 9 AM to 5 PM Pacific Time

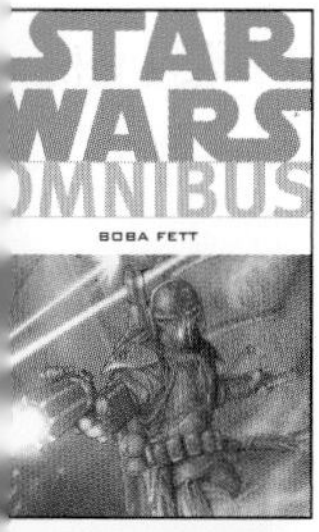
STAR
WARS
BOBA FETT
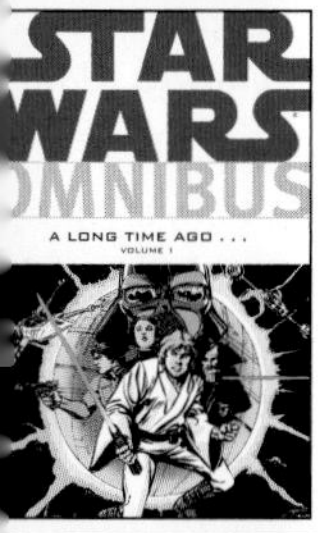
STAR
WARS
A LONG TIME AGO . . .
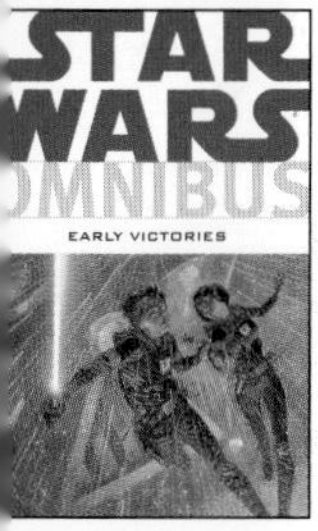
STAR
WARS
EARLY VICTORIES
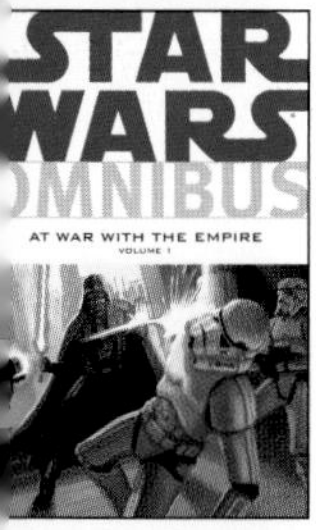
STAR
WARS
AT WAR WITH THE EMPIRE
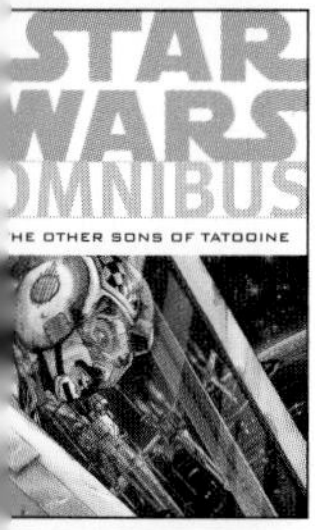
STAR
WARS
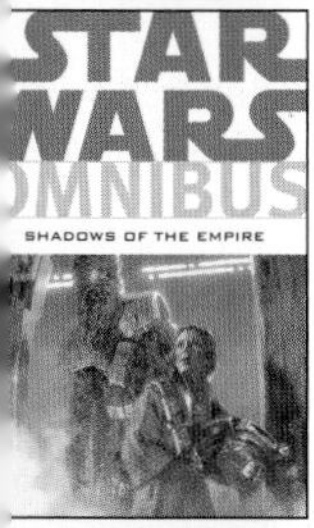
STAR
WARS
SHADOWS OF THE EMPIRE
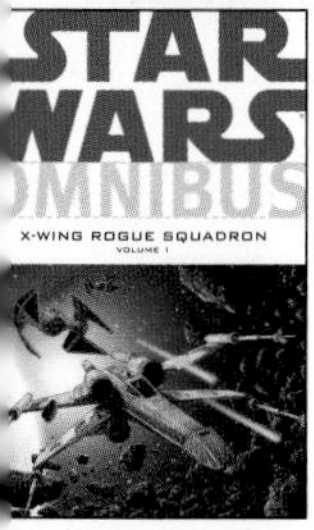
STAR
WARS
X-WING ROGUE SQUADRON

STAR WARS OMNIBUS COLLECTIONS

STAR WARS: BOBA FETT

Boba Fett, the most feared, most respected, and most loved bounty hunter in the galaxy, now has all of his comics stories collected into one massive volume!

ISBN 978-1-59582-418-9 | $24.99

STAR WARS: INFINITIES

Three different tales where *one thing* happens differently than it did in the original trilogy of *Star Wars* films. Luke Skywalker, Princess Leia, Han Solo, and Darth Vader are launched onto new trajectories!

ISBN 978-1-61655-078-3 | $24.99

STAR WARS: A LONG TIME AGO. . . .

Star Wars: A Long Time Ago. . . . omnibus volumes feature classic *Star Wars* stories not seen in over twenty years! Originally printed by Marvel Comics, these recolored stories are sure to please Star Wars fans both new and old.

Volume 1: ISBN 978-1-59582-486-8 | $24.99
Volume 2: ISBN 978-1-59582-554-4 | $24.99
Volume 3: ISBN 978-1-59582-639-8 | $24.99
Volume 4: ISBN 978-1-59582-640-4 | $24.99
Volume 5: ISBN 978-1-59582-801-9 | $24.99

STAR WARS: WILD SPACE

Rare and previously uncollected stories! Contains work from some of comics' most famous writers and artists (including Alan Moore, Chris Claremont, Archie Goodwin, Walt Simonson, and Alan Davis), plus stories featuring the greatest heroes and villains of *Star Wars*!

Volume 1: ISBN 978-1-61655-146-9 | $24.99
Volume 2: ISBN 978-1-61655-147-6 | $24.99

STAR WARS: EARLY VICTORIES

Following the destruction of the first Death Star, Luke Skywalker and Princess Leia find there are many more battles to be fought against the Empire and Darth Vader!

ISBN 978-1-59582-172-0 | $24.99

STAR WARS: AT WAR WITH THE EMPIRE

Stories of the early days of the Rebel Alliance and the beginnings of its war with the Empire—tales of the *Star Wars* galaxy set before, during, and after the events in *Star Wars: A New Hope!*

Volume 1: ISBN 978-1-59582-699-2 | $24.99
Volume 2: ISBN 978-1-59582-777-7 | $24.99

STAR WARS: THE OTHER SONS OF TATOOINE

Luke's story has been told time and again, but what about the journeys of his boyhood friends, Biggs Darklighter and Janek "Tank" Sunber? Both are led to be heroes in their own right: one of the Rebellion, the other of the Empire . . .

ISBN 978-1-59582-866-8 | $24.99

STAR WARS: SHADOWS OF THE EMPIRE

Featuring all your favorite characters from the *Star Wars* trilogy—Luke Skywalker, Princess Leia, and Han Solo—this volume includes stories written by acclaimed novelists Timothy Zahn and Steve Perry!

ISBN 978-1-59582-434-9 | $24.99

STAR WARS: X-WING ROGUE SQUADRON

The starfighters of the Rebel Alliance become the defenders of a new Republic in these stories featuring Wedge Antilles and his team of ace pilots known throughout the galaxy as Rogue Squadron.

Volume 1: ISBN 978-1-59307-572-9 | $24.99
Volume 2: ISBN 978-1-59307-619-1 | $24.99
Volume 3: ISBN 978-1-59307-776-1 | $24.99

AVAILABLE AT YOUR LOCAL COMICS SHOP OR BOOKSTORE!

To find a comics shop in your area, call 1-888-266-4226

For more information or to order direct: • On the web: DarkHorse.com • E-mail: mailorder@darkhorse.com • Phone: 1-800-862-0052 Mon.–Fri. 9 AM to 5 PM Pacific Time •

STAR WARS HARDCOVER VOLUMES

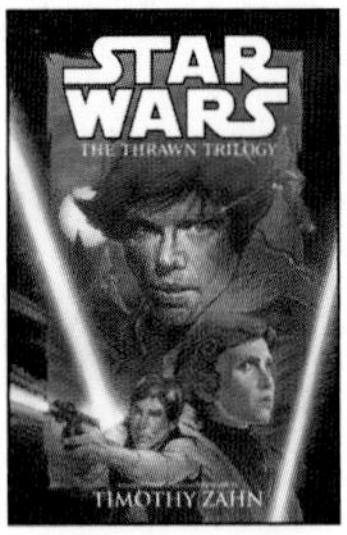
STAR WARS
THE THRAWN TRILOGY
TIMOTHY ZAHN

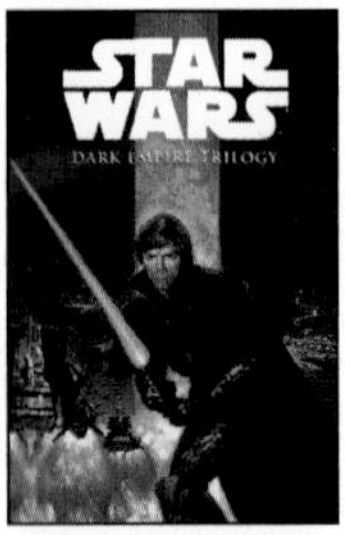
STAR WARS

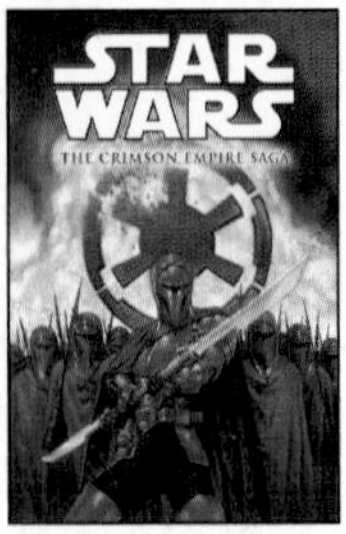
STAR WARS

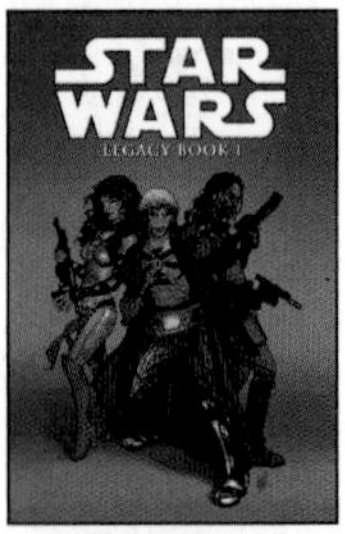
STAR WARS

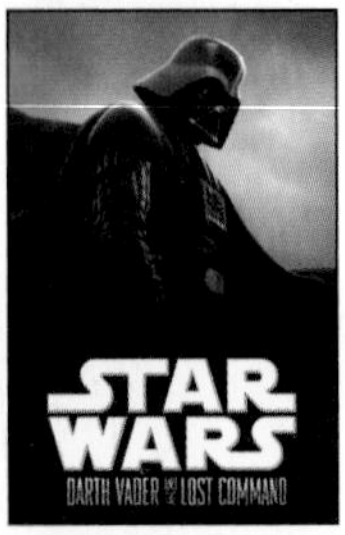
STAR WARS

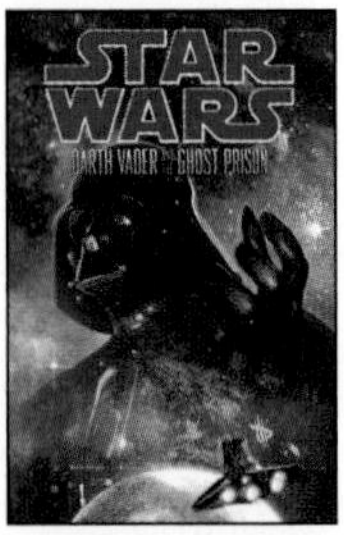
STAR WARS

STAR WARS: DARTH VADER AND THE CRY OF SHADOWS

Clone trooper Hock, left for dead by his Jedi leaders in the Clone Wars, now believes he has found a truly great warrior worthy of his loyalty—Darth Vader!

ISBN 978-1-61655-382-1 | $24.99

STAR WARS: THE THRAWN TRILOGY

The comics adaptations of Timothy Zahn's best-selling novels *Heir to the Empire*, *Dark Force Rising*, and *The Last Command*. The last of the Emperor's warlords, Admiral Thrawn, is ready to destroy the New Republic—and the odds are stacked against Luke, Leia, and Han!

ISBN 978-1-59582-417-2 | $34.99

STAR WARS: DARK EMPIRE TRILOGY

Six years after the fall of the Empire in *Return of the Jedi*, the Empire has been mysteriously reborn . . . Princess Leia and Han Solo struggle to hold together the New Republic while Luke Skywalker is drawn to the dark side . . .

ISBN 978-1-59582-612-1 | $29.99

STAR WARS: THE CRIMSON EMPIRE SAGA

The blood-soaked tale of the last surviving member of Emperor Palpatine's Royal Guard! From revenge to redemption, the story of Kir Kanos takes him from the deserts of Yinchorr, to the halls of Imperial power, and to the inner circle of the New Republic.

ISBN 978-1-59582-947-4 | $34.99

STAR WARS: LEGACY

The future of Star Wars and the future of the Skywalkers is told in John Ostrander and Jar Duursema's acclaimed *Star Wars: Legacy*. A Sith legion has conquered the Empire, the Jedi have been scattered, and the galaxy is divided. Into this comes Cade Skywalker, hei to the Skywalker legacy . . .

Book 1: ISBN 978-1-61655-178-0 | $34.99

Book 2: ISBN 978-1-61655-209-1 | $34.99

Book 3: ISBN 978-1-61655-260-2 | $34.99

STAR WARS: DARTH VADER AND THE LOST COMMAND

Still haunted by the death of Anakin Skywalker's beloved Padmé, Darth Vader must locate a lost Imperial expeditionary force—led by the son of Vader's rising nemesis, Moff Tarkin. Vader's journey is compounded by traitors and the mysterious Lady Saro.

ISBN 978-1-59582-778-4 | $24.99

STAR WARS: DARTH VADER AND THE GHOST PRISON

An uprising against the Galactic Empire leaves Emperor Palpatine close to death. Saving the Emperor—and the Empire—appears to be a lost cause . . . unless Darth Vader and a young lieutenant can locate the Jedi Council's mysterious "Ghost Prison."

ISBN 978-1-61655-059-2 | $24.99

STAR WARS: DARTH VADER AND THE NINTH ASSASSIN

Eight assassins hired to murder Darth Vader—eight assassins dead. Now the man who enlisted them seeks a ninth assassin. When it comes to avenging his son, no sacrifice is too great to acquire the one man who can kill the Dark Lord of the Sith . . .

ISBN 978-1-61655-207-7 | $24.99

DARK HORSE BOOKS

AVAILABLE AT YOUR LOCAL COMICS SHOP OR BOOKSTORE!

To find a comics shop in your area, call 1-888-266-4226

For more information or to order direct: • On the web: DarkHorse.com • E-mail: mailorder@darkhorse.com • Phone: 1-800-862-0052 Mon.–Fri. 9 AM to 5 PM Pacific Time